Lou von Salomé

Lou von Salomé

*A Biography of the Woman
Who Inspired Freud,
Nietzsche and Rilke*

Julia Vickers

McFarland & Company, Inc., Publishers
Jefferson, North Carolina, and London

LIBRARY OF CONGRESS CATALOGUING-IN-PUBLICATION DATA

Vickers, Julia, 1957–
    Lou von Salomé : a biography of the woman who inspired
Freud, Nietzsche, and Rilke / Julia Vickers.
      p.   cm.
    Includes bibliographical references and index.

    ISBN 978-0-7864-3606-4
    softcover : 50# alkaline paper

    1. Andreas-Salomé, Lou, 1861–1937. 2. Authors,
German — 20th century — Biography. 3. Andreas-Salomé,
Lou, 1861–1937 — Friends and associates. I. Title.
PT2601.N4Z93   2008
383'.809 — dc22   2008036018
[B]

British Library cataloguing data are available

©2008 Julia Vickers. All rights reserved

*No part of this book may be reproduced or transmitted in any form
or by any means, electronic or mechanical, including photocopying
or recording, or by any information storage and retrieval system,
without permission in writing from the publisher.*

Cover photograph: Lou Andreas-Salomé

Manufactured in the United States of America

*McFarland & Company, Inc., Publishers
  Box 611, Jefferson, North Carolina 28640
    www.mcfarlandpub.com*

Acknowledgments

I would like to give special thanks to the following people:

To my family, who mean so much to me; to A.V., to whom I am grateful for improving my life beyond words; to all those who showed enthusiasm for and interest in my subject, providing me with hours of wonderful conversation; and to T.N., who taught me the value of inspiration.

*Fortunate is the man whom the Muses love;
sweet words flow from his lips.*

— Hesiod

Table of Contents

Acknowledgments   v
Preface   1
Introduction   3

PART I. GOD THE FATHER

  1. A Russian General's Daughter   9
  2. *Ecco Homo*   18
  3. Girl Genius   25
  4. The Nietzsche Experience   32
  5. *Any Third Person*   47
  6. The Birth of a Tragedy   53
  7. Divine Inspiration   59
  8. The Mysterious Mr. Andreas   66

PART II. MUSES AND WRITERS

  9. Marriage — and a Life   75
  10. In Nietzsche's Shadow   81
  11. *L'homme Eternal*   87
  12. The Inspiration of a Young Poet   105
  13. Love and Other Difficulties   115
  14. To Russia, with Love   130
  15. Together, Alone   137
  16. The Land in Between   145

PART III. FATHER FREUD

    17. Oedipus Rex — 157

    18. Ego and Eros — 164

    19. The Beautiful Narcissist — 172

    20. That of Loss — 178

    21. Return to the All — 188

Afterword — 193
Chapter Notes — 195
Bibliography — 205
Index — 207

Preface

In Europe, particularly France and Germany, Lou Andreas-Salomé is hailed respectively as a great muse and a brilliant scholar. During her lifetime she seemed to appear on the scene of every major event of intellectual history. She created a living link to the most influential thinkers of her time, and her wide-ranging contribution to the intellectual world is clear in books on Nietzsche, Rilke and Freud; yet biographies about her are few.

Lou von Salomé's legacy is viewed with both awe and mistrust, reverence and condescension. Of the few volumes in English, Rudolph Binion's *Frau Lou*, published in 1968, stands out as a monument to research. I relied on it a great deal, for above all others it expresses a full view of this multifaceted woman. However, Mr. Binion believes that Andreas-Salomé fabricated some of the details that she put into her memoir. While in my own research I have also found her fiction gives more insight into her life than her memoir, I cannot fully agree with Binion's treatment. I feel it is important to admit that no biographer knows the exact details of the past and we are left with only numerous, and sometimes conflicting, perspectives. We often have to rely on our intuition and the knowledge of an individual spirit to guide us through. There is a certain element of unreliability in every biography and autobiography, and when I found conflict in "facts" I attempted to reconcile the conflict through a mixture of knowledge and intuition. Through the analysis of letters passed among the various participants in the story, my understanding of the Nietzsche affair in particular exposes deceit and manipulation from others, rather than from Lou herself, as Binion argues.

During her lifetime Lou von Salomé utilized a number of monikers that may be confusing to the reader. Born Louise von Salomé, after her mother, she was given the Russian nickname Ljolja as a child. As a teenager she adopted the more masculine form of her name: Lou. Her passport to Germany lists her name as Lou von Salomé, but she soon dropped the von and became known as simply Lou Salomé. When she married F.C. Andreas she became Lou Andreas-Salomé, but because of the length of that name she often told people to simply call her Frau Lou. In the book I refer to her more often as Lou von Salomé, being that it retains her original character, which even in marriage she never surrendered.

It has been an exciting challenge to understand such a complex and unique woman, and this challenge drove me on. Lou von Salomé inspired many in her lifetime, and the inspiration continues.

Introduction

No woman has radiated a stronger or more direct influence in German-speaking lands in the last 150 years than this Lou Salomé from Petersburg.[1]

— Kurt Wolff

Become who you are! was the advice Friedrich Nietzsche often gave to his brilliant friend Lou von Salomé. But discovering who Lou von Salomé was is not an easy task. "The course of Lou Salomé's life," says translator Stanley A. Leavy the introduction to von Salomé's *Freud Journal*, "was one of ceaseless determination to be true to the image of herself and to reject all influences that might have limited her."[2] She has been labeled a catalyst to genius, a collector of geniuses, a genius of life, and a near-mad, near-genius, the first modern woman and a person worthy of hero worship. She has been called an intellectual *femme fatale*. "Men longed for her, suffered for her, and it is possible one or two even died for her"[3]; she was "cerebral, bewitching and heartless"[4]; she was "a vestal virgin combined with a she–Narcissus."[5] "She may have destroyed lives and marriages," one admirer said, "but her presence was exciting. One felt the spark of genius in her. One grew in her presence."[6] She was a muse, or as close to these mythical goddesses as any mortal could ever come. She inspired the most brilliant men of her time — poets, playwrights, philosophers, and psychoanalysts. She stimulated thoughts on philosophy, religion and psychology, as well as volumes of love poetry and prose. Her effect on creative people was seemingly as magical and spontaneous as fruit falling from a tree. Whenever she passed through one's life, a great work was sure to follow.

She was an extremely active and creative force in the artistic culture of nineteenth century Europe, but most important to her was her role as an insatiable intellectual conquistador, who followed her instincts and curiosity into the realms of the intellect and conquered her numerous fields of interest. "My life," she wrote, "has been a wonderful mixture of inner logic and outer impromptu." She was an "artist and philosopher, thinker and poetess, a strong personality yet so much a woman in every trait of her being."[7] She was a best-selling author of dozens of novels and short stories. She wrote hundreds of influential essays on literature, philosophy, religion, women, sexuality and psychology. In her twenties she was a girl-philosopher worthy of Nietzsche's fascination. In her thirties and forties, she was a cultural critic, writing about, befriending and inspiring some of the most important European writers of her time. In her fifties, she was a dear friend to Freud and became a lay psychoanalyst and worked with patients sent to her by him. In none of these endeavors was she a dabbler or a dilettante, but an intense, serious, tireless genius of a woman.

It's worth noting that Lou von Salomé was not a beauty by today's standards. Far from glamorous, she nevertheless cast a spell with her genius and charm on all who met her. In her youth, she was striking, with penetrating blue eyes. She was a Nordic type — tall, long-legged with dark blonde hair — and her figure was slimmer than the full-figured ideal of her time. She dressed like a nun, in the high collared habit of a University of Zurich co-ed, her hair pulled back tight. In middle age, she wore simple Russian-style dresses that often looked dowdy, if not disheveled. Her outer appearance was of no interest to her whatsoever. And yet she was one of the most tantalizing and sought-after women of her era.

She was considered a phenomenon in her own life time. Feminists of Germany and Scandinavia debated over her works and lifestyle and wrote a multitude of admiring and challenging words about her. She had the "seriousness of a man, the lightheartedness of a child and the devotion and love of a woman,"[8] an early feminist wrote. Her writing was unique among the women writers of the Victorian age. She confronted bold subjects — chiefly God and sex — without fear and offered rare insight into the soul of a woman. Rainer Maria Rilke saw her as the spiritual guide of his poetic breakthrough and the love of his life: "Lou — how splendid You are, what space You have opened up in me."[9] She had a childlike, Russian directness that was at once disarming and endearing. Men who met her were often surprised at her ease and candor when discussing love and sexuality. But despite her intellectual openness, she was ever-elusive, and becoming *who she was* — as Nietzsche had instructed — without any social restrictions became her lifelong quest.

The story of Lou von Salomé is not only the story of an exceptional woman; it is the story of European cultural history. It includes many of the best-known characters, but also the equally important figures who were lost in time. It is the story of genius and madness, of creativity and desire, of the erotic and the intellectual, of the great and the egotistical: it is the story of the intellectual Titans who helped to shape our modern world and the woman to whom they paid homage.

Lou von Salomé's extraordinary life followed another dictate that Nietzsche gave to her: *Turn away from half measures and resolve to live wholly, fully and beautifully.*

I
GOD THE FATHER

I do not wish to flee from pain
Nor ask that love be true
All I want is some broad plain
To kneel upon beneath you.

— Lou Andreas-Salomé,
Looking Back: Memoirs, p. 8

1

A Russian General's Daughter

Lou is a Russian general's daughter ... sharp as an eagle and brave as a lion, and yet still a very girlish child.[1]
— Friedrich Nietzsche

On a Sunday in May 1880, a secret initiation took place in a small country church in Holland. To the observers it was a confirmation, unusual only that the initiate was a little older than confirmation age and a Russian. Conducted in Dutch before the initiate's mother and a small local congregation, the ceremony had a hidden meaning known only to the pastor and the girl who knelt before him.

The nineteen-year-girl was Nordic in appearance, with pale blue eyes. Her dark blonde hair was pulled back tightly, exposing a candid face that was charming in its directness.

The strong and clear voice of Pastor Hendrik Gillot reverberated through the small wood paneled room. "Fear not, for I have chosen you, I have called you by name: you are mine."[2] To which the girl answered, "You bless me, for I do not leave you."[3]

But leave him, she would. The ceremony was performed for just that purpose. She couldn't obtain a passport in Russia without being confirmed in a faith. But Lou von Salomé had lost her faith in God. She wanted to leave her Russian homeland and seek out a world of intellect at the University in Zurich. What was thought to be a confirmation of faith was actually the initiation into an extraordinary life, ministered by a man who loved her and would deny her nothing. Her mother, who didn't speak a word of Dutch, was none the wiser. It was the end of a long hard battle she had fought with her daughter over religious confirmation. Louise — or Lou as Pastor Gillot affectionately called her — thought it an assault on her integrity to profess a belief she no longer held. But she made an exception when it came to deceiving her mother and Mother Russia. It was all for the best. And she would have her freedom.

The von Salomé family has been traced back to the French Huguenots, who with their mad love of religious freedom fled France to Baltic Germany in the 1600s. As Napoleon marched through Prussia early in the 19th century the von Salomé family fled again to Russia's Imperial capital, St. Petersburg, the luminous Nordic city. Alexander I ruled Russia and Napoleon was on the move in an attempt to capture the great bear of a country. But the French, though battled-hardened, were no match for the iron will of the huge Eurasian empire. Russians were strong, hardy people who endured one of the harshest climates in the world. Hardship was not only a common part of life, the Russians were proud of their ability to endure suffering. It was this fierce and proud Nordic people that Tolstoy would celebrate in *War and Peace*.

Lou's father, Gustav von Salomé, was eight years old at Napoleon's defeat, but quickly grew into a tall, handsome young man, eager to become a military officer. Face to face with world history, he was energized with military dreams and ambitions. Exceptionally bright and fervent, the young man distinguished himself and was awarded medals for valor in the storming of Warsaw in 1830. Von Salomé rose to the level of colonel at the phenomenal age of twenty-five, and soon rose to the rank of general. Tsar Nicholas I, who became very fond of the valiant young man, awarded him with nobility. Growing up, Lou would gaze with pride upon the Russian coat of arms, dedicated by the Tsar, with its helmet icon and two slanting bands of gold and red beneath it.

"In his youth," Lou would write of her father, "he enjoyed all the pleasures of life in the splendid imperial city."[4] Such pleasures included all the accoutrements of the court elite — the best food, the finest entertainment, the most brilliant conversation and the prettiest women. The capital was home to many literary icons of the age, and Gustav von Salomé befriended Russia's two of Russia's greatest poets — Pushkin and Lermontov.

In 1844, at the late age of thirty-seven and at the height of his illustrious career, General von Salomé married a twenty-one-year-old blue-eyed blonde named Louise Wilm. Louise was the daughter of a well-to-do sugar manufacturer, of northern German and Danish heritage. Meticulous and dutiful, the young woman wrote in her diary soon after her marriage that she would dedicate her life to "her husband, her family and her God — in that order."⁵ It was this sense of duty and self-sacrifice that stood out most about her character, and it would be the trait that would cause a decade-long clash with her only daughter. She gave birth to five sons (the first and the fourth died young); then, on February 12, 1861, General and Frau von Salomé became the parents of a golden-haired girl. The general named her after his wife — *Louise* — but the beautiful little girl was called by a Russian nickname, *Ljolja*. General von Salomé was, by that time, fifty-seven and the Inspector of the Army, a less strenuous administrative appointment. In his youth he had been commanding and authoritative, dictating to his sons what professions they would pursue, regardless of their interests or talents. Now he had softened into a kindly older man who used his authority wisely and justly. He was then and had always been the unconditional monarch of his home, but with the birth of little Ljolja, a child queen would soon reign. She would rule her father not by strength and power, but by charm and an innate sense of self-determination.

The family lived in the majestic, sweeping General Staff Building in the very heart of Imperial Russia, directly across from the Romanov Winter Palace. During the summer months they stayed at their private estate in Peterhof, a beautiful town off the coast of Finland, a town where the Tsar and his family also spent summers at one of the many royal palaces.

The St. Petersburg that Lou would remember from her childhood had an eerie magnificence. Set against the blue and white winter sky, it seemed to Ljolja a colossal celestial city, the city of God, hovering in space. Its opulent buildings with their luminous onion domes glowed like the golden flame of a candle against a crystalline winter background; swirls of pastel and primary colors — turquoise and green, pink and gold — adorned the palaces and churches. Despite the multitude of people on the streets, there were no loud noises. The human voices and the jingling bells of the sleighs sounded like a far-away song, muffled by the voluminous white snow. Even in the daytime, the lights of the shops shone like muted yellow beacons in the vastness of white.

The white nights of summer, too, were strange and dreamlike. To little Ljolja, the stone buildings seem to float weightlessly, as if arising from a dream state. The city interwove an Eastern and Nordic mystique while remaining uniquely Russian.

There was a broad cultural gap between cosmopolitan St. Petersburg and the peasant villages on the vast, bleak Russian plains. Both of Lou's parents were of German heritage, and German was the first language of the household. French (the language of Russian aristocracy) was the second, and Russian came in a distant third. Her father, however, instilled in her a reverence for Russian peasants — he became emotional when he spoke of them. Little Ljolja knew few of them personally, except for her beloved and pretty Russian nanny. She would reach middle age before she discovered the true Russia, when she would return blissfully with her husband and her young lover in tow. But during her childhood she lived in a cocoon of privilege that had little in common with the rest of Russia. And yet, as if through the air, she absorbed the dreamy, exotic atmosphere giving her otherwise German character a mysterious Eastern essence. She was endowed with a German mind and a Russian soul, two conflicting traits that would later make her character distinctive and fascinating to some of the greatest minds of the Western world.

Lou's father impressed her as a loving, godlike figure. Because of his age, he was more grandfatherly than fatherly. At this later stage of life he was warm and demonstrative, lavishing his golden haired daughter with hugs, kisses and presents. "I was deeply moved by the nature of his devotion,"[6] she wrote. His strong, manly presence was accompanied by a humble, childlike warmth. Though he seldom expressed it, he had become deeply religious by the time Lou was born. It was through his intercession that the Tsar allowed a German Reform Church to be established in St. Petersburg.

Lou was the only girl in the von Salomé family, and her three older brothers had a tremendous influence on her. Alexander, called Sasha, was the oldest. Kind-hearted and full of life, he had great sense of humor and an infectious laugh. "He was my security,"[7] Lou wrote. The second brother, Robert, was, according to his little sister, artistic and sensitive but became an engineer because their father commanded it. The third brother, Eugene, whose Russian nickname was Zhénya or Jenia, was her closest companion in her youth. Jenia taught Lou healthy lessons in her childhood, lessons she heeded throughout her life. Once when she was angry she attempted to throw a cup of hot milk on him, but instead spilled it on herself. *See what happens when you attempt to hurt someone else*, he told her sagaciously, *it always comes back on you*. This lesson in reciprocity no doubt helped build her empathetic and understanding nature for which she was later noted.

She considered Jenia a born diplomat, but the patriarch of the family forced him to become a doctor. Jenia obeyed his father's edict and became a pediatrician. He fulfilled his obligation well, developing a special rapport with children and the highest respect within court. Tall and thin, he was somewhat unattractive, but women were nonetheless magnetically drawn to him. Yet he never married and lived with their mother until his early death at forty.

Even though her brothers were away at school or had married and moved away during her childhood, their existence gave Lou a sense of security, a comfort level that she took everywhere with her. She would always be at ease in a man's world. "Fraternal solidarity was so much a part of experience within the family, as the youngest sibling and the only sister," she wrote in her memoirs, "that it continued to exercise its influence upon my relationship to men throughout my life."[8] Years later she would feel at home in the assemblage of the Freudian circle, where she was often the only woman present. So deep was her respect for her brothers that whenever she had self-doubt she comforted herself with the thought that she came from the same family as those admirable men.

Although her fraternal solidarity with her brothers and father was strong, she felt quite remote from her mother. The open affection she shared with her father always ceased when her mother entered the room. Her father would always rise and bow to his wife chivalrously. Lou's mother didn't approve of public displays of physical affection, but graciously accepted her husband's courtesy at a distance. Neither would the elder Louise von Salomé take her husband's gallantly offered arm in public, while little Ljolja was proud to be escorted by him. Lou's childhood memories, written in her old age, came after years of study with Sigmund Freud. Her account of a time when she requested that her mother, while swimming in a lake, would "please drown"[9] must have fit into what she saw as a female version of an Oedipus complex. But it seemed to Lou that the sense of rivalry with her mother began at her birth. She tells us that although General von Salomé was thrilled to have a little girl after so many boys, Mushka — as they called their mother — would have preferred "a round half dozen boys."[10] Frau von Salomé preferred things to be uniform and unvarying. She had a sense of order and duty which she never questioned. As an adult, Lou felt her mother had repressed her own independent nature in taking on the role of wife and mother, and expected others to have the same high level of self-sacrifice and self-control as she did.

Ljolja most certainly inherited her mother's disposition for self-sacrifice, and throughout her lifetime would work excessively, despite physical illness. But mentally, she was as free as a bird, and intended to let no cage hold her. Soon she would be questioning everything her mother held sacrosanct — most notably the unequivocal obedience to parents, husband and God.

Lou's parents had different points of view on some things, but they were in complete agreement about religion. They were both extremely pious and instilled Lutheran values into all their children. Prayer meetings were a regular feature of family life. God was an ever-present entity in the daily life of the little girl. Beyond family life, in the streets of St. Petersburg, the chants and prayers of religions from all over the world could be heard in the multi-national city: Russian Orthodox, Muslim and Buddhist. Lou grew up in a world rich with God's presence.

Despite the large and loving household, Lou spent long hours of solitude during which her remarkably vivid imagination took free rein. She made up stories spontaneously, inspired by the people bustling around the Palace in St. Petersburg, or by the nature walks she took at the summer estate off the coast of Finland. She created characters and stories that took on a greater reality to her than reality itself. Feeling so godlike in her creation, she once worried: what would happen to her fantastical creations if something happened to *her*? She arranged her world of fantasy not chronologically, but based on her perceptions. A passing schoolboy and an old man going by would be transformed into the different stages of life in one individual. Thus, all people, and experiences became part of the tapestry she was weaving, uninhibited by the fabric of time and space. Once, lost in one of her make-believe stories, she noticed a bunch of violets while walking in the woods. Upon returning home, she realized she had gathered them into a bouquet, without any recollection of doing so. Her heart was filled with gratitude for this small miracle she felt God had bestowed upon her. Whenever beauty came into her life she felt a deep sense of appreciation. These gifts from God, as she saw them, gave her a sense of wonder and gratitude that stayed with her throughout her life.

It was the strength of her imagination and the awe she felt for her father that caused Lou to have what she described as a "deep primal intimacy"[11] with God from a very young age. Rather than turn to the outside world, Ljolja relied on her inner world as reality. She devoted herself to her intimate God and shared in his role as creator. She was not only a creator of stories but a co-creator of worlds. Each night she would recount everyday occurrences and her fantasy stories to God. Despite knowing that God already *knew*, she felt this communication was a necessity, "to provide God with the entire world which paralleled our secret one."[12] She lavished in the maternal warmth and the fatherly power of a god who made her own parents — even the whole of the external world — almost superfluous. And while she felt she was every bit as powerful and omnipotent as God, she was not quite as perfect as God was.

Years later when she found this poem among her childhood mementos, Lou felt she was reading an unknown poet:

> I do not wish to flee from pain
> Nor ask that love be true;
> All I want is some broad plain
> To kneel upon beneath you.[13]

Written at their summer home in Finland, "under the magical glow of the white summer nights,"[14] the sentiment expressed was not a schoolgirl's reciting of what she believed was required of her, but a deeply felt conviction, one that continued, in one form or the other, throughout her life.

But what made her accept such a fantasy as real? she queried herself in old age. And then she gave an answer that reveals her Freudian training: Arrested development, brought on by "an all-too-religious upbringing."[15] Unable to accept any realistic boundaries enforced on her, she remained in her world of fantasy far too long.

To illustrate her inability to accept life's restrictions, she gives an example of her relationship to her own image in a mirror. As a child she hated to look in mirrors because the reflection was not how she saw herself in her imagination. The image was limited and separate from her world at large. Disliking the feeling of being a finite being, limited by her own outline, she avoided the mirrors. Unlike Narcissus who so loved his own image that he drowned in it, Ljolja refused to accept that she was merely a small being. She knew herself to be greater than this simple outline — she who secretly ruled over the Russian general's court. And it was the flat refusal of limitations that would become the most powerful characteristic of her life.

But the loss of her all-powerful faith in God came to Ljojla in early adolescence, swiftly and without warning. An otherwise innocuous event triggered the major crisis of her life, an event she would later recount in a short story, "The Hour without God," and her memoirs.

One cold winter day a servant delivered eggs from their country home to their Petersburg residence. Teasing the sheltered and impressionable child, he told her a man and a woman had appeared at the country estate, standing before the door of her playhouse, wanting to come in from the cold. But he told them to go away. Excessively worried that they may have frozen to death, the next time she saw the servant she asked if the homeless couple were still standing out in the cold. No, he told her, a strange thing happened. They grew thinner and thinner until they collapsed and disappeared, leaving nothing behind but the buttons from their clothes, and where they had stood "the ground was still covered with frozen tears."[16]

Not realizing that the servant was referring to a snowman and woman, the susceptible girl believed that real people had disappeared before her playhouse. Distraught she turned to God, seeking his guidance as to what happened to the man and woman — and how could it be that people disintegrated in this manner? That night, distraught with fear, she asked God what had happened to those poor people who stood before her playhouse. Then she waited for his answer. If only the explanation that the servant was playing a trick had come into her tortured mind, she would have been appeased. But all she heard was a deathly silence. A horrifying realization came to her. It was as if a door had opened in her mind to reveal something too horrible to face. In an instant she was plucked from the benevolent world of her magnificent imagination and she saw her aloneness in the world. But this was not simply a personal catastrophe; God was lost to the whole universe as well. She would look back on it as a second birth, as if she had been thrust into the world a second time, to be confronted with sobering reality.

Ironically, the adolescent Ljolja became better behaved after losing God. She felt pity for her poor parents who continued to believe so strongly in the illusion. She discontinued changing the little weekly calendar in her room, with 52 biblical sayings, leaving it on a week a saying that advised her to *Study to be quiet and to work with your own hands*. She had left the calendar unturned — and it would remain in her room on that page for years — because of her estrangement from God. And yet, after looking at the words day after day in her youth, they became emblazoned in her mind, so that they seemed to be the last word God sent before his departure. She held those words as her motto until she later replaced them with a new motto from a man she would see as "the prophet of a new religion, one who recruits heroes as disciples"[17]: *Turn away from half measures and be resolute in living, wholly, fully, beautifully.*

At seventeen, Lou had few friends among the girls of the Romanov court. She didn't attend social functions and felt she had little in common with her peers. Her only confidante was a maiden aunt named Caro, an intelligent and charming woman with strong opinions. Unlike the elder Louise von Salomé, who believed women had one option in life, and that was to be devoted to her husband and family, Caro believed strongly that a woman could choose unrestrained freedom over family life. She conceded that women had natural drives to form relationships, but by asserting her will, she could retain a sense of individuality, rather than being submerged by others. An original thinker, Caro didn't consider herself a feminist but believed in personal development and conscious choice nonetheless. It was a way of thinking that would strongly influence her young niece who was fervently searching for answers.

Ljolja had been receiving instruction for her religious confirmation from the family pastor, Herman Dalton. Dalton had become concerned with the girl's religious development when, after he stated to her Sunday school class that one could not conceive of any place without God, the precocious girl answered, oh yes, one can — in Hell! Dalton was not pleased.

Although Ljolja had no intention of confirming herself in a faith she no longer believed, she let Pastor Dalton talk her into continuing her instruction during her father's illness. But the teenager was biding her time until she figured out a way to get out of the prescribed confirmation ceremony, which to her would be hypocrisy.

Visiting with Caro in Berlin that summer, Lou confessed her loss of faith and the feeling of isolation it caused her. Caro knew of an extremely popular if somewhat independent-thinking clergyman named Hendrik Gillot, from the Dutch Reform Church in St. Petersburg. He was considered one of the most important men in St. Petersburg, as well as an opponent of the von Salomé family pastor, Herman Dalton. In Gillot's country of origin, Holland, he had published a book titled *The History of Divine Worship, According to Liberal German Theologian Otto Pfleiderer*. As a proponent of the Reformed Protestant movement, Gillot believed in sound intellect rather than blind faith. He was considered a nonconformist (albeit a beloved one) as well as a leader of the Reform movement within the community. Caro believed this could be the right person to help Lou in her desperate state. But she had no idea how strong an effect this man would have on her niece's life.

2

Ecce Homo

It was as if he were Lord and instrument in one, educing and seducing me toward my own deep inclinations.

— Lou Andreas-Salomé
Looking Back: Memoirs

Upon returning to St. Petersburg, Lou went to hear the 40-year-old Gillot speak at the Dutch church. He was a boyish-looking Dutchman with fine, almost delicate features and pale blond hair. As he began to speak and gesture in his comfortable yet enthralling style, she was struck to the core with a feeling of simpatico. His apparent strength of character appealed to her more than his words. She knew right away he was a kindred spirit, who would release her from her isolation. This is the person she'd been searching for, she told herself: *I must speak with him.* She promptly wrote him a letter that hardly seems to have been written by a seventeen-year-old girl to a 40-year-old man. It has a sort of directness that is undaunted by convention — the first indication of the bold and earnest personality to come. Treating him as the confessor of her innermost feelings, she told him of her loss of faith, her all-too-powerful inner world and her feelings of isolation.

> The person writing to you, Herr Pastor, is a seventeen-year-old girl who is lonely in the midst of her family and surroundings, lonely in a sense that no one shares her views, let alone satisfies her longing for fuller knowledge. Perhaps it is my whole way of thinking that isolates me from most girls of my age and of our circle....[1]

No one in her family suspected her loss of faith, she told him. But now the time had come to be confirmed and she couldn't go through with it. "For even in a girl there can be a wild, untamable longing for everything ideal."[2]

2. Ecce Homo

Her letter touched him and he responded with the instant affection that Ljolja aroused in many. *Yes*, he wrote back, *come to see me.*

When she entered his house he put his arms around her. For Gillot, it was the warm embrace of brotherly love. For Ljolja it was the life-saving rescue from a life of fantasy that too soon was disrupted by the loss of God.

Years later, Lou looked back on this significant moment in her life and stressed the enormous importance of idealized love in youth. She asked: Don't such feelings arise from our souls' mingling with the primal life force itself, a merging of inner and outer reality? Aren't our fantasies the fuel of our existence — and when they come into being, isn't that what gives our life *meaning*? Gillot was the embodiment of her wishes and dreams — and as such the real man was secondary to what he represented to her, and the heights of ecstasy to which she rose. What others might have undervalued as simply a schoolgirl crush, Lou saw as the magic, the alchemy that propelled her into the world of intellect.

Alone with Gillot in his study, she felt as if his pale brilliant eyes penetrated her thoughts and feelings, making her feel naked before him, more than naked — as if he could see into her soul.

Nervous and shaking, she poured out her feelings in a polite but unrestrained way. She had no one she could talk to, she confided, no one who could understand what she felt. She wanted to escape the fantasy world of her childhood, to be guided into the real world with a firm hand and intelligent mind. She didn't want to continue with the dogmatic confirmation instruction with Pastor Dalton. She wanted something more. But she couldn't reveal such feelings to her family, particularly her beloved father.

Pastor Gillot agreed to help her. But he warned her that his training would be thorough and rigorous. She would have to give up wasting her time on fantasy stories and learn to think and write rationally. In her words, he intended to *de-Russianize* her. First, he rid her of the Russian nickname, Ljolja. Since he couldn't pronounce the Russian jumble of consonants in her name, he gave her a simple if somewhat masculine name: Lou. It was a name she would adopt and keep the rest of her life. She even preferred the masculine sound of it — didn't she want to be a boy as much as her mother had wanted the even half-dozen? And Gillot had given it to her, as if she were being reborn in his image.

She arranged to meet with him again, and they began her secret lessons.

As her private teacher, Gillot took the girl's trust seriously: he aimed to cleanse her of fantasies and help her develop clear and rational thought. This enlightened, dynamic, supremely confident man seemed to be the only human on Earth to match — and even surpass — the willfulness of young Lou. His intensity and drive thrilled her and even though it took a great deal of her strength, she submitted completely to his rules. "I must know and hear everything that passes through this fantasy-filled, useless head,"[3] Erik, a school teacher modeled on Gillot in her autobiographical novel *Ruth*, tells her. At first, Lou was defiant and refused to hand over her autonomy to this tyrannical man. But in an almost brutal fashion Gillot demanded that she submit to his instruction, and his strength of mind inflamed her; she found herself drawing pleasure from her forced subservience.

Gillot's demand that she bring her make-believe world into the light of reality was a dangerous mixture of talk therapy, intellectual enlightenment and erotic stimulation. He demanded that she tell him everything. He required that she give up the tyranny of her own ego — her sheltering inner world of fantasy — and submit to him, thereby rising to her higher self.

"How difficult this yielding must have been," Caro wrote her, "especially for you; I know you so well!"[4] "[T]he more difficult I found it," Lou confessed, "the more passionately I listened to him." [5] In the novel *Ruth*, Ruth's teacher, Erik, tells her the secret desire of every man: to rule over, to love and be responsible for a woman. This is what brings happiness to a man. As much as Lou fought it, she was seduced by it. And even though Gillot was a stern and demanding teacher, he was fueled by his desire to mold this marvelous genius of a girl. "It was as if he were Lord and instrument in one," Lou would later write, "educing and seducing me toward my own deep inclinations."[6]

Playing God with her nebulous mind, Gillot began instructing her in a rigorous study of philosophy and religion. He assembled great philosophic works before her. To his great surprise the seventeen-year-old could quickly absorb anything he gave her. She studied Descartes and Pascal in French. She learned Dutch in order to study Gillot's copy of Kant. She wrote copious and insightful notes on Kierkegaard, Rousseau, Voltaire, Spinoza and Schopenhauer. Gillot exposed her to the great religious texts of the world and many of the great writers. The Dutch God-intoxicated Spinoza became her favorite philosopher and Goethe her favorite writer.

So confident was Gillot in her intellectual abilities that he allowed her to write some of his sermons — until she included a passage from Goethe's *Faust* that seems to be more about her feelings for Gillot than about religion:

> Call it Bliss! Heart! Love! God!
> I have no name for it!
> Feeling is all;
> Name is but sound and smoke
> Shrouding the glow of heaven. —[7]

According to Lou, it brought him a reprimand from the Dutch ambassador, who probably was somewhat leery of Gillot's cutting edge sermons already.

In February 1879 — the same month she would turn eighteen — Lou's beloved father died. If a world without God was to be endured, she would now have to face a world without her father's strong and loving presence. But, no longer harboring the fear that she might disappoint him, she decided to let her true feelings be known. She firmly decided she would not go through with the confirmation with Pastor Dalton that she had been putting off for several years. Worse yet, she told her mother about the covert lessons with Pastor Gillot.

Lou's mother was at wit's end. To Louise, and to Petersburg society, conformation was not a choice but an essential. She wrote to Caro expressing the helplessness she felt before her daughter's refusal to be confirmed by the family pastor. "You ask me to treat her lovingly, but how is that possible with such a stubborn person who always has to have things her own way in everything?"[8] She complained that Lou refused to go through with the confirmation because it would be "a lie and a crime," yet had no problem being less than scrupulous about her secret meetings with Gillot. In April she told Caro she wanted to meet with Pastor Gillot and discuss her daughter.

The handsome pastor arrived at the von Salomé residence and went into the visiting room with Lou's mother, leaving Lou no choice but to listen through the door. Though outwardly decorous, Frau von Salomé feared her daughter would be compromised. Gillot informed her that their actions were respectable and, as Lou put it, "It was impossible to do wrong."[9] Lou heard her mother warn him, "You bear the responsibility for harming my daughter." To which he replied, "I want to be responsible for this child."[10] The struggle was short-lived. Frau von Salomé gave in to Gillot's persuasive argument that this young genius of a girl needed his specialized intellectual guidance.

But no sooner had she agreed, than another storm was looming on the horizon.

That there was an erotic element in the teacher-pupil relationship was quite obvious to Lou. But she loved him in an idealized way — he was her lost god, a father figure. She and her aunt Caro openly discussed erotic implications of the relationship: "how heavily he must suffer from a conflict of feelings raging within him ... but what strength of will this man must possess!"[11] Lou was not secretive about her own love for this older, married man; neither was she morally conflicted. She believed in the absolute purity of their love. She worshipped Gillot and felt she would do anything he asked her to do. But when during one of her lessons he suddenly, as she put it, *approached the subject of marriage* (though, given her reaction, it seems more likely he approached her physically), a shock came over her. Just as sudden as the disillusionment she had experienced with God was her sense that a veil had lifted now: she saw Gillot as a mere man rather than the exalted being she had imagined. She was overwhelmed by the revelation and rejected him out of shock.

> All of the sudden that which I had worshipped dropped from my heart and feelings and became something foreign — something that made its own demands, something that no longer brought my own fulfillment, on the contrary, threatened it....[12]

Her sudden and horrified disillusionment makes more sense when being caused by the mad kisses of a middle-aged married man of God — as she depicts a similar scenario in a novel years later — rather than by a man simply "approaching the subject" of marriage. While it probably wouldn't have bothered the free-minded Lou to admit that *Ljolja's* love story had what we now consider *Lolita* elements, she most likely wanted to protect herself, Gillot and her family and even her own idealization from the more prurient details of her chaste first love. Her horrified reaction wasn't caused by the fact that he was married, she tells us in her memoir. It was because someone she had worshipped like a divine being had fallen to earth. Her fantasy collapsed under the weight of reality, and like her childhood vision of God, it left her feeling cold and alone. In the novella, called *Deviations*, she reexamines the pivotal moment in her life, concluding that both characters suffered from delusions about one another. Delusion and love become synonymous in this tale. Gillot was a confident man, and he had little doubt about the intensity of his protégé's love for him. What he didn't know was the strength of his own delusion. If the situation had been brought to what Lou called a *human conclusion*, her fantasy image of him as a god-man would certainly have been destroyed.

In her memoir Lou accounts a time in childhood when her father bought her a present, telling her there were splendid dresses made of gold inside. When she was told they were actually made of paper trimmed with gold, she refused to open the box, thus retaining her fantasy vision forever: "Thus the clothes remained golden in my mind."[13]

"Still," she later wrote, "my deification of [Gillot] had been right for me," because she needed him in order "to come to terms with myself."[14] The desire to be guided by and adhere to her inner world rather than the outer one was at once strange and brilliant, a trait that would make her a unique force in the world of intellect.

The universe seemed always to collaborate with Lou's inner world, and the shock and disillusionment of losing her defied love now prompted her to take a new path. Lou was inspired by her *Lord and instrument*. She wanted to escape Russia and embrace the Western world of intellect, the world which Gillot represented to her. It was Gillot's teachings that had inspired her desire for freedom. Rather than cling to the illusion she had of Gillot, she chose to enter his world. Rather than cling to the love of her life, which would have caused difficulty for her and others, she let his love inspire her to a unique and genuine life. In a critique on Ibsen's plays she wrote years later, she drew out a notable quote that clearly applied to her movement away from Gillot: "The transformation came when you let me choose freely."[15] Never in her life would she regard love as a possessive emotion. Never would she enslave herself to the love of one man, nor would she be possessive of others. Hers was a generous, bounteous offering, and the world would give back in equal measure. A poem she wrote at this time expresses the excitement she felt for life:

> *A Prayer to Life*
>
> Indeed I love you as a friend
> Loves a friend, in all your mystery —
> Whether I wept or laughed again,
> Whether you brought pain or joy
>
> I love you even for the harm you do;
> And if you must destroy me,
> I'll tear myself from you
> As I would leave a friend.
>
> I embrace you with all my might!
> Let your flames set me on fire,

> And in the glow of that last fight
> I will explore your riddle's depths.
>
> To be for centuries! To live
> Wrap your arms around me once again:
> If you have no more joy to give —
> At least you still grant pain.[16]

Friedrich Nietzsche, whom she would meet within a year, would call her poem heroic in attitude: "[I]t sounds like a voice for which I've waiting and waiting since childhood."[17] Sigmund Freud, whom she will befriend later in her life, will teasingly tell her that a bad head cold would have cured her of such enthusiasm for life's pain. Biographer Angela Livingstone calls the poem "a prayer without God"[18] and writes that Lou "sent her love out not to one man but to something far more vast and diffuse, something she could think of as wholly and uniquely intoxicating; life itself, the very sensation of it."[19]

The Sunday in May, in the simple Dutch church, was the most significant moment in Lou von Salomé's life — a life that seemed to be full of significant events. The ceremony changed Gillot "from a God into His priest," and he "became he who confirmed me in my quest for all things great and beautiful."[20] It was important not only that Gillot loved her but that he sent her off into the world with an armor of intellect, what Lou would call "a boyish readiness."[21] What Gillot had intended to be a Pygmalion story, Lou had transformed into the birth of Athena, the virgin goddess who aligned with the heroes of Ancient Greece. Just as Athena was the patron goddess of Odysseus and Jason, Lou would align herself with the intellectual heroes of Europe — Nietzsche, Rilke and Freud were only a few of the luminaries.

She had a vague goal at the moment: she wanted to study among intellectuals and she wanted to be free to pursue her intellectual quest. Gillot was the major muse of her life, and she wanted to devote her passions to the world in the loving and demanding way he had devoted himself to her. She would soon become one of the most inspirational women Europe had ever known.

3
Girl Genius

[Lou von Salomé] is a phenomenon that scarcely seems possible.... She is a person of genius.[1]
— Ferdinand Tönnies

In September 1880, Lou von Salomé and her mother settled in at a charming country home with the Brandt family, friends of the von Salomé family, just outside of Zurich. Her mother had insisted on escorting her, but Lou wasn't about to let that hinder her freedom. The University of Zurich was the first European university open to women, and there were many young, serious-minded women from Russia seeking an intellectual freedom that was wasn't possible in their homeland.

Lou began the study of her two great passions: religion and philosophy. In her class readings she studied philosophers and theologians of both East and West. She read the sacred texts of the world — the *Rig-Veda*, the *Tao Te Ching* and Confucius. She took on Goethe and Victor Hugo in her spare time. Her intense desire to learn caught the attention of her professors. She developed a special rapport with theologian Alois Biedermann. Biedermann wrote to Lou's mother of his "heartfelt interest in the spiritual and intellectual life of this most unusual girl ... pure and genuine being ... an unusual woman possessing both childlike purity and integrity of mind as well as unchildlike, almost unfeminine direction of spirit and independence of will. In both, she is a *jewel*."[2] Biedermann gave Lou a copy of his book, *Christian Dogmatic Theology*, in which in which he denied the historicity of the Gospels while upholding the eternal ideas which they embody. He inscribed it, "For the Spirit searcheth all things, yea, the deep things of God."[3]

In a feverish state Lou filled notebooks full of comments and observations. Her mind was bursting into bloom in the intellectual atmosphere that had previously been forbidden to women. Biedermann's lectures fused with her own opinions: "In the religious act we cannot imagine God except personally, indeed according to our own personality. But we can *think* him absolutely. Light falls into a room in the form of the opening through which it enters."[4] She entered a poetry circle led by one of her professors, Gottfried Kinkel, who was charmed by her poems and even more by her.

During that first year Lou drove herself to the breaking point, obsessively studying beyond endurance, just as she had done with Gillot. She transferred the pain of her lost love — and lost illusion — into a fiery energy. She drew perverse pleasure from her state of feverish bliss — "the way after the break with Gillot, I *fell* ill in full joy and life-affirmation."[5] Throughout her time in Zurich she suffered from severe coughing and headaches. Zurich was too damp and cold. At the end of the 1881, her mother decided she needed to be in a warmer climate to restore her health. In January of 1882 she took her daughter on a trip to Italy to recuperate. There Lou would have an encounter that would affect her for the rest of her life.

After traveling through several health resorts, with her health improving, Lou and her mother settled in Rome. Lou was less impressed by the ancient ruins than the brilliant Italian sunshine that highlighted them. The manmade world of crumble and decay was less important to her than the inspiration of ever-renewing nature.

By the grace of Gottfried Kinkel, Lou had brought with her a note of introduction to Baroness Malwida von Meysenbug, the famous author of the *Memoirs of an Idealist*. Meysenbug was 65 around the time Lou arrived in Rome, a small elderly woman, simple in bearing and dress, with clear blue eyes, a quick, calm smile and a gentle, kind expression. Meysenbug looked more like a doting grandmother than the radical thinker that she was. Her memoir emphasized the declining power of organized religion in Germany and the escalating influence of German intellectuals and free-thinkers, many of whom were her close friends.

An encounter at Meysenbug's salon would be the first link in a chain of events that would draw Lou closer to the intellectual epicenter of Europe.

In February, Lou was invited to join Meysenbug's philosophical gathering of young educated women known as the Roman Club. Like everyone else who met Lou, Meysenbug was immediately charmed by the brilliant and vivacious young scholar. Soon after meeting Lou, Meysenbug wrote her: "It is long since I have felt such a warm tenderness for a young girl. When I first met you I felt as though my youth was re-arising."[6]

The two women, although far apart in age, shared a similar background of class and religious restrictions, against which they both rebelled. Like Lou, Malwida often expressed an ecstasy of being alive as well as a rapturous desire for knowledge: "To seek communion with stars on bright, lonely nights, to step boldly into the most difficult labyrinth of thought...."[7] After reading some of Lou's poems, Meysenbug wrote,

> They disclose what I behold with ever purer delight: your inner life, which is meant for blossoms so noble that you must keep it most holy.[8]

Lou greatly admired Meysenbug and her accomplishments. But the fundamental differences in their social views quickly came to the fore.

The event that would alter Lou's relationship with Meysenbug began innocently. One evening in March, she and some of the other young ladies were gathered in Malwida's home when the door bell rang. After answering the door Malwida's servant ran in and whispered something to her mistress. Malwida then hurried to her desk, scraped some money together, and then left the room. After a tittering among the girls, Malwida returned with the young Paul Rée, a friend Malwida "loved like a son,"[9] who had come from Monte Carlo in a rush to repay a debt after having "lost everything, literally every penny, gambling."[10] Lou was immediately intrigued by the unconventional entrance and focused her laser-like interest in Rée's direction.

Starting a conversation with him, she quickly discovered he was a writer and philosopher with ideas that excited her. He had a doctorate from Halle and had written a dissertation on Aristotle's ethics. He had published a book of psychological musings and had a special interest in the study of moral conscience. Their conversation was so engrossing they spent several evenings this way, talking excitedly while meandering through the cobblestone streets of Rome to the *pensione* where she and her mother were staying. It was considered scandalous for a young woman to be alone with a man at night, but Lou didn't care what others thought. In fact, she got a certain thrill out of shocking the *bourgeois*. The Russian general's daughter was on a personal crusade, forging a path uniquely her own, and if people wanted to whisper about her behavior, *let them*.

Lou saw in Rée's eyes "a mixture of humorous contrition and superior kindness."[11] She and Rée developed an immediate rapport, discussing philosophy as well as deep personal feelings in the piercing clarity of the Roman moonlight. Rée spoke of Positivism, a philosophy he embraced. He spoke of his friend, Fritz, a philosophical genius whose thoughts on religion and psychology were highly similar to Lou's.

Lou spoke candidly to Rée about her experience with Gillot, explaining how it had turned her away from the conventional pursuits of a woman of her class — romance and marriage — and had set her on a quest for something altogether unusual for a girl of twenty.

She revealed to Rée a secret dream she harbored, a dream that was as shocking as it was provocative. The radical ideas of the Russian women at the university whom Lou had coyly observed had certainly helped her create such a fantasy. It was a vision of living together with intellectual men — comrades in her philosophical quest. She wanted to go a broad step beyond Meysenbug's co-education salons. It would be noble and emancipated, daring and stimulating.

Rée was at once taken aback and intrigued by Lou's bold vision. But he was not as adventurous as she. By all accounts, he was a reticent and affable man who preferred exercising his radical ideas on paper only.

After several weeks Rée went to Meysenbug and confessed about the nightly walks, fearing that such behavior would compromise the reputation of the salons. Clearly the nightly talk of living together had caused a mixture of emotions within him. He felt unable to resist Lou's magnetism, he told Meysenbug, and thought it best for him to go away. He asked her to make up an excuse for him — his mother was ill or something — but Meysenbug refused. She felt betrayed and offended by the nightly excursions of two of her favorite protégés. She wanted her salons to be thought of as a place where nothing "but the noblest emancipation was encouraged."[12] "And what," she later asked Lou about the midnight walks, "would Rée have done had an officer or anyone else been unpleasant to you — fought a duel?"[13] No, as far as she was concerned Rée had to face up to his behavior.

Despite Rée's predicament and Meysenbug's reservations, Lou persuaded Rée to continue their philosophical discussions, "through the streets of Rome, under the moon and stars,"[14] and managed to convince Meysenbug and her mother that it was all perfectly innocent. However, Rée found it frustrating to be with a girl who at once offered her whole self and yet gave nothing. Wouldn't it be better if they simply got married? And here we get the first glimpse of just how unusual her life will be: She told him she intended to share her life with him, but the convention of marriage was tedious to such an unconventional young woman, who longed to rise above the common and the sensual, to experience the ecstasy of the intellectual. She wanted to fulfill her dream; she wanted a collection of passionate scholars who could guide her inner passions — inspire her as she would inspire them — into intellectual achievement. She had already seen in her mind the house which they'd share, "a pleasant study full of books and flowers, flanked by two bedrooms" where, after an exhaustive day of intellectual effort, they would part to their separate rooms at night, "colleagues, working together in a joyful and earnest bond."[15] This Platonic idyll seemed to be a replay of her childhood with her loving brothers all around, only now she was handpicking her intellectual brothers.

Earlier both Meysenbug and Rée had written to Fritz Nietzsche about Lou, whose radical thinking seemed simpatico with his. "[A] very remarkable girl," Meysenbug had written, recommending that he "spend some time together with this remarkable creature."[16] Rée's letter to Nietzsche about Lou did not survive, but Nietzsche's reply was typical of the philosopher's dramatic and mischievous style: "Greet the Russian girl for me, if you think there is any sense in doing so; I lust after souls of this kind. I even plan to go on the prowl for one soon — I need them because of what I plan to do in the next ten years. Marriage is another matter...."[17]

Lou was eager to meet the genius whose philosophy sounded so close to her heart. Now Lou wondered: what if Nietzsche joined them in their study plan for the coming winter months? Rée considered. Perhaps the esteemed professor *would* give the living arrangements respectability.

When Meysenbug and Lou's mother found out about Lou's talk of setting up house with Rée and Nietzsche they rose to a new level of outrage. Although Lou expected, even anticipated, her mother's disapproval, she was disappointed by Meysenbug's opposition. The mother of revolutionary ideas had no real courage in her thinking, Lou protested. Her "idealism" stifled Lou's "impulse towards a totally unrestrained freedom."[18]

Her impulse towards unrestrained freedom. It's a phrase she heeded throughout her life. It was more of a wild compulsion than an impulse. Her impulse for freedom drove her every thought, feeling, and desire. And not only was she determined to defend her freedom, but she was driven to make her private dreams into public statements. Anyone who stood in her way was doomed to disappointment. She seemed to be announcing to the world, "I will live and work with whomever I choose, and that has nothing to do with my moral character." She did not intend to tip-toe around the issue of men and women working together as Meysenbug did, but to ram it head on. Of course, Meysenbug's disapproval did nothing to dissuade her. Idealists lacked courage, Lou griped.

Frau von Salomé, beleaguered and distressed by her daughter's latest campaign, wrote to Pastor Gillot back in Petersburg, hoping he might have some sway over his former protégée. But apparently he had no sway whatsoever. After receiving his warning that her plan to live with the two older men was preposterous, Lou wrote back:

> I can neither live according to models, nor will I serve as a model for anyone else; but I will structure my life in accordance of myself, no matter what the consequences. This is not a principle I'm following, but something more wonderful — something that exists inside me, hot with life, something that wants to burst....
>
> You also write: you had always thought of this wholehearted devotion to purely intellectual goals as a "transition" for me. Well, what do you mean by transition? If any other goals are supposed to stand behind it such as would make one give up the most magnificent and most hard-won thing on earth, namely freedom, then I want to stay forever in transition, for I shall not give that up.[19]

Gillot had no counter argument to this declaration. Despite the maturity she showed in pursuing her goals, in that same letter we are reminded she was a coquettish teenager. She made a point of detailing how she had persuaded Rée to go along with the plan: "...on our nightly walks between 12:00 and 2:00 in the Roman moonlight ... I expounded it to him more and more successfully." If this detail was meant to reassure Gillot of her pure-mindedness, it was off mark. If it was meant to make Gillot jealous, then she was on target.

No one could be happier than she was, she told him:

> because the bright, pious, and joyful battle for that freedom which is now beginning does not scare me, on the contrary, let it begin! ...But I would be shocked if you didn't give me your spiritual support. You write with some annoyance that your advice won't do much good. "Advice"— No! What I need from you is certainly exceedingly more than an advice: it is trust.[20]

He should be singing her praises, she exclaimed. Look how well she'd learned her lessons from him. She was not indulging in fantasy, but making her dreams a reality — and what a reality. Could he have picked anyone more brilliant than Friedrich Nietzsche? That she saw his letter as provincial and pedantic is clear. "I became what I am through you," she concludes and signs it, "Your girl."[21]

In March 1882, Friedrich Nietzsche set forth on what he called a Columbus-like voyage, sailing first to Messina. His end goal was not so clear, but he planned on stopping off at Rome to meet with Rée and his Russian discovery. When Rée had not received word from Nietzsche by

April 20, he sent a letter, encouraging him to come to Rome soon. By delaying his arrival, Rée told him, he had "stricken the Russian girl with astonishment and distress. She has in fact grown eager to see and speak with you."[22] He goes on, as if to entice Nietzsche into speeding up his voyage, "She is a forceful, unbelievably clever being with the most girlish, even childlike qualities. She would so much, as she put it, like to make a nice year of it...."[23]

Soon afterwards Nietzsche arrived in Rome, the dazzling city that held ancient ruins, the throne of Catholicism, brilliant sunshine and the extraordinary Russian girl, Lou von Salomé.

4

The Nietzsche Experience

A real man wants two things: danger and play. Therefore he wants woman as the most dangerous plaything.
— Friedrich Nietzsche
Thus Spoke Zarathustra

To the modern world the name *Nietzsche* has a taint of the ominous, the mystifying and the misunderstood. In the movie *2001: A Space Odyssey*, we witness the birth of the space age *Übermensch* accompanied by the commanding music written in Nietzsche's honor, with its soul-stirring drum beat and heralding trumpets. We associate him with the evolutionary coming of the higher man, as well as the farthest reaches of genius and madness.

Lou von Salomé would later call him a mystical philosopher of the will, a prophet who sought heroes for disciples. His writings were explosive, and yet profoundly creative, bursting with life, with a bold flair that was unsurpassable: "I am not a man, I am dynamite."[1] A great lover of music, he infused his work with a poetic rhythm and power that could only be matched by a Wagnerian opera. Like an alchemist, Lou wrote, "he had the creative gift for transposing the most sober or ugly thought into an inner music.... Nietzsche's transformation of mere thought into something really experienced was like no one else's...."[2] His inner life was so alive that the outer world became superfluous: "[Y]ou sudden sparks and wonder of my solitude," Lou quotes him from *Beyond Good and Evil*, "you, my old beloved, wicked thoughts!"[3] His thought, she says, "enthralled his entire person: more than thinking an idea through, he lived it with passion and with such measureless abandon that it exhausted him."[4]

Nietzsche's prose is almost a living organism and he plays the trickster god behind it. If you take his writing too literally, he mocks you. If you take him too seriously, he'll make a fool of you. If you don't heed his words, he has contempt for you. If you don't grasp his complexities — well, then, you have his pity. History is speckled with dangerous men who took Nietzsche too literally and failed to grasp his complexities.

Walter Kaufmann, a leading translator of Nietzsche, points out in an introduction to Nietzsche's works how far and wide Nietzsche's influence has been. While all 20th century philosophers, especially Jean-Paul Sartre, have registered his impact since his death, Kaufmann believes that Nietzsche's influence on literature and psychology is even greater. Kaufmann's list of writers and poets that show a sharp influence of Nietzsche is extensive: Camus, Gide, Malreux, Thomas Mann, Hermann Hesse, Rilke, Stefan George, Christian Morgenstern, Gottfried Benn, Shaw, Yeats, Joyce and Eugene O'Neill. Lou's encounter with Nietzsche affected her whole body of her work in various ways. During her lifetime, she became a sort of personal spokesperson for his significance and resonance in the world of intellect. Lou called Nietzsche "the solitary genius of mankind, who alone is capable of interpreting the totality of the past from the vantage point of the present ... deciding the future as a totality with its goal and significance — even into the far reaches of all eternity."[5] She generates an image of him standing atop the highest mountain with an infinite overview — from ancient to modern man and beyond: this is Nietzsche's legacy.

As a child, Lou had enjoyed a fantastical Russian childhood sheltered by the rich court life of St. Petersburg. By stark contrast, Nietzsche learned about madness and death at an early age. His father, a Lutheran pastor from a long line of distinguished pastors, developed a brain disease when Nietzsche was only five. He watched his father suffer, bedridden and insane, for months before his death.

Within a year of his father's death, his younger brother died, leaving Nietzsche to be raised in a solely female household, which included his mother (who was the daughter of a pastor as well), his paternal grandmother, his younger sister, and two maiden aunts. Piousness was serious business in the Nietzsche household and all these devout women doted and focused on the religious development of the brilliant little boy. Nietzsche was nicknamed "the little pastor" because of his serious and religious nature. It was presumed he would follow the path of his father and both his maternal and paternal grandfathers, who were pastors as well.

He showed early signs of genius in writing out the details of everything that interested him, even his childhood games with playmates. At age fourteen, he precociously wrote his autobiography. In his account of his brother's death he says he dreamed he saw his father taking a child in his arms into his grave with him. Within hours, he says, his brother died. The sense of guilt or responsibility for the death of loved ones is a common feature in children. There is an echo of collective responsibility and guilt in his most famous statement: *God is dead,* and its lesser known follow-up: *We have murdered him.*

The precise period of Nietzsche's loss of faith is difficult to pinpoint, but perhaps the early loss of his father may have planted the seed, an "act of God" which would seem senseless to his young probing mind. The mind that would not be satisfied by religion's vague answers to life's hardest questions began to surface in his teenage years. At fifteen he wrote a versed drama about the Titan Prometheus, who defied the gods in favor of human freedom and power. In adolescence he became preoccupied with the search for knowledge. When he read the Germanic sagas, he reported that "every word was like lightning, powerful and full of significance."[6] He recognized that language could exert a magical power to move its audience and "pierce its way into life. Nietzsche sought to infuse his own writing with the words that would wield the magical power to 'shatter his audience.'"[7] It is the *piercing* and *shattering* quality of his work that is most striking. Biographer Safranski writes that Nietzsche "took pleasure in quoting a verse from a saga: 'We have fought beautifully: we sit on corpses/That we felled, like eagles on branches.'"[8] Utilizing the power of a religious sermon, Nietzsche became a priest of the pre–Christian world — the myths of the Ancient Greeks and the early Nordic tribes. As his philosophy developed, Nietzsche advocated sloughing off what he considered the slave mentality of the Judeo-Christian religion and replacing it with the ancient Greek or the Germanic hero, whom he called "the blond beast of prey."

While Lou's battle cry in her teenage years was for unrestrained freedom, Nietzsche's was for self-mastery. His early loss of his male role model and his subsequent upbringing among doting, extremely pious women caused him to search all of history and mythology for masculine idols. In addition to his admiration for the Nordic warriors, he defiantly worshipped the Greek god of ecstasy, Dionysus, whose lust for life was so much the opposite of Christian ideals. In the earthly realm, he admired men like Goethe and Wagner, whose art rose to the level of epiphany.

While in adolescence Lou sought to escape the fantastical world of her own making, young Nietzsche strove to conquer the academic world with its own weapons. After distinguishing himself in boarding school and college, Nietzsche had become a professor in the Classics department of the University of Basel at the unprecedented age of 24.

A talented amateur musician himself, Nietzsche met and became a devotee of Richard Wagner in 1869. In letters written to friends, Nietzsche proclaimed his admiration of Wagner's visionary genius. Like Nietzsche's philosophy, Wagner's operas looked back to the cult of the Nordic hero as a new world myth.

Wagner's wife, Cosima, was the illegitimate daughter of Franz Liszt. Nietzsche became infatuated with her, but his devotion to Wagner was strong. Inspired by Wagner, Nietzsche wrote his first book, *The Birth of Tragedy*. It establishes him as more than a remarkable scholar. In psychological insight, the work prefigures the archetypal work of Freud and Jung. As a philosopher, he establishes his ability to view the breadth and depth of western culture, from the ancient Greek to the modern European, in one grand sweeping motion. The struggle within the human being, *The Birth of Tragedy* explains, is the struggle between the Apollonian and Dionysian elements within, and from this dynamic struggle, art emerges. Art, then, replaces religion as the true redeemer of mankind.

Apollo is the Greek god who brings light to the world every morning as he ushers the sunrise. He is the god of rationality, laws, order, and patriarchy — the hallmarks of early civilization. His main dictates are *Know thyself, nothing in excess* and *keep women under rule*. But he is also the Greek god of the arts and he presides over the nine Muses, like a conductor of musicians. "The deity of light," writes Nietzsche, is also the ruler "of the inner world of fantasy."[9] Apollo rules over the land of dream and prophecy. This land, Nietzsche says, is the land of the poet. For a poem, as C.G. Jung would later put it, is a dream dreamed onward.

By contrast, Dionysus is the god of ecstasy and divine madness. His ancient celebrants, predominantly women, escaped to the wilderness, where they enjoyed wine and other intoxicants and danced wildly to primitive music that drove them into a state of unrefined rapture. Dionysian music evoked "awe and terror,"[10] Nietzsche says: "at the moment of supreme joy we hear the scream of horror or the yearning lament of irretrievable loss."[11] This is the concept that would later deeply influence the poet Rainer Maria Rilke. Rilke will poetically phrase it: "beauty's nothing but the start of terror we can hardly bear.... Every angel is terrifying."[12] Pain is born of joy, Nietzsche tells us. In a moment of ecstasy we cry out in sounds of agony. When at the greatest point of pleasure, the human being suffers unbearable anguish, because he is conscious of the knowledge that the joy *will not last*.

Dionysus unites us with our animal nature, where we are one with nature and the soul of our race. Dionysus is the spontaneous dance or beating of the drum to express the beauty of life and the horror of loss.

Apollo, Nietzsche says, is the *principium individuationis*, the individual inner life. The Apollonian part of our nature loves beauty, form, and structure. It is the drive behind the Parthenon, Homer's *Iliad* and Michelangelo's *David*.

In Greek mythology, every winter Apollo traveled to the land of the Hyperborean, so Dionysus took over Apollo's shrine in Delphi during the three winter months. Because the two gods alternately shared the same dwelling, Nietzsche concludes that in the Greek psyche these two polar opposites had arrived at reconciliation in the form of artistic expression.

European society had embraced the Apollo archetype, the god of laws and structure, while rejecting Dionysus, who represents the wild lust for living. Even in his academic studies of the ancient Greeks, Nietzsche found that the academic world had repressed the true nature of the Greeks and represented them as all sweetness and light. But, as he points out, the very greatness of the ancient Greeks lies in their ability to embrace this combative duality within, to be fully human and *transcend it through art*. Art verifies that we are animal, human and god all at once. The ancient Greeks who created the magnificent sculptures and structures were the same people who could be utterly cruel and barbaric. They valued laws and democracy, but instituted slavery and fell into decadence. They spoke of equality, but the strong would absolutely dominate the weak. It is the dynamic struggle of the opposing forces in the human being that gives tragic art its deep, emotional resonance. In Homer's *Iliad*, Achilles is at once a great hero, admired by generations of Greeks, and a bloodthirsty warrior who drags Hector's dead body behind his chariot in celebration. The tragedy of Oedipus highlights man's desire to escape his fate as a human animal — a fate of killing and copulating at will — only to find himself ensnared within the murderous and incestuous trap that he sought to escape.

Birth of Tragedy suggests that *both* energies dwell within us and must be honored at their proper time, just as Dionysus was honored at Apollo's shrine. European culture had for too long honored the Apollonian and turned away from the Dionysian in disgust.

In her book on Nietzsche, Lou describes his concept of Dionysus:

The Dionysian he took to be the orgiastic element as it is lived in blissful raptures, in the mixture of pain and lust, of joy and horror, and in self-obliterating drunkenness of Dionysian festivals. In them the conventional barriers and boundaries of existence are broken, so that the individual seems to melt into the totality of nature again.[13]

Nietzsche's personal approach to art came from a Dionysian source within him. "Mind? What is 'mind' to me? What does knowledge matter?" he would later write to Lou. "I treasure nothing except *impulses*, and I would dare say that we have that in common."[14] "Nietzsche," Lou would write, ""during his Dionysian intoxication, sensed something homogeneous in his own nature — a mysterious unity of being in woe and bliss, self-wounding and self-deification — a life of the emotions heightened into excess, in which all things become mutually dependent...."[15]

The significance of ancient Greek culture, Nietzsche believed, was that it reconciled the disharmony of the Apollonian and Dionysian forces *through art*. Putting it simply, the ancient Greek "was saved by art."[16]

This idea resonated through Wagner's music, Nietzsche believed. It would later resound through the psychological and literary worlds of the late 19th century and into the 20th. It would open the door to the study of Greek myth as key to the human mind and as a psychological path to give meaning to life — from Sigmund Freud's Oedipus complex to James Joyce's *Ulysses*. Lou would write of Nietzsche's first philosophical phase:

> His artistic instinct luxuriated in the revelation of Wagnerian music; his strong predisposition for religious and moralistic exaltations thrived in the metaphysical interpretation of that art and its uplifting potentials; his comprehensions and thorough knowledge, mirrored in his conceptions of Greek culture, served the new-world view as well. Just as in Wagner's person the genius of art and the releasing redeemer had become a reality, so the role of the knower and scientific mediator fell to Nietzsche, for that reason, he saw his mission to be that of the philosopher.[17]

Wagner, who had embraced his intense passions through his art, was to Nietzsche an artist-hero who transcended this basic struggle of the human psyche. His operas were an expression of the terrible beauty of being human, the *overcoming* of the volatile mixture of animal, cultural, intellectual and creative lusts that brew within us all.

The Birth of Tragedy was the sign of things to come from Nietzsche: phenomenal and highly original work that not only influenced two other people who would figure prominently in Lou's life — Rilke and Freud — but cast a long shadow over the 20th century.

Despite his praise of Wagner in *The Birth of Tragedy*, Nietzsche would later lose faith in his idol when he sensed that Wagner's operas began to take on an artificial Christian morality, no doubt influenced by Cosima, whose piety had taken on shades of anti–Semitism. While Nietzsche was staying in Sorrento with Paul Rée, Malwida von Meysenbug and the Wagners, disagreement broke out between Nietzsche and Wagner that caused a permanent rift. When Nietzsche published *Human, All Too Human*, he "took to task geniuses like Wagner, who retain religious incense in their music and art," as Siegfried Mandel, translator of Lou's book on Nietzsche, so aptly puts it. "He put a scalpel to the [anti–Semitism] of his time, exemplified by the Wagners, and declared that the ostracized Jew is an essential 'ingredient for the breeding of the most strong, European race ... to whom one owes the noblest human (Christ) and the purest philosopher (Spinoza) and the greatest book.'"[18] The "life-denying and Catholic-romantic *Parsifal*"—Wagner's latest opera—"stood in contrast to Nietzsche's life-affirming ideals."[19] To Nietzsche it was an intellectual step backwards, taken by a man who he had believed was leading the way to a new consciousness. The loss of faith in his idol was a terrible blow to Nietzsche, and one he lamented throughout his life.

Paul Rée first met Nietzsche in 1873, when he attended Nietzsche's lecture at Basel; he was 23 and Nietzsche was only 26. Rée was in awe of the young scholar who philosophized "with a hammer," who "proclaimed that God was dead, Christianity was a disease and democracy a sham."[20] He enrolled in Nietzsche's pre-platonic philosophy course. The two young philosophers became close friends, and Nietzsche invited Rée to spend winter leave with him in Sorrento, at one of Malwida von Meysenbug's villas. Von Meysenbug took on a motherly role, cooking and cleaning for them while they worked—Nietzsche was writing *Human, All Too Human*, while Rée worked on his ideas on moral philosophy.

At thirty-four, Nietzsche resigned his position at the University of Basel because of his bad eyesight and debilitating headaches. After leaving the university he spent his time traveling from one European retreat to another as he struggled with poor health and loneliness—all the while writing bold and brilliant philosophical works that would echo far beyond his century.

By the spring of 1882, when he arrived in Rome, he had just published *Daybreak* and was completing *The Gay Science*. His restless wandering had become a way of life, and he had most likely given up on the idea of someone relieving his intellectual and spiritual loneliness.

4. The Nietzsche Experience

On April 25, Paul Rée arranged for his two best friends to meet in St. Peter's Basilica. Even though both Lou and Nietzsche had lost their faith in the Christian god, walking through massive slanted rays of sunlight pouring down through the cathedral rotunda clearly heightened the anticipation for them both. Lou recorded her first impression: His appearance was unremarkable, she noted. He was "a man of average height, dressed modestly, but with evident care, of tranquil demeanor, and with plain brown hair combed back," and his mouth was almost completely concealed by his "great, bushy, combed moustache."[21] His nearly blind eyes gave "his features a special kind of magic,"[22] revealing a mind that was both searching within and looking into the future. His eyes stood "like the guardians and protectors of his treasures — silent secrets — not to be glimpsed by the uninvited."[23] Most striking was "his studied, elegant posture."[24] He seemed like a prophet who came out of the mountains, she thought, wearing a mask of civilization. Discovering what lay beneath the mask intrigued Lou.

Bowing in a courtly fashion, he asked, "From what stars have we fallen together here?"[25] Awestruck, she replied, *I came from Zurich*.

After the brief but fateful meeting, Nietzsche retreated to his room with an attack of his reoccurring illness.

Nietzsche had plans to travel to the Italian lakes in the north, and Rée agreed to accompany him. Lou, anxious to meet with Nietzsche again, entreated Rée to make arrangements for her and her mother to meet them there. It was difficult to ask and nerve-wracking waiting for Nietzsche's reply. Lou was so nervous about everything going smoothly, she wrote to Rée pleading, "see to it that our trip comes off—please, please!"[26] Rée wrote back reassuringly. Her wish was his command. "Most commanding Miss Lou! We will travel tomorrow at noon, reaching the lakes Saturday in the morning. Monday in Milan you find a wire *poste restante* on our place of sojourn."[27]

Nietzsche had insisted on meeting Lou's mother before they left for the rendezvous. Rée accompanied Nietzsche to meet Frau von Salomé. Nietzsche was full of praise for her daughter. Frau von Salomé expressed her thanks to the highly esteemed professor for his interest in her daughter's intelligence. But, setting aside any motherly pride, she was concerned about Lou's intellectual pursuits. Perhaps he would consider her old-fashioned, but she believed women belonged in the home. She was also compelled to warn Nietzsche of her daughter's willfulness, a characteristic of which he was well aware by this time. Lou lives by her own rules, her mother lamented. However, she held the two scholars in the highest esteem and hoped their maturity would be beneficial to Lou's child-genius.

Nietzsche's trip to the lakes was postponed for a brief period when he had another of his attacks which included headaches so severe that he often took opium to relieve them. Malwida told a friend, "He [spent] almost his whole time in bed and saw nothing of Rome apart from Villa Mattei and St. Peter's."[28] But he did find the strength to meet again with Lou and Rée. He read parts of *The Gay Science* out loud to them. The text must have seemed like a philosophical call to arms to the Russian general's daughter. In *The Gay Science* he called for preparation for the next step in man's evolution. In a call for what he called *preparatory men*, Nietzsche wrote, "I welcome all signs that a more manly, a warlike, age is about to begin, an age which, above all, will give honor to valor once again.... To this end we need many preparatory valorous men who cannot leap into being out of nothing — anymore than out of the sand and slime of our present civilization and metropolitanism: men who are bent on seeking for that aspect in all things which must be *overcome*."[29] This is the preparation for the *Übermensch*, the person who *overcomes* his own weakness, and does not need the crutch of religion to threaten and reward him, but acts out of a superior sense of morality, who rises above the level of mankind, as man rose above ape. The book calls for the courageous: "For, believe me, the secret of the greatest fruitfulness and the greatest enjoyment of existence is: to live dangerously! Build your cities under Vesuvius! Send your ships into uncharted seas!"[30]

Lou was immediately captivated by Nietzsche's divination of a heroic, manly age. She was seduced into an intellectual ecstasy by his brilliant and daring mind, just as she had swooned before Gillot as a great man of knowledge: *ecce homo*. Here was a man to idealize. Here was a man who would be part of her destiny.

Nietzsche was equally impressed with Lou. Her ability to grasp his ideas, even those unspoken, amazed him. "Lou is the daughter of a Russian general," he wrote a friend, "as shrewd as an eagle and brave as a lion.... She is most amazingly well prepared for *my* way of thinking and my ideas."[31]

While Nietzsche had playfully discussed the plan for an intellectual commune with Lou in his letter to Rée, Lou now begin to pursue it more seriously. Nietzsche wasn't totally convinced a triangular friendship could work — and yet tellingly he pursued the idea with an enthusiasm equal to Lou's. Falsely, Lou later recorded in her memoir that Nietzsche *unexpectedly* inserted himself into their plan to set up an intellectual household. But the letters among Rée, Nietzsche and Lou show clearly that she pursued him with all her might. Her mind was made up: Nietzsche *had* to be the other man in her intellectual fantasy.

Within one week of their first meeting Nietzsche abruptly told Lou — using Rée as his messenger, according to Lou — that if they were to carry out their study plan, he would feel duty-bound to "offer you my hand so as to protect you from what people might say." [32] Though biographer Rudolph Binion believes Nietzsche's comment was misconstrued by Lou as a real proposal as opposed to a gallant gesture, it was not the first time Nietzsche had proposed to a woman after only knowing her for a short time. And although Lou may not have known it, Meysenbug and Rée may have put the thought in his head in their previous letters. Lou tells us in her memoir she was taken aback by Nietzsche's sudden proposal. She tactfully declined, explaining she would have to give up the pension she received as the daughter of a Russian general if she were to marry. The matter seemed to be dropped. But it was — only a week after their meeting — already the first thread of the relationship's unraveling.

The foursome met in Orta, the northern lakes area of Italy, in the first week of May. They ventured to Monte Sacro, a site which would leave a beautiful and sacred memory for both Lou and Nietzsche. When the two showed a desire to climb the mountain, dotted with the ruins of numerous 16th century chapels, Rée stayed at the foot with Lou's mother.

The gentle climb, fresh alpine air and the religious ruins made the event magical to them both. Exactly what transpired no one would ever know but them, but it deeply affected Nietzsche and afterwards he referred to it as "the most exquisite dream of my life!"[33] He imparted something of his philosophy that, until that moment, he had entrusted to no one. It may have well been his early formation on ideas that would go into *Thus Spake Zarathustra*. Later he would write her of the effect of this moment, "Back in Orta I conceived a plan of leading you step by step to the final consequence of my philosophy—*you*, as the first person I took to be fit for this."[34] Later he would linger over the memory of his "Lou of *Monte Sacro.*"

From that moment on Nietzsche regarded her as a soul mate, sharing what he called a brother-sister brain. He could speak about things with her that he dared not say to anyone else. And she would receive his ideas with radiance and enthusiasm. In old age, Lou would coyly tell the editor of her memoir, "I no longer remember if I kissed Nietzsche on Monte Sacro or not."[35] If there was an erotic element in Nietzsche's sermon on Monte Sacro, it merely fueled their mutual philosophical epiphany. Both had learned, years before, to repress their sexual passions by channeling them into intellectual pursuits. If a kiss passed between them, it's easier to imagine Lou kissing his hand in reverence than a passionate embrace.

Rée and Lou's mother were not pleased when the two wanderers returned hours later. The restless period of waiting had aroused Rée's jealousy and the mother's worries. Still elevated by the fresh Monte Sacro air and what had transpired between them, Lou and Nietzsche smoothed things over quickly.

Lou, who felt she had only brief moments of freedom as it was, had clearly made the most of their time alone. Nietzsche made urgent plans to meet with Lou alone again and she excitedly agreed.

After a trip to Basel to visit his friends the Overbecks, Nietzsche returned and met with Lou on May 13 in Lucerne. At the Löwengarten, they spoke under a stone relief of a sleeping lion. According to Lou's memoirs he proposed a second time. Again she tactfully declined but continued to beseech him to be part of the intellectual commune, what she called the "trinity." She believed working together they could inspire another to the greatest heights; to succumb to something as ephemeral as emotion would cause it to dissolve away. And Nietzsche was game for anything involving danger and play — and the world's most dangerous plaything: *live dangerously! Build your cities under Vesuvius! Send your ships into uncharted seas!*

It was right after their meeting at Lucrene that an infamous photograph was taken of the three friends, a photograph that would cause quite a stir in the 19th century intellectual world.

Set in the photographer's studio before the background of a fake mountain and sky, the picture shows Lou crouching in a cart with a small whip fashioned with sprigs of lilacs, while Rée and Nietzsche hold the handle of the cart as if pulling her forward. Nietzsche biographers tend to believe the photo was Lou's idea. Lou wrote that *Nietzsche* insisted on the photograph, and that she and Rée participated reluctantly. In a letter to Lou, Nietzsche seems to put the blame on the photographer: "—Oh, that naughty photographer! And yet: what a lovely silhouette perches there on

Intellectual trinity: Lou von Salomé, Paul Rée, and Friedrich Nietzsche, May 13, 1882 (Wikimedia Commons).

that delightful little cart!"³⁶ Whoever thought of the idea — and it seems more like Nietzsche's style of mocking humor — Lou looks mischievous, but at the same time a little awkward, unwilling to place herself fully in the cart. Rée tries to retain some dignity by striking a traditional pose, while Nietzsche offers a defiant three-quarter profile, looking off dramatically into the future. No matter whose idea it was, the message is clear: Lou is the driving muse and the two men are more than willing to be at her command.

By the end of May Lou won the final battle with her mother. Frau von Salomé agreed to return to St. Petersburg without her — on the contingency that Lou would stay with Rée and his mother at Stibbe. It was a major victory for Lou's crusade for *unrestrained freedom* despite the fact that her physical health continued to be precarious. The mother and daughter traveled to Hamburg, where they visited with other relatives, including Lou's brother Jenia, who would escort her mother back to St. Petersburg. Before leaving she received a letter from Nietzsche who had devised a suitable plan for him and Lou to be alone — or at least apart from Rée. He arranged for Lou and his sister Elizabeth to attend the debut of Wagner's *Parsifal* Bayreuth in July; then the two of them would travel to Tautenburg, where she could stay for several weeks. Once in Hamburg she wrote Nietzsche. She approved his idea, but perhaps in the interim they could meet in Warmbrunn, where they could be together and work as a team. Flirtatiously, she added that his book *The Dawn* "entertains me in bed better than visits, shopping and travel dust."³⁷ It could only lead to Nietzsche wondering, which parts entertained her interest most? Could it be his courageous affirmation of sexuality? In *The Dawn* he had reinstated the powers of Eros and Aphrodite, proclaiming, "In themselves sexual feelings, like those of pity and adoration, are such that one human being thereby gives pleasure to another human being through his delight; one doesn't often encounter such beneficent arrangements in nature. And to slander it and to corrupt it through bad conscience! To associate the procreation of man with bad conscience!"³⁸

Lou also wrote Nietzsche that he and Rée were "two prophets, turned towards the past and the future." Rée "discovers the verdict of the gods," and Nietzsche "destroys the twilight of the gods." She admires Nietzsche as the heroic thinker: "you say somewhere 'If you have to disregard the happy life, only the heroic life is left.'... We are good travelers," she adds cheerfully, "and will find the path even in the undergrowth."³⁹

"When I'm alone, I often, very often, say your name out loud — to my greatest pleasure!"[40] he wrote her. A couple days later he wrote to Rée, "I often laugh about our Pythagorean friendship...."[41] And to his friend Franz Overbeck he wrote that he was such a trusting fellow that "I'd put my head in a lion's mouth, not to mention...."[42] The summer plans were not definite, he told Overbeck, but nonetheless, mum was still the word in effort to hide the projected *ménage à trois* arrangement from his saintly mother and sister. He also stressed to Lou in a letter to keep their plans secret, lest there be "a European-wide chain of gossip."[43]

She was at the same time receiving letters in Hamburg from Rée that could only be described as lovesick. The day they parted he wrote, "I thought I would expire from pain and longing."[44] While attempting to work, he confessed his thoughts kept turning back to her. It occurred to him

> that I am not so wholly open and honest in my relationship to Nietzsche especially since a certain little girl has bobbed up from abroad.... I am and shall remain your friend alone; I have no scruples about behaving a little crookedly, a little falsely, a little mendaciously and deceitfully towards anyone except you. Out of my friendship to you I make a cult; I regard as a sin ... if I did or said anything false, dishonorable, unfriendly, crooked with respect to you, I would have a feeling just like the one believers may have after committing a great sin. [45]

Before leaving Hamburg, Lou saw her mother off to Petersburg, escorted by Jenia. Lou left alone and thrilled by her hard-won freedom on a night train to Stibbe.

Nietzsche had asked his friend Ida Overbeck to find housing for the intellectual "trinity." When Frau Overbeck found a place that had certain rules accompanying it, Lou wrote her explaining that the aforementioned residence wouldn't work, because there were too many conditions that would block "my freedom with reference to visiting terms and social intercourse." That is, if she wanted Rée and Nietzsche to sleep over, that was her business. Theirs was a noble cause, she reassured Frau Overbeck, but it might take the world some time to catch up with them. She understood, Lou wrote, that the landlady had no reason to trust an unknown girl. She understood that trust had to be "won slowly with patient conquest of natural prejudices. We will get there — it is with confidence and courage that I face life; which until now has always led me through all obstructing difficulties, if not without combat, at least with happiness."[46]

Nietzsche upheld the ideal of a mentally passionate non-marital relationship to Ida Overbeck, but didn't deny there was passion between Lou and himself. That was why Rée was necessary, he explained. Ida believed Nietzsche saw Lou as his alter ego and hoped to work with her towards his monumental goals.

It's difficult to imagine that any of them truly believed that this would work.

5

Any Third Person

I often laugh about our Pythagorean friendship.... It gives me a better conception of myself to be really capable of such a friendship.— Yet it is still something to laugh about, isn't it?[1]

— Nietzsche, letter to Paul Rée

Once she returned to Stibbe, Lou informed Nietzsche that *yes*, she would join him *sans* Rée in Tautenburg after attending the Bayreuth festival with Nietzsche sister, as he had arranged. "Now the sky over me is bright!" he rejoiced. "Yesterday at noon I felt it was my birthday. You sent your acceptance, the most lovely gift anyone could have given me now...."[2] Nietzsche envisioned his sister as an unobtrusive chaperone, but knowing her as he did, it seems unlikely that he believed she would stand by idly watching the cerebral seduction of her brother.

Elizabeth (called Lisbeth) had nurtured and was devoted to her brother's genius since a young age. For years she had played the role of secretary to him, and he referred to her as his "faithful llama." In bringing the two women together, he hoped his sister would strengthen his ties with Lou. But if Nietzsche imagined that Lou and Lisbeth would become fast friends he couldn't have been more wrong. Whereas Nietzsche's thinking burst forth like fireworks, Lisbeth was narrow-minded and bigoted. She was proud of her ancestry of religious men, and saw her brother as a paragon of virtue and genius. It was just the sort of thinking that Lou detested. And if Lisbeth's account of the event is to believed (and that's the only detailed account we have) then Lou would make it clear to the uptight clergyman's daughter that Nietzsche was like any other man when it came to women. He had one thing on his mind — sex.

On July 21 Lou set out for Bayreuth. She met Lisbeth en route and rode the train into a village wholly dedicated to Wagner. Malwida von Meysenbug was also there for the grand event and she introduced Lou to

Wagner's inner circle. Though Lou didn't have much of an ear for music, she certainly took pleasure in meeting the cultural elite. Backstage she enjoyed herself thoroughly with set designer Count Paul von Jukovsky, a close personal friend of Wagner. From Stibbe, Rée wrote about her latest flirtation:

> You will find out that I am the most ridiculous jealous man you've ever met, but this time it is really a more understandable kind of jealousy, my dear, I'm afraid I could be deprived of you and that I could not take…. For surely, he'll want to marry you. Finally, Lou, even then I will remain your friend —[3]

In closing he adds, "Dearest little snail, if I only would have you back again."[4]

At first, the 36-year-old Lisbeth was charmed and impressed by the younger woman, as were so many others. But the good will between them would quickly collapse.

Lou was most certainly a great success with the Wagner crowd, while Lisbeth found herself on the outside. Lisbeth felt snubbed by the Wagner circle — perhaps, she believed, because of her brother's rift with the composer. Lisbeth glowered from the sidelines while Lou charmed and was charmed by some of the greatest artists in Germany. According to Lisbeth, Count Jukovsky sewed the hem of Lou's dress for her — while she was still wearing it! She also claimed Lou flaunted her power over Nietzsche by showing everyone the infamous photograph of her wielding a whip over Nietzsche and Rée, taken in Lucrene. She bragged, said Lisbeth, about having Nietzsche and Rée wrapped around her little finger.

No doubt Lou enjoyed herself. She was very young, and despite the maturity of her intellect, she loved to flirt and couldn't help enjoying her extraordinary power over men. Lisbeth seethed in anger at being slighted by Wagner's group, and she vented it on Lou. In her view, Lou was betraying her brother by consorting with those who had done him wrong. But wasn't that why they were there — to enjoy the best of European culture?

As the festival wound down, with Lou in high spirits and Lisbeth in a restrained rage, an argument broke out at the hotel room between the two women. Taking a haughty pose, Lisbeth scolded Lou: How *dare* she flaunt herself with Nietzsche's enemies and discuss openly her plan to live with him and Rée! Lou must have bristled at the older woman's admonishment. She had managed to get rid of her own mother. She certainly didn't need another obstacle to her unrestrained freedom.

Offended by Lou's indecency, a traumatized Lisbeth recounts, she managed to pack her clothes and leave for Tautenburg where Nietzsche awaited them. Lou remained behind in Bayreuth with a head cold.

The first thing Lisbeth did when she arrived in Tautenburg was to tell Nietzsche the awful details of Lou's flirtatious behavior, framing Lou's friendliness with the Wagner circle as an insult directed at Nietzsche. He was, of course, horrified by Lisbeth's account. His great expectations about his intellectual dream girl, his Lou of *Monte Sacro*, were suddenly deflated. She had betrayed him not only to his sister but to the Wagner circle! Apparently aware of the volatility of the situation, Lou sent a polite note thanking Nietzsche for arranging for Lisbeth's companionship in Bayreuth: "her presence was a great support for me and I am sincerely grateful to her."[5] She awaited his word as to whether she should come or not. On August 4, in another telegram, he told her: "Do come, I'm suffering too much for having made you suffer: we shall bear it together."[6]

Nietzsche sent Lisbeth to pick Lou up at the train station while he found a room nearby for her stay. But the quarrel between Lou and Lisbeth was refueled when Lisbeth found that the man to whom she was secretly engaged — Bernhard Förster — had shared a train car with Lou. Lou, not knowing of Förster's engagement to Lisbeth, had enjoyed a jovial conversation with him *en route*. How much more could Lisbeth bear from this temptress?

When the two women arrived at the house of Heinrich Gelzer, where Nietzsche had secured a room for Lou, another argument broke out. How could Lou go about flirting with every man she met? How could she jeopardize the Nietzsche name this way? Didn't she know Fritz was a revered man — noble and pure? Lisbeth wildly wrote to a friend that Lou laughed irreverently and replied: "Who first soiled our study plans with his low designs, who started up the mental friendship when he couldn't get me for something else, who thought of concubinage ... your noble pure-minded brother!"[7] And "men all wanted only that, pooh to mental friendship! and she knew first-hand what she was talking about, because she had been caught *twice* already in that kind of relationship."[8] (Assuming the first was Gillot, it's unclear if Lou — for it had to have been Lou who told Lisbeth this — was referring to Rée, or if Lisbeth had just thrown in a second lusty fellow for good measure.) When Lisbeth demanded that Lou "stop this indecent talk"[9] she has Lou saying, "[W]ith Rée I talk a lot more indecently."[10] Lisbeth wailed to her friend in prudish indignation, "Oh, what martyrdom for my sensibility the whole story was!"[11] Clearly, Lou had pursued the relationship with Nietzsche—it was *her* dream originally and only later became his.

Ernst Pfeiffer, Lou's friend in her old age, says Lou told him she had become irritated by Lisbeth's constant assertions that Nietzsche was a saint and merely repeated to Lisbeth something Rée had told her. Rée had given Lou an underhanded warning before she left for Tautenburg which would prove the undoing of the trinity. Rée slyly told her that Nietzsche had subtly suggested that if he couldn't have Lou in marriage then "wouldn't it be better to live *together without marriage?*"[12] (Was it Nietzsche's intention to imply a sexual liaison or did Rée merely use the statement to his own advantage?) But, when Lou repeated the quote to Lisbeth, the pastor's daughter vomited out of piousness, had to lie down and "compresses were necessary."[13] Rudolph Binion says Lou's "impish impulse to make Lisbeth squirm in her straight laces" would certainly have the intended effect. "Lisbeth was indeed shocked," he wrote, "shocked for life."[14]

When Lou arrived the next morning, Nietzsche confronted her with Lisbeth's accusations. They quarreled. Lou bristled at his domineering attitude. According to Lou, Lisbeth's version "had no basis in fact"[15]—a polite way of saying it was exaggerations and lies. Lisbeth says that Lou was then asked to leave but *pretended* to be ill, to extend her stay. With Lou sick in bed, Nietzsche's angry tone of voice changed to a plea for her to stay. He slipped notes under her door. He had been dreaming of this time he would spend with her and no one, not even Lisbeth, would rob him of that.

Lou played down the scene in her memoir: "It seems Nietzsche and I argued a bit at first about all sorts of nonsense…. But soon we put it behind us, and our subsequent experience was a rich one, undisturbed by any third person."[16] Gracefully, Lou would not even stoop low enough to utter Lisbeth's name—*any third person*. Throughout her lifetime, Lisbeth would continue to attack Lou, but Lou flatly refused to engage in an argument, implying only that the accusations were false.

For now, Nietzsche was determined to put the mess behind them. Ignoring the *third person* in the house, he took Lou for a walk through the lovely village, showing her the site where the village elders planned to erect a plaque that would pay tribute to a number of his books. Alone again, they spoke of their most intimate feelings about philosophy and life. Alone again, they were free to talk on a level of a daring intimacy they shared with no one else. "I was able to penetrate Nietzsche's thought much more deeply,"[17] Lou wrote suggestively. Their discussions were provocative and took them to the very brink of intellectual passion, resulting in mutual excitement and inspiration. They talked all day long and well into the night. They would sometimes discuss such forbidden subjects that they were unable to look one another in the eye afterwards.

Rée had asked Lou to keep a diary of her time spent with Nietzsche. It was perhaps Rée's way of wedging himself between them. In it Lou recorded her observations of Nietzsche and his ideas. On August 14, they managed to slip away to a dark pine forest where they walked through the dappled sunlight, talking for hours with only the rustling squirrels to overhear them. "Conversing with Nietzsche is uncommonly lovely,"[18] she wrote in her notebook. They were in complete simpatico, taking the words out of each other's mouth, and sometimes communicating without speaking at all, through knowing glances. "We often recollect our time in Italy," she wrote an already jealous Rée. Nietzsche told her "softly, '*monte sacro*— I have you to thank for the most bewitching dream of my life.'"[19] Telling Rée such intimate details of their conversations points to Lou's strange need — as opposed to simply being cruel — to have a second man bear witness to her relationship with another. It was a theme that would show up again and again in her fiction.

For Nietzsche — who had spent most of his time in solitude, or in the company of those who could not fully comprehend his philosophy (especially his faithful sister) — Lou was an epiphany. She was creatively forging her life. Lou inspired Nietzsche, and would inspire others, by her very spirit. Here was a bold heroine, as engaging and as profound as any character from a Russian novel. And yet she was also flesh and blood, and yearning for experience. Nietzsche wanted this phenomenal girl as the heir to his philosophy, his Mary Magdalene, his partner. It would be a shame, he told her, "if you did not carve out a memorial to your innermost mind in the time you have left to you."[20]

Lou recognized his importance in intellectual history clearly. "In Nietzsche's character lies such a heroic trait. It is such an essential part of him and gives unity and structure to all his other properties and drives. We shall yet witness his becoming the prophet of a new religion and it will be one that seeks heroes for disciples."[21] Zarathustra was fomenting: "Nietzsche the God-seeker, who came from religion and was moving towards religious prophesy."[22]

Nietzsche edited essays she'd written, and his notes on her writing style reveal the strength and beauty of his own: "Of prime necessity is life: a style should live.... Style is out to prove that one believes in an idea; not only thinks but also feels it.... The more abstract the truth which one wishes to teach, the more one must entice the senses...."[23]

If, Lou wrote Rée, "anyone [were] listening to us would think two devils were conferring."[24] Funny she should mention it — someone *was* listening. Lurking in the shadow of these profound and daring conversations was Lisbeth, again left on the sidelines of the main action, while Nietzsche — like the Wagner crowd and her own fiancé — fawned over Lou. Lisbeth's eavesdropping and bitter reporting of the conversations would show how little she understood her brother and his philosophy.

After three weeks of intense day- and night-long conversations, Lou and Nietzsche said goodbye. Both were invigorated by the encounter. As she left, they made urgent plans to reunite.

The moment she was gone Lisbeth was on the attack. How dare he associate with that awful Russian! Was he so infatuated that he didn't care what happened to his own good name? You have no eye for greatness, he told her. But Lou just used his philosophy to dress up her own egotism and immortality, Lisbeth asserted. You're just jealous, he shot back. Jealous? Lisbeth protested, why would I be jealous of a girl who reminded me of *a monkey*?

Sister and brother continued to quarrel fiercely. When it came time for them to visit their mother in Naumberg, Lisbeth refused to accompany him. Nietzsche, distraught and bewildered, went home alone.

6

The Birth of a Tragedy

[W]hat should I say: it's all over now.[1]
— Nietzsche to Lou von Salomé

To say that the relationship between Lou, Rée and Nietzsche was a simple triangle is to undermine the network of complexities that entangled them. Comrades, non-sexual lovers, rivals, soul mates, friends — they were all of these things, yet they were none of them. Rée and Nietzsche were rivals for Lou, but neither of them admitted it openly to the other. Lou openly played on the jealousy of both men, but somehow expected them all to get along.

The three-way relationship was less like a triangle and more like a mobile, dancing and rocking, its parts colliding in any number of dynamic ways, sending wild undulations through their independent lives.

This would be the first of many similar relationships Lou would have throughout her lifetime, relationships that would boggle the mind as well as defy any sort label or definition. After all, words were mere boundary lines; they stifled her *urge towards unrestrained freedom.*

While Nietzsche had been the brilliant star of the academic world, Lou was a metaphysical wonder who seemed to defy the laws of physics. Since her childhood days of fantasy, against the backdrop of St. Petersburg court life, she had created her own world. Now the outside world seemed to be collaborating with her in fulfilling her secret daydreams. She wanted to live and work with philosophers, and lo, the most brilliant philosopher of her time seems to fall from the sky and into her life. *From what stars have we fallen?*

But Lisbeth's meddling had filled the dark space between them with mutual suspicion. And Rée had already played his part. By subtly suggesting to Lou that Nietzsche's intentions were not so innocent, he had rocked the mobile and set its parts spinning. He knew full well that it would be an affront to Lou to be any*one*'s any*thing*— be it mistress, concubine, lover, disciple or wife.

Returning to Stibbe and to Rée, Lou escaped into the world where she felt safe — the world of intellect. She poured her Nietzsche-zeal into studying his works. "[Lou's] all buried in books and works,"[2] Rée wrote to Nietzsche. Through September she read *Human, All Too Human*, which became her favorite of Nietzsche's books, and *The Gay Science*. She excitedly began a draft of a work on his philosophy and character, a work which later would be the first published book on Nietzsche's thought. She read day and night, to the point of exhaustion. And when she fell ill, she took Nietzsche's books to bed with her.

Fell ill. It was a common pattern by now. Lofty thought led to earthly passions, earthly passions led to escape through obsessive study, and obsessive study led her to a mysterious illness. Whether the illness was brought on from studying too much, a physically frailty, or a neurosis, she would always manage to come back all the stronger: *That which does not kill me makes me stronger.* This time she came back as part Lou, part Nietzsche, just as she had left Russia as part Gillot. That which she loved she absorbed wholeheartedly. But at the same time her wariness of losing her unrestrained freedom amounts to near-paranoia. She, after all, had become intellectually obsessed with Nietzsche, and the threat of being dominated by *his* way of thinking was all too real.

While Lou lounged in bed voluptuously surrounded by Nietzsche's works, Lisbeth was busy escalating her attack on Lou via mail — scathing letters to her brother, their mother, Rée's mother, Frau Overbeck, Malwida von Meysenbug and anyone else who would listen. How could he allow that terrible Russian to soil his reputation? "You can imagine with what zeal the Russian girl took up his philosophy," Lisbeth wrote, "for her it was the finery in which her evil, egotistic, and immoral nature looked most passable."[3] She went on to say she had lost faith in her brother's philosophy after encountering Lou. "She is really, I cannot deny it, my brother's philosophy personified: that raging egotism which knocks down anything in its way and that utter want of morality."[4]

By the time the besieged Nietzsche arrived in Naumburg his mother had already been saturated by Lisbeth's accusations by mail. Mama Nietzsche admonished him by uttering the words that he was never able to forgive: *he was a disgrace to his father's grave.*[5] With that, Nietzsche had had enough of the "Naumburg virtue," as he called it. He packed his bag (did he even get a chance to unpack?) and went to Leipzig. His relationship to his mother and sister, from then on, would be strained.

Meanwhile back at Stibbe, Rée was relieved to have Lou all to himself. He knew that she had not been swayed by Nietzsche's attempt to wedge himself between them. Although Lou was intensely affected by Nietzsche on an intellectual level, emotionally she had become weary of him. Lurking deep within her psyche were visions of an entanglement between servitude and sex, via the philosophy of her aunt Caro and her encounter with Gillot. Rée offered her a supportive relationship; he was non-threatening and offered little resistance to her unrestrained freedom, apart from some jealous whimpering. He was the weakest of the three and was easily absorbed into her orbit. Nietzsche wanted to be the sun in this universe. He offered only devotion to *his* genius and *his* mission. But Lou had her own mission, even though it was a deeply personal quest rather than an earth-shaking philosophy.

In September Nietzsche sent a polite note to Rée saying, "I think that the two of us, the three of us, are intelligent enough to remain good friends...."[6] He had spent too much time alone, he explained, and had to re-learn how to be with others.

Ironically, Rée replied that "*nothing* can part us, as we are bound by a third party to whom we bow down — not unlike medieval knights, only with better cause."[7]

In early September Rée and Lou quarreled over his addiction to gambling, which had reared up in her absence. In a heartfelt letter he wrote to her the next day, he lamented that while she had stayed up nights talking with Nietzsche, he had roamed the streets of Berlin trying to conquer his compulsion for gambling. "Exhausted I finally gave up the battle.... [W]eakness of character is now part of my being, indeed it is almost key to my being."[8] Fearful that she had lost respect for him and ashamed of doing anything disagreeable in her eyes, he attempted to withdraw from the anxiety-ridden situation: "I'm afraid we must part company.... [L]et us go our separate ways to our graves."[9] "No, absolutely not!" Lou wrote in the margin of his letter. "Let us live and strive together until you have retracted this!"[10] Rée lamented: "You are the greatest loss that I ever suffered in my life, or ever will suffer."[11] Clearly, he considered her friendship more of a loss than a gain.

From his self-imposed exile in Leipzig Nietzsche wrote Lou, "Come to Leipzig very, very soon! Why wait until October 2nd?"[12] His letters emphasized that they were far more alike than she and Rée. He repeatedly referred to their "brother-sister brain." They were indeed more alike. What he did not realize was that Lou didn't want a man whose iron will and strength of character matched her own.

To his friend Peter Gast he wrote that Lou was coming on October 2 and that a few weeks later they were headed to Paris. There is no mention of Rée.

But when Lou did arrive in Leipzig she was escorted by Rée and his mother. They began a three-week stay during which the three of them conversed, worked and attended the theater together. Once Nietzsche got Lou alone, he again intimated that she alone understood him and his philosophy.

A close friend of Nietzsche, Peter Gast visited while they were there. He had an hour-long discussion with Lou. He described her as a long-legged, well-proportioned blonde with the penetrating stare of an "ancient Roman."[13] He agreed with Nietzsche on her intelligence and strength: "She is definitely a genius of heroic character" and "[h]er ideas show that she has dared to travel to the farthest horizons of the thinkable world as well as to those of the moral and intellectual worlds — as I said, a genius in spirit and disposition."[14]

There were floating anxieties among the three participants in the meeting. Lou wrote in her diary that even the "most ideal love can become sensual again, precisely because, in its purely ideal state, all the great emotions are unleashed.... I do not love the feelings when they return this way because that is the point of *false pathos*, where they lose their truth and candor," adding, "Is it this which estranges me from N.?"[15] Lou's irritating habit of vagueness makes it impossible to discern whether she's talking about Nietzsche's sensual feelings or her own — although it at least suggests the feelings are mutual. Nonetheless, Nietzsche must have detected her feelings of estrangement and lack of candor. No definite plans for Paris or Vienna were made, and at the end of the Leipzig visit, Lou returned with Rée and his mother to Stibbe.

After the Leipzig visit there is a change in Nietzsche's letters. Though few of Lou's letters survive, it can be deduced from Nietzsche's that he had begun to realize that she felt closeness to Rée that made him feel like the odd man out of the trinity. His correspondence vacillates between extreme anger and deep disappointment.

In November, in a letter he wrote to Rée, Nietzsche seems to bow out of the situation altogether:

> But my dear dear friend, I thought you would feel just the contrary and would secretly be pleased to be rid of me for a time! This year there were a

hundred instances, beginning in Orta, where I found that your friendship with me "came at too high of a cost to you." I took possession of far too much from *your* Roman find (I mean Lou)—and it always seemed to me, especially in Leipzig, that you had a right to be somewhat unforthcoming toward me.[16]

Longing to fully grasp the situation, he asks Rée to give him an indication of "precisely what is that 'comes comes between us' as you say."[17] He then wrote to Lou, "And now, Lou, dear heart, clear the air! I want nothing else than a pure, clear sky over every aspect: otherwise I will fight my way through, you can count on that, no matter how hard it is. Yet a lonely man suffers frightfully when he suspects something about the two human beings he loves — particularly when it involves a suspicion of the suspicion they entertain concerning his very essence."[18] Nonetheless, they shared a special bond: "I feel every tremulous motion of the *loftier* soul in you, I love nothing else in you but these stirrings. I will gladly renounce intimacy and closeness, if I can be sure of one thing: that the two of us feel as one in regions where vulgar souls will never dwell."[19] Then added, "Be what you must be."[20] In a letter that exists only in his own draft, he was more revealing: "what should I say: it's all over now[.] Shall we quarrel with one another? ...I wanted clear skies between us. But you? You're a little birdie perched on a gallows! And to think I once believed you were virtue and honesty incarnate."[21] In old age, Lou told the inheritor of her memoirs, Ernst Pfeiffer, that she and Rée were puzzled by Nietzsche's suggestion to clear the air of suspicion amongst them. But clearly Lou had a good idea — and Rée knew all too well where the problem lay. Even though Lou was still anxious to make the study plan go through, it was clear to Nietzsche that she no longer trusted him. Seemingly still unaware that Rée had a role in Lou's mistrust of him, Nietzsche confided to Rée the most painful slight: what Lisbeth told him Lou had said about him soiling their plan with his sexual motives. "Every since Tautenburg," he wrote in a draft of a letter to Paul Rée, "I undertook to *torture* myself by *loving* her!"[22] Around December 20, he wrote a draft of letter addressed to them both:

> Don't get too unnerved by these irruptions of my delusions of grandeur or my wounded vanity: and if one day I myself should, as a result of the above-mentioned affects, take my life, there would not be too much to mourn. What do my raving fantasies matter to you I mean you and Lou! The two of you should discuss with one another at some length the possibility that ultimately I am halfway gone to the nuthouse, sick in the head, and that my loneliness will take me the rest of the way — To this from my point of view

altogether comprehensible insight into my state of mind I have come after taking a huge dose of opium out of desperation. However, instead of losing my understanding on account of it, it seems my understanding has finally *come* to me.[23]

There would be no Vienna, no Berlin, no Paris: the trinity was over forever.

Though neither of them knew it at the time, Leipzig was the last place Lou and Nietzsche would see another again. But the impact on each others' lives would reverberate for years. It would be more than a year later that the truth would become clear to Nietzsche. He would spend most of 1883 casting Lisbeth-inspired aspersions against Lou — stooping so low as to calling Lou "a nasty-smelling monkey with her false breasts."[24] But eventually Nietzsche's anger toward Lou would evaporate and he would once again be writing her praises in his letters to friends, years after they last saw one another. By then he realized that it was the meddling of *third persons*— namely sister Lisbeth and friend Rée — who had inflicted the true and irrevocable damage.

7

Divine Inspiration

Das Ewig-Weibliche zieht uns hinan.[1]
The Eternal-Feminine entices us ever upward.
— Goethe

Inspiration for a man, according to Goethe, lies in the sphere of the *eternal-feminine*, the ideal vision of Woman. She drives man to create and to destroy. She motivates him to greater heights, and ignites his imagination, where all things are possible. But perhaps an even greater stimulus is the *loss* of the feminine.

Once Lou and Nietzsche's short but powerful encounter was over, the inspiration began for them both. Nietzsche, suffering alone in Sils Maria: "If I do not discover the alchemical trick of turning this muck into gold, I am lost."[2] He wanted to believe, he wrote, that "all experiences are useful, all days are holy, all people divine!"[3]

Though Nietzsche was the first major figure in intellectual Europe that Lou inspired both creatively and romantically, it was only the beginning of her reign of influence. She had left a dark and powerful wake in his life. And both of them would be guided by one another's spirit in their subsequent works. In "the wake of ten absolutely clear and fresh January [1883] days, my 'Zarathustra' came into being, the most liberated of all my productions."[4] He wrote it in fevered state and completed the first two parts in nine months.

Zarathustra, in Nietzsche's vision, is a prophet who, after spending ten years contemplating in a cave, descends the mountain into the pool of common humanity, with whom to share his philosophy. He searches for outstanding individuals, persons who are genuinely hungry for something more in life than the fulfillment of mediocre desires. He sets out to teach the concept of the *Übermensch*, the human being who overcomes his human limitations. "Man is something that is to be overcome."[5] By accepting that the comforting belief in God is an illusion, the higher man bases his belief in himself and creates his own moral system. This is not a system based on threats of the reward of Heaven or the punishment of Hell, but on individual truths (and herein lies the danger of Nietzsche's philosophy.) As demonstrated in Kubrick's *2001*, the *Übermensch* is the next step in human evolution. The common English translation of *Übermensch* is *superman*. But this has associations of a man with superpowers; a better way to translate it might be *higher man*. Nietzsche stresses that the *Übermensch* is a human being who *overcomes*, rises above the loss of God, who courageously lives with the emptiness that faces him in a godless universe, as Nietzsche attempted (but failed) to do. The *Übermensch* transcends his own human limitations, beyond the realm of religion and morality. It was the spirit which came to life in his talks with Lou. She breathed life into Nietzsche's creation.

In 1884, Nietzsche referred to Lou's influence on his work and reprimanded Lisbeth for cutting the encounter short. In a draft of a letter he wrote:

> One thing is certain, of all acquaintances that I have made, the one with Fraulein von Salomé is the most precious and the most fertile to me. Only after my encounter with her, I was ready for my Zarathustra. I had to cut this encounter short *because of you*.... Lou is the most talented, most thoughtful creature one can imagine — of course, she also has questionable qualities. *I, too,* have such qualities.... You can not imagine what comfort Dr. Rée has been to me for years —*faute de mieux*, it goes without saying how incredibly beneficial my encounter with Fraulein Salomé was to me.[6]

From the first month of 1883 and to the end of 1888, Nietzsche would write eight books, his genius reaching its apex over these years.

In *Beyond Good and Evil*, published in 1886, he gives us the free spirit. Woven through the numbered aphorisms in Part 4 of this work are harsh and sometimes puzzling verdicts on women and profound statements on love that demonstrate the depth of his frustration and loss: "The sexes deceive themselves about each other — because at bottom they honor and love only themselves (or their own ideal to put it more pleasantly). Thus man likes woman peaceful — but woman is *essentially* unpeaceful, like a cat, however well she may have trained herself to seem peaceable."[7] "In revenge and in love, woman is more barbaric than man."[8] "When a woman has scholarly tendencies, there is usually something wrong with her sexually."[9]

On the first day of the New Year, 1883, Lou wrote in her journal a summary of 1882. She spoke of the rejuvenating sunshine she experienced in Rome, the nightingales singing on Monte Sacro, and the beauty of Lucerne. She wrote of her friendship with Paul Rée and how, after her mother returned to Russia, they "entered into that strange friendship-relationship on which our whole lives have depended ever since."[10] "[T]hen came the day when we left Stibbe together, hand in hand, entered into the 'big world' like two comrades."[11] Her dream of living with *both* Nietzsche and Rée died in silence, for she doesn't mention the original "winter plan" or the conflict with Nietzsche.

But Lou began living out at least part of her daring dream. She and Rée did leave Stibbe hand-in-hand to take an apartment in Berlin. There they began working on their independent projects. Lou began writing her first novel, a work inspired by her talks with Nietzsche called *Struggling for God*, and Rée was working on a philosophical book, titled *The Origin of Conscience*. The two friends held regular salon-type meetings for scholars — among them philosophers, historians and cultural experts. It was an exciting and brilliant atmosphere. The group half-jokingly referred to Lou as "Her Excellency,"[12] a reference to the title on her passport, and to Rée as her "maid of honor,"[13] an emasculating title that seemed to him accurate enough. Lou's unique presence took center stage and the men were mesmerized by her discourse. H.F. Peters wrote of the group:

> They admired her strength of character, her sovereign contempt of all petty virtues, her indifference to middle-class morality, fully as much as the unusual quality of her mind and her distinguished origin. Although she was the youngest member of the group and often the only woman present, she was the vital center, sparkling with ideas, daring in her speculations, and entirely free of cant, pretence and prejudice.... Small wonder that this brilliant and exotic Russian fascinated them all.[14]

Although she was an attractive, tall and well-proportioned blonde, as Gast had described, her appearance was not where her ultimate charm lay. Her true beauty lay in the youthful boldness of her thoughts and ideas, the intensity of her discourse, and the strong sense of self and purpose that seemed unshakeable. Her bright blue eyes sparkled with candor and genius — with a dash of tomboyish mischief. She was intellectually fearless, and would discuss openly any matter that men would discuss. As Peters had commented, it was her exotic *Russianness* that made her seem so unique and charming among the intellectual Germans. She was ever-longing for comrades-at-arms against the world of banality. Still, there was a part of her that was a traditionally feminine presence — extremely receptive and nurturing to ideas, the respectful German *fräulein*.

Binion describes the Lou of Berlin as "beautiful and emotionally bewitching."[15] Once again she began collecting admirers. One was Ferdinand Tönnies, a brilliant young pioneer of sociology. Tönnies writing to a friend described Lou at this time:

> She is really an altogether an extraordinary being; so much cleverness in a twenty-one-year-old girl would make your flesh creep were it not for her truly tender disposition and utter demureness. She is a phenomenon that must be viewed up close to be believed. And a single look suffices to annihilate any thought of a "woman of loose ways," as the preacher says.... [H]er power of expression is significantly rich. She is a genius.[16]

Another admirer was an older man, Baron Carl von Schulz, who sent her notes begging, "I must see you again: *please, please* do not refuse me this."[17] Still another man, a professor, proposed to her at the Berlin zoo — despite the fact that, she semi-modestly told a female relative, "I was so frightfully unlovable."[18]

Regardless of the all the male attention she received, Lou was still haunted by the image of Nietzsche. Not everyone in their circle knew who Nietzsche was, she later wrote, but "nonetheless he stood, like a hidden shadow, an invisible figure in our midst."[19] None of them came close to matching his unique and hot-blooded genius.

In this atmosphere of the intellectual and the erotic — an atmosphere in which she thrived like a rare, exotic hothouse plant — Lou wrote a three hundred-page novel. Inspired by her month long stay with Nietzsche, Lou utilized notes from her Tautenburg journal for the novel. There is a great deal of Nietzsche's biography in the novel's hero. The protagonist of her story, Kuno, is a preacher's son. He was once fiercely religious but had lost his faith in God, which leaves him with a sense of guilt for having "murdered God."[20] The three female characters who fall in love with Kuno are clearly the conflicting aspects of Lou's own character that express both her deadly fear of and intense desire for sex. Biographer H.F. Peters describes the three female characters — Märchen, the dreamy child; Jane, the worshipful adolescent; and Margherita, the independent co-ed — in *Struggling for God*:

> Jane, a pale but passionate girl, is an extreme idealist. She feels a strong need to admire, to worship, to kneel before an ideal, to deify it. This she calls a woman's religion. Margherita's need is for personal freedom. She becomes a

student because she wants to live a fuller and freer life. Finally Kuno's [illegitimate] daughter, Märchen, who lives in a world of her own amidst the wonderful creatures of her vivid imagination, is a shy and sensitive child.[21]

The author of *Frau Lou*, Rudolph Binion, points out that the three female characters represent Lou's three phases of her selfhood (childhood, adolescence and young adulthood), as well as the three men that inspired each stage of her development. From her God to Gillot to Nietzsche, her transcendence was possible only through the separation from these godmen. Kuno's relationship with Märchen (*Märchen* means *fairy tale* in German; it was a nickname Nietzsche gave to Lou) is the young Lou in the fairy tale world of her St. Petersburg upbringing. Kuno teaches Märchen, but does not tell her he is her father out of wedlock. Like Gillot's, Kuno's teaching is authoritarian and harsh, an attempt to break her will, encouraging her to "fight with life, with Promethean defiance, for an ideal of her own."[22]

Kuno, who vacillates between piety and promiscuity, seduces both Jane and Margherita. His behavior causes him great shame. Sex in *Struggling for God* is a powerful force, always with negative consequences. Rather than emancipating her heroines from social restraints, Lou seems to move from identification with the female characters in the story to identification with the masculine character. Livingstone writes:

> Kuno is Nietzschean [but he] also seems to represent the author herself, for there is nothing very male about him, and the break with the family, the glorification of freedom, the switch from pious religious fervor to pious fervent celebration, the mixture of devotion with principled infidelity, the very deliberate and conscious amorality, the highly charged sexuality along with horror of sex — all these things belong to [Lou's] own biography.[23]

By identifying with the Nietzsche-like Kuno, she seemingly transcends the fate of her female characters, who suffer the consequences of loving or being seduced by a man. Though she lost Nietzsche as a friend, she absorbed him as an alter ego. And by attempting to deny her own femaleness, she hoped to escape the social and biological consequences of female sexuality.

Published in 1884, *Struggling for God* (*Im Kampf um Gott*) became a best seller, followed by enthusiastic reviews and devoted fan mail. It was particularly popular among educated young ladies who enjoyed the seductive mix of philosophical profundity and sexual drama. They became the core audience of her future novels and many wrote her letters praising her work well into her old age. The subjects Lou discussed in the novel — love, sex, philosophy and God — were the author's major concerns. The intense philosophical conversations that took place between Lou and Nietzsche were voiced by Kuno and Jane. "The pattern for five or ten pages of action is followed by ten or twenty of moralizing," wrote biographer Binion, as if she had alternately written "the former 'dreamingly' by moonlight and the latter thinkingly by sunlight."[24] It was the very charm of her paradoxical personality. Many found in *Struggling for God* Lou's unique spirit — her radiant golden personality and the piercing blue-white light of her intellect. In the book she reveals her surprising candor and thoughtfulness, as well as her personal struggle. Franz Overbeck called it the most astonishing book he had read that year. Overbeck sent a copy to Erwin Rohde, also a friend of Nietzsche's, who read it with great eagerness and saw plenty of Nietzschean inspiration in it. Paul Deussen, a friend of Nietzsche's from his school days and an attendee of the Lou and Rée circle of scholars, wrote, "I must admit, that while reading it my love for Lou blazed up in bright flames. With its various suicides, adulteries, and the like, it is diversely judged. My friend Ebbinghaus maintained that they were 'a nun's daydreams' but I found much of her spirit in the book and fell in love with the spirit."[25] Another mutual friend of Lou and Nietzsche, Henrich von Stein, discussed the book with Nietzsche, who "praised the semi-novel of his *soeur inséperable* von Salomé."[26] "There is a loftiness in it," Nietzsche wrote Overbeck, "and even if it's not the eternal feminine which draws this pseudo-maiden ever onward then perhaps it is — the eternal masculine. And there are a hundred echoes of our Tauntenburg conversations in it."[27]

Throughout the years of 1883 through 1885, Lou and Rée continued to live and work together. They spent summers in the nearby mountain resorts where they were often joined by other intellectuals who had become enamored with the bewitching Fraulein von Salomé.

Behind the scenes, the "Naumburg virtue" was still at work. Lisbeth found an ally in Malwida von Meysenbug, Lou's former mentor, who had lost faith in her protégée. In letters they vented their annoyance about her, condemning her current living arrangements with Rée. Even Nietzsche (still under Lisbeth's influence) chimed in, writing to a friend that Lou was "shrewd and fully self-controlled in respect of men's sensuality; heartless and incapable of loving."[28] When under her spell, Friedrich Nietzsche considered her as sharp as an eagle, brave as a lion and yet gloriously feminine. Now she had a "cat's character: that of beast of prey posing as a domestic animal"[29] and "a brain with only the rudiment of a soul."[30]

Lou queried their mutual friend Henrich von Stein about a reunion with Nietzsche, but Nietzsche told Stein that he preferred to remain a hermit in a cave.

Meanwhile Nietzsche labeled Rée's book boring and empty. The public must have felt the same, for Rée's work sank into obscurity. Even Lou would later write that it was "somewhat narrow-minded and utilitarian."[31]

Not long after publishing his book to meet with a renowned lack of interest (in sharp contrast with Lou's ever-growing fan club), Rée decided to give up philosophy altogether and began to pursue a degree in medicine. The intellectual salon became less important to him. He took a room in a separate boarding house to study and saw Lou on weekends. Lou continued to insist that their platonic marriage would last forever. But along with philosophy, Rée had given up on a fuller relationship with his pseudo-girlfriend Lou.

Throughout his relationship with Lou, Rée suffered from anxiety and self-hatred. Lou tried to support him by reassuring him of her love. But her nonsexual love only intensified his anxieties. Lou was constantly being circled by admirers, and Rée's fear of losing her ironically drove him further away. From the other side of Berlin Rée wrote woefully to Lou, asking what would happen to their relationship if one of them got married.

Right on cue, a mysterious man stepped up to fill the space that Rée had so apprehensively opened. Legend has it that he sought Lou out after reading *Struggling for God*— her book so endowed with her spirit and so drenched in God and sex — and appeared unannounced one day at her door. His name was F.C. Andreas, and she would marry him within a year.

8

The Mysterious Mr. Andreas

My love for my husband began — I can't express it otherwise — with an inner command.[1]

— Lou Andreas-Salomé
Looking Back: Memoirs

It's easy to imagine Friedrich Carl Andreas as an Arabian prince, with his broodingly intense stare that exposes a fierce and fervent mind. It's easy to cast Lou as a Russian Scheherazade, enticing him with her intellectual banter and seductive tales. But their story is far from an Arabian fantasy, and would have little to do with traditional gender roles. If anyone were to end up being a member of a harem, it would be Andreas himself.

Born in 1846 in Java, Andreas was forty years old when he showed up at Lou's door. A short, bearded man with flashing eyes, he was a fascinating blend of eastern and western cultures, which made him appear at once cultivated and wildly exotic. His maternal grandfather, Lou tells us, was a German physician who worked in Java and married a beautiful Malaysian woman. From his father's side, he was a member of the Persian royal bloodline, but the family was ousted in a feud and ended up in Germany, taking on the Nordic name Andreas. He was a brilliant teacher of eastern languages. And the list of other languages he studied, many of which he mastered, is long: Greek, Latin, Aramaic, Old Norse, Sanskrit, Hebrew, Javanese, Dutch, French, Scandinavian languages, Turkish, Hindi and English. Along with this he had an in-depth knowledge of the literature, history and art of these civilizations, particularly the ancient ones. He was a vegetarian, abstained from alcohol and had a special affinity with animals — characteristics which Lou found endearing and contagious. Like Lou, money meant little to him: learning and love were his driving passions.

Andreas had a following of brilliant students who were captivated by his special style of teaching. They often stayed up all night, deep in intense conversation, drinking tea, which Andreas made in the style of an oriental tea ceremony. Like Lou, he was highly intuitive and lived each moment to its fullest; but he also saw himself as an explorer, ever looking forward towards a scholarly goal. It was a paradox of personality that they shared — at once lovingly mystical and coldly rational.

Lou's choice of mates, after offers from so many highly accomplished men, seems curious. Like Brunhilde, whose father preserved her in a ring of fire, Lou seemed to have been awaiting a true hero. But Andreas was no Siegfried. Neither was he Nietzsche. By all accounts he was a kind and fiercely loving man, brilliant but without high achievements. He was forever planning a book he never completed. He never distinguished himself at the university, despite his personal impact on his students. Andreas was never fully appreciated by the university, Lou tells us, because his oriental style of teaching could not be measured or evaluated by occidental standards. Like Lou, his true genius lay in his personal effect on others. Like both Gillot and Nietzsche, Andreas was an intellectual, willful, older man, but unlike them he never fulfilled his intellectual promise.

Lou felt that Andreas had a paradoxical nature created by the tension between the goal-oriented western European part of him and the eastern part that simply wanted to experience life. Unlike the fluctuating Apollonian and Dionysian drives Nietzsche wrote about in *The Birth of Tragedy*, the duality within Andreas found no art form that served as referee for the warring factions. He lacked ambition and seemingly had no desire for the public fame Lou had achieved. His impact as a teacher, however, was impressive.

Lou gave almost no concrete details of their courtship. We know that they met sometime in 1886. She does offer us the surprising fact that in November 1886, "the evening before our engagement,"[2] he attempted suicide before her eyes by plunging a knife in his chest. Some biographers believe that the near-fatal accident on the evening before their engagement was the impetus to her marrying him. But she wrote of it as if the marriage were preordained. "My love for my husband began" she wrote a year after marriage, "— I cannot express it otherwise — with an inner command. It is not at all a question of a binding together, but of already being bound."[3] And in her memoir she wrote, "Only someone who knew him intimately and fully, who loved him intimately and fully in character and nature, can know what the word compulsion meant in this case. What brought about this compulsion was the power of something irresistible to which my husband himself succumbed."⁴ Further: "There's no point in trying to describe this to anyone who didn't know my husband"; he had a quality that "I never saw in any other human being." The power of his character and his love overwhelmed her. He embodied both the "colossal, powerful forces, [along] with the unrestrained actions of huge animals," in combination with "the effects of the most delicate, helpless creatures, like a little bird one cannot bear to step on...."⁵ It was this mysterious mixture of overwhelming force and heartbreaking vulnerability that compelled her to love and marry him.

But it leaves us with the question: why did he attempt suicide in front of her? Which in turn leads to an even greater mystery: Though Lou agreed to marry Andreas, she would never consummate the marriage. One theory as to his attempted suicide is that she may have explained to him that it was her intention to remain a virgin forever. Though she uses words such as *compulsion* and *irresistible* in describing her attraction to her husband, the impact of her overwhelming love for Gillot was a deadly threat to her. Her fear of sexuality was both personal and societal.

In an attempt to understand her unwillingness to consummate the marriage, we must start from the general attitude towards sexuality—female sexuality—in this era. Throughout Europe, young women were under tremendous pressure to behave according to the accepted moral code. Sex before marriage was strictly forbidden for women, and there were almost no mitigating circumstances that made it otherwise. On the other hand, marital infidelity in the upper classes where the courtly love exemplar still thrived was considered *de rigueur*—as long as it was handled discreetly. Aristocrats, artists and writers of this age looked down on the middle class as prudish and judgmental. Nonetheless, in all classes, the cult of "pure" womanhood was deeply engrained in the collective psyche. From adolescence onward, young women were steeped in the doctrine of virginity. At home, in church and even in school the *virgo intacto* was held up as a model of noble womanhood. In a weak attempt to explain her decision not to consummate her marriage, Lou wrote about how her girlhood admiration of the virgin warrior, Joan of Arc, intensified when an overexuberant teacher exclaimed, "There's nothing that a pure virgin cannot do!" To Lou's impressionable adolescent mind it must have registered as a doorway to heroic activity—the freedom of the male world that her brothers enjoyed. The armor of virginity would allow her movement in this world. But it hardly explains her resolution against marital sex.

Nineteenth century science considered female sexual desire to be an anomaly — in fact, deviant. Most women don't even have sexual feelings, gynecologists of the time claimed. But because women are compelled to suffer, they must endure the demands of their husbands. The belief that masochism was normal and sexual desire was abnormal in women naturally created a great deal of conflict in the psyche of 19th century women.

Helene Stöcker, in reviewing a character in one of Lou's stories, sums up very well the conflict within Lou. The character has "a passionate desire to be conquered as a woman, and at the same time the outspoken urge to develop herself further in individual freedom."[6] Lou saw sexuality — the Victorian image of a man "conquering" a woman — as the largest threat to her unrestrained freedom. Having absorbed Aunt Caro's philosophy, she believed that women had to choose between sexuality and unrestrained freedom, because by their nature they were biologically inclined to be submissive to men. Lou's healthy sexual drive most certainly would have been treated as a threat to the social order in which she lived, and she viewed it as a personal threat as well. Years later, in her fiction, we will see her questioning her own worthiness, based on society's view of woman's sexuality.

In a disturbingly significant childhood memory which sheds another small ray of light onto her view of sexuality, Lou tells us she witnessed her Russian nanny, a woman she loved dearly, being beaten by her husband. Lou clearly remembered how the woman looked up at her husband with servitude and love in her eyes. Biographer Binion aptly names it a masochist's primal scene. Lou's fear of sexuality may have been the fear of what she saw as the "normal" masochism in the wifely role. She came to associate this behavior with the Russian — particularly Slavic — model of marriage.

In her parents' marriage, although it was neither violent nor abusive, Lou saw her mother had submitted completely to her father's will. But in turn, her father submitted to Lou's will. This remarkable family dynamic most certainly made Lou view her mother's submissive state as inferior and undesirable, as well as giving Lou the impression that her own power was even greater than that of the god-like father figure.

In a diary entry a year after her marriage, she wrote, "The only person I ever loved and yet never criticized was Gillot, although, I really loved him as an ideal."[7] But her youthful way of thinking was over and she no longer sought "a god-man," she wrote. "Were I to love another man as I did Gillot, I would have run from him, because I would have believed in the possibility of passion but not in the possibility of marriage and A

Life."[8] It was the power of Gillot's personality — a man who "wants to rule and affect others with his energy"[9] — that made it possible to love him, but impossible to marry him. In her diary she argued that *married* love and *sexual* love were separate things. She didn't understand why "people who are in love in a predominantly sensual way, *get married.*"[10]

She felt she had symbolically knelt before Gillot the way one kneels before a God. But her relationship with Andreas was not "one person kneeling before another, but two kneeling together."[11] A marriage based on one being subordinate to another threatened her. But it wasn't society that she fought but her own innate desire to subordinate herself, as her mother had to her father and as she had to Gillot.

In childhood Lou couldn't bear to look into a mirror, because it showed her, not as the infinite being she felt herself to be, but as a finite creature with boundary lines. Because of this, she tells us, she avoided mirrors, to keep intact her vision of omnipotence. Throughout her life, she refused to accept limits. Furthermore she believed she could disregard those limits forced upon her. Her mother, Petersburg society, the church: these are all things she escaped quite easily. Now faced with what she saw as the most powerful limitation — a marital sexual union — she refused.

But a marriage without sex wasn't the only stricture she placed on their union. Lou agreed to marry Andreas on the condition that Rée would continue to be part of her life. Andreas eventually agreed and Lou spent an evening explaining the arrangement to Rée. As he was about to leave, he realized it was raining too hard and returned to the warmth of Lou's apartment. They continued talking — for so long that Lou was surprised to see it was light outside when he left. She turned to see a note on her table: "Have mercy — don't look for me."[12] There was never a time she needed Rée's friendship more, she wrote.

While her diary entry makes the early years of her marriage sound serene, they were far from it. The first year was a battle of wills. Headstrong Andreas was sure he could overcome his young bride's sexual inhibition; her childish reticence would pass. After all, he had won her hand through the intensity of his own will. But this was one battle he would not win. Like her decision to refuse conformation by the church — influenced by a reoccurring dream in which she said *No!* to the ceremony — Lou recognized that her prohibition on sexual union came from her unconscious, and saw no choice but to obey it. The two incidences of resistance to tradition point out a key element in Lou's character: she heeded not her conscious, rational, daylight self but her unconscious, that lurked in the realm of dreams and mysterious inner dictates. Like the famed Oracle of Delphi, this interior dictator gave puzzling statements that nonetheless had to be treated with reverence because they were believed to be messages from a god. Giving in to her inner demands made many of her decisions inexplicable and baffling to herself and others. It also put her on the lifelong quest to uncover the meaning of these revelations.

Aside from these conflicts, the young married couple's lives revolved around their independent scholarly studies and general work around the house. Lou says she easily adapted to her husband's lifestyle and began eating a vegetarian diet, wearing simple clothes, taking barefoot walks in the woods and observing animals. They socialized little.

From the outside it appeared the independent, willful Lou von Salomé was a thing of the past. Frau Lou, as she now called herself, settled into her domesticity without any qualms. But the self-determined daughter of the Russian general was merely regrouping her forces. She was a famous author before she was the wife of a scholar, and her independent identity — although in a state of flux early in the marriage — would emerge again, defiant as ever.

II
MUSES AND WRITERS

Although we may first experience the Muse through an external figure, we must remember the Muse's energy is transpersonal and cannot be possessed. The Muse is mysterious — an inspirational, interior source of creativity.
— Linda Schierse Leonard,
The Call to Create, p. 30

...the beloved is scarcely more than the bit of reality which moves a poet to his poem.
— Lou Andreas-Salomé,
Looking Back: Memoirs, p. 16

9
Marriage — and a Life

> *Were I to love another man as I did Gillot, I would have run from him, because I would have believed in the possibility of passion but not in the possibility of marriage and a Life.*[1]
> — Lou Andreas-Salomé
> *Looking Back: Memoirs*

After living in Andreas' bachelor apartment for a short while they bought a house in Tempelhof, a suburb of Berlin. A large old house with huge rooms, surrounded by elm trees, it reminded Lou of her childhood dwelling in St. Petersburg, though far less opulent. They would live there for five years. It marked a new stage in Lou's interests. Rather than the philosophical types who had orbited around her and Paul Rée, she now felt herself instinctively drawn to the writers and artists among whom they lived in the outskirts of Berlin.

By that time many of the writers and artists throughout Europe had been hit by the powerful wake of Nietzsche's announcement, *God is dead.* Following his lead from *The Birth of Tragedy,* writers began to see art as the new religion. The loss of a faith in God caused a shift among educated Europeans. No longer was the life of the soul to be entrusted the church. Now it was the responsibility of the writer to speak for humankind, or as James Joyce put it in *Portrait of the Artist,* like a smithy of the soul, he sought to forge the conscience of his race. It was precisely this urge to look to the writer as priest that drove Lou to quote from Goethe in one of the sermons she wrote for Pastor Gillot. And Nietzsche himself had held Goethe up as a shining example of the god-man, the *Übermensch.*

In 1889, Lou and her husband began attending an independent theater known as the *Freie Bühne*, and after several years of no literary output at all, she began her most prolific era. Lou began writing articles for the journal associated with the *avant-garde* theater, also called *Freie Bühne.*

The theater had been formed to produce works free of censorship and free from making a profit. Plays were produced purely on their artistic merit, and the *Freie Bühne* showcased the works of some of the greatest writers in Europe. She befriended many of the great playwrights of the time who had not yet met with worldwide fame. They included Gerhart Hauptmann, later a recipient of the Nobel Prize; Arne Garborg, one of the most important figures in Norwegian literature of his time; the Hart brothers — Julius and Heinrich, both poets and literary critics; August Strindberg, the Swedish playwright; Arno Holz, author of the Naturalist play *Die Familie Selicke*, which was hailed by critics after its performance at *Freie Bühne* in 1890; and Eugen Kühnemann who later, in a letter to Lou, dedicated his book *Herder's Life* to her.

As a literary movement, Naturalism had started with French writer Émile Zola, whom the German Naturalists admired. Zola's work was inspired by 19th century scientific experiments in heredity and environment and began a new type of novel that would probe deeply into psychology and sociology of human existence. August Strindberg, Henrik Ibsen, Leo Tolstoy and Gerhart Hauptmann ranked among the best European Naturalistic writers. Hauptmann was later considered a leader in the Naturalist movement.

Lou attended rehearsals at *Freie Bühne* and extolled the theatrical offerings through her articles on Hauptmann and others in literary journals. Hauptmann was a young, sensitive intellectual. Lou befriended both him and his wife, Marie. Lou considered his work the center point of the literary community. He "brought something to the stage which was to aid in the triumph of that new direction in art and literature,"[2] she wrote. Hauptmann was a follower of Nietzsche in seeing man's nature as a precarious balance between Dionysian and Apollonian forces.

Within a year of his meeting Lou, Hauptmann's work began to show Lou's influence. In 1890, the independent theater premiered Hauptmann's *Lonely People* (Einsame Menschen). Though inspired by his brother's marital predicament, Hauptmann admits the husband and wife in the play turned out to be his own wife and himself. The character of Anna, the Russian intellectual, most certainly was strongly influenced by Lou.

Lonely People depicts a young intellectual artist, Johannes, married to a less intelligent woman who has little understanding of his artistic sensibilities. When Anna, a Russian philosophy student from the University of Zurich, arrives he begins to see new hope in his life. The family — which includes Johannes' mother-in-law — at first greatly admires the young woman who seems so selfless and dedicated to her work. But Johannes is most fascinated by her. Johannes and Anna discover that they are kindred spirits and spend a lot of time together discussing intellectually exciting subjects, to the dismay of his wife and her mother. Peters describes the story with its familiar tones:

> Her coming has a very stimulating effect on the young artist. At last he has someone to talk to. The stultifying atmosphere of his bourgeois home is lifted from him. Anna's presence releases new and unexpected energies in him, making him feel he is experiencing an artistic rebirth. But the point of the play is that during this process other than purely intellectual forces are also aroused.[3]

As Johannes' obsession with Anna becomes clear, his mother-in-law begins to criticize the girl student, who cares so little about her outward appearance that she goes around with a hole in her sleeve.

Eventually Anna, realizing that her presence is having a destructive effect on the family, leaves. In the final scene, lovesick Johannes leaves a note behind, then exits towards the lake, suggesting he intends to drown himself. But Hauptmann does not show the final act, leaving the audience with the question — is his path towards the lake representative of suicide or escape? Does Anna bring death or rebirth? It is a question that would be ever-present in Lou's life as well. Was she a creative or destructive force — or was she beyond such terms: beyond good and evil?

Intellectual stimulation leading to inspiration, inspiration leading to desire: it was becoming a worn path in Lou's life. The drama gives us a glimpse into the effect Lou had on the writers around her, how her insights into the artistic soul could lead to artistic rebirth. But it also shows us her curious way of dealing with this magical influence off-stage: she reviewed the play herself for a literary journal. She praised *Lonely People*, but in her detached way she comments that the playwright doesn't fully comprehend the character Anna, who represents "the modern woman." (That she becomes a critic of those she inspires will later be a feature in her relationship with Rainer Maria Rilke as well.) If Lou didn't recognize herself in Anna, she missed out on the compliment. She was "a new kind of female character for the German stage," wrote Warren Maurer, "[m]aking her own way in the male world ... without sacrificing her femininity."[4] Although Anna is "subject to the same temptations as Johannes, she vacillates briefly and then follows her better moral instincts by withdrawing her disruptive influence...."[5] While many a muse would be pleased with this depiction, it is significant that in Lou's analysis she didn't seem to see an image of herself, but looked *alongside* the artist to uncover a greater work of art — *two kneeling before something rather than one kneeling to the other*. Like being both the garden and the gardener, she was art object and art critic, preferring the latter role, for it gave her self-rule. Lou's ability to look objectively at works she had influenced made her friends believe she had a total absence of vanity — who wouldn't be affected by such flattery? But it may well have been another of Lou's mysterious inner commands, a need to detach herself from objectification, the ever present urge towards unrestrained freedom.

Naturally, Lou's critical approach to the inspired work did not always please the inspired artist. Hauptmann later commented that he was too dumb for Lou's tastes.

If men behaved flirtatiously towards his wife, it probably didn't seem unusual to Andreas. He certainly knew he had married a very rare and charming woman. But such flirtations were only the beginning of the long, strange journey they would take together.

In 1892, not long after the rebirth of Lou's literary productivity, a new man proclaimed his love for Lou. He would be the first of many in the Andreas marriage. His name was Georg Ledebour. Unlike the sensitive, artistic types that circled around the theater that Lou frequented, Ledebour was a defiant and dynamic man, a political activist and an editor and journalist for a Social Democratic newspaper. After World War I he would become a leader of a socialist movement. His politics were extreme as his character was strong and fearless. Although Lou had little or no interest in politics — she was far too individualistic for that — his strong will made him just the type of man to whom she was attracted.

When he asked her why she didn't wear a wedding ring, she coyly replied that they had "forgot to buy rings, and now decided to leave it that way."[6] Ledebour found this preposterous. Detecting that her marriage lacked fulfillment, he told her she was not yet a woman. Lou was surprised by his insight into her marriage. They quickly fell in love. Lou found herself overwhelmed by the experience. They met secretly whenever possible — even though their relationship remained chaste. His presence in her life "meant salvation from an almost unbearable loneliness."[7] She considered divorcing Andreas. But when she informed Andreas of her new love and her intension to leave him, Andreas replied with finality, "I can't stop *knowing* that you are my wife."[8] Ledebour insisted on talking to Andreas, but Lou did all she could to keep the two men apart — first telling Ledebour that Andreas was ill, then, that he was insanely jealous: "The excitable state of my husband, who wasn't blind, but preferred blindness, insofar as he would rather simply stab the other person to death than talk things over with him, was the determining factor."[9] Fearful of what Andreas might do, she claims to have felt helpless, and remained with Andreas even though her strongest inclination was to flee. In her memoirs she sounds uncharacteristically passive in the situation. She felt "rubbed raw"[10] by her conflicting desires and the external pressures from the two willful men.

In the end, she gave into her husband's demand never to see Ledebour again.

After a year of these dramatic scenes, the strange yet incomplete bond with Andreas was somehow strengthened in her mind. "[H]ow weak the bonds of sacrament or society seem in comparison with the *indissoluble* bond created by my husband's character and nature, which would not admit of the slightest loosening,"[11] she wrote years later.

As she'd once clung to Rée to protect her from Nietzsche's power over her, she now clung to Andreas, to protect her from *all* other men, forever.

When Ledebour was jailed for political reasons, Lou sent him letters, but they were promptly returned unopened. He never spoke to her again.

What is most significant about her relationship to Ledebour was that it marked a change in their marriage. Andreas refused to let her go — "there still could be no talk of divorce" but "it was not humanly possible to go on as we had...."[12] Although she accepted his demand to remain married to him, "a new arrangement was settled upon. Nothing would change outwardly. But inwardly everything would."[13]

All through this tumultuous period, Lou never ceased writing. Strongly influenced by her exposure to the plays shown at the *Freie Bühne*, Lou had become interested in the plays of Henrik Ibsen. Andreas translated Ibsen's plays into German for her: *A Doll's House*, *Hedda Gabler*, *The Wild Duck* and others. She was impressed by Ibsen's fully human portrayals of women, women who longed for something outside their domestic confines. She began writing a book that would later be called *Ibsen's Heroines*, which presents a psychological examination of the women in his plays, who seek freedom from the narrow 19th century definitions of womanhood. Published in 1892, *Ibsen's Heroines* established Lou — who was already a famous novelist — as a literary critic.

One reviewer called *Ibsen's Heroines* "the best book yet written on

Ibsen."[14] Another wrote, "[I]t is only right and delightful that it is a woman who has so well understood old Henrik's praise of women."[15]

In a study of Lou's work, Biddy Martin sums up *Ibsen's Heroines*: "Salomé's interpretation of Ibsen's female characters is first and foremost a study in their psychology and an effort to work through certain key questions about love and sociality...."[16] Using a parable of a wild duck forced to live in an attic, Lou demonstrates Ibsen's insights into the conflict between one's true nature and social and domestic constraints.

Soon after the publication of her critique of Ibsen's work, she began writing the first book length study of Nietzsche to be published, based on an early sketch she had shown to Nietzsche in 1882.

10

In Nietzsche's Shadow

After Buddha was dead, his shadow was still shown for centuries in a cave — a tremendous, gruesome shadow.[1]
— Friedrich Nietzsche
The Gay Science

In the early part of 1888, while in Nice, Nietzsche expressed to a friend his emotional anguish, calling himself "a sufferer who is ashamed to betray how much he suffers."[2] He lamented that his books were not fully recognized and his "relentless and underground struggle" against everything "revered and loved"[3] had driven a part of his psyche underground to a frightening and lonely place. He stated prophetically that he was "something decisive and doom-laden standing between two millennia."[4]

In December of 1888 and January of 1889, while Nietzsche was staying in Turin, Italy, his friends began receiving strange letters from him. Nietzsche's letters had always reflected his sharp mood swings, generally influenced by his state of health. But the letters of late 1888 and early 1889 were marked sharply by delusion. Later dubbed the *Wahnbriefe* (madness letters), the letters demonstrate his literal identification with his most profound ideas. A letter to Jakob Burckhardt read: "I bear the tedium of having created a world. Now you are — thou art — our great greatest teacher: I, together with Ariadne, need only be the golden mean in all things, having in every respect such superiors...."[5] It was signed *Dionysus*. To August Strindberg, who had written to Nietzsche in admiration of his work, he wrote, "I have convoked a conference of princes in Rome, I intend to have the young Kaiser face a firing squad." He signed it "Nietzsche Caesar."[6] To the King of Italy, Umberto I, he sent a message that he would come to Rome; he signed it "The Crucified."[7] In a gesture that suggests the level of importance Cosima Wagner played in his imagination, he wrote a short note, addressing her as the mythical wife of the god of ecstasy: "Ariadne, I love you. Dionysus."[8] Another note to her is even more disturbing: "It is mere prejudice that I am a human being. Yet I've often dwelt among human beings, from the lowest to the highest. Among the Hindus, I was Buddha, in Greece Dionysus — Alexander and Caesar were reincarnations of me.... However, I now come as Dionysus victorious," adding at the end, "I also hung on the cross."[9]

Franz Overbeck wrote to Peter Gast that he had become increasingly concerned in December when Nietzsche's letters began to reflect feverish exaltation. Overbeck tells Gast that from the letters it became clear to him that "N[ietzsche] had gone out of his mind. He was not only a king, but also the father of other kings (Umberto and others), had been to his own funeral (and that of his son Robilant), and so on, and all this in a frenzied tone of a madman."[10]

On a cold January day, after witnessing a horse's beating by a cruel owner, Nietzsche rushed compassionately to the aid of the helpless animal, threw his arms around its neck, then collapsed in the street. When he regained consciousness, he was speaking incoherently. From that point, it is said, he never recovered his sanity. His landlord, seemingly more concerned with avoiding public scandal than preserving Nietzsche's well-being, contacted Franz Overbeck. Soon after, Overbeck traveled to Turin to find Nietzsche "crouching and reading in the corner of a sofa — the last proofs of *N[ietzsche] contra Wagner,* as I later found — looking horribly worn out." Nietzsche recognized his friend and rushed to embrace him, breaking into a flood of tears. Overbeck was "so shaken" by his friend's condition he could barely "stand upright."[11]

Nietzsche, however, conducted himself with great dignity when Overbeck took him to the psychiatric hospital, and even recognized the doctor who greeted him, Dr. Wille. Nietzsche had consulted him years before, when researching religious insanity. Nietzsche greeted him, recalling that he was "doctor for the insane,"[12] not attaching the significance of this to his own situation. Subsequently, Nietzsche's condition stabilized in the institution and eventually his mother took him home to care for him.

Though one doctor told Overbeck in confidence that he suspected Nietzsche's insanity was caused by syphilis, there is no concrete evidence of this. And the fact that Nietzsche's father went insane due to what doctors then mysteriously called "softening of the brain" may be the most probable link to Nietzsche's condition. Lou would be the first person to write a book on Nietzsche, and would offer fascinating insight on his pending insanity, which seemed woefully obvious to her from the time she met him.

Nietzsche himself believed that Lou had a unique ability to understand him — and it is not a belief to be taken lightly. During their summer of "trinity" talks, he had written to Lou, exploring a thought "about whether or not I had some predisposition for madness.... But when you read this you will in the end say *yes!* And will make a note of it in your sketch of me."[13] This pronouncement was probably more prophetic than he realized.

After Nietzsche's collapse came the interpretations of his work. "Nietzsche's philosophical history ended in January 1889," wrote biographer Rüdier Safranski, "[t]hen commenced the other history, the history of his influence and resonance."[14]

Lisbeth Nietzsche had, in 1885, married Bernhard Förster and together they traveled to South America where they intended to start a colony dedicated to the purity of the German race. When Nietzsche collapsed, Lisbeth returned to Germany. There she began the process of archiving Nietzsche's writings to reflect her own narrow views, as well as falsifying some records — efforts that would later enable Adolf Hitler to utilize Nietzsche's work to foster his own will to power. In 1893, Elizabeth established the Nietzsche Archive using one of the rooms in their Naumburg house. She began a series of arguments with Overbeck and others in her version of Nietzsche's legacy.

In 1894 Lou completed the first book-length study on Nietzsche and his philosophy. She makes a strong case for her belief that Nietzsche's philosophy and his insanity fed one another and drove him over the edge. She relates the intricate interweave of Nietzsche's philosophy and his mental and physical health, and demonstrates that Nietzsche himself saw this as a sound approach to his thoughts and works. She points out that "[s]uffering and loneliness were the two great lines of fate in Nietzsche's biography."[15] Throughout his works, she says, are references to "*the value of suffering for the gain of knowledge.*"[16] He acknowledged "the influence of mood upon a person who is ill and the influence of recovery upon one's thinking."[17] After each episode of illness, Lou reports, he arose triumphantly from his own ashes:

> All things became new, even to the mind — "*neuschmeckend*" or "new tasting," as he called it tellingly — and to one's eyes the most common and everyday assumes a new cast. Everything absorbs something from freshness and dew of a morning's beautiful dawn because one morning has separated it

from the preceding night. And so ever recuperation becomes his own rebirth and with it all life around him — and as always the pain is "entwined with the victory."[18]

She points out that his famous line, "That which does not destroy me makes me stronger,"[19] was no clever boast, but an essential element in his creative genius. (It was this form of intellectual masochism that the two shared. The young Lou von Salomé derived *pleasure* from driving herself to the point of illness: she fell *ill* in *full joy*.) Lou illustrates that Nietzsche saw suffering as the mother of the soul, when she quotes from *Zarathustra*: "Spirit is that life which itself cuts into life: with its own suffering it increases its own knowledge.... You only know the spark of the spirit but you do not see it as the anvil, nor see the gruesomeness of the hammer."[20] And from *Beyond Good and Evil*, she quotes:

> That tension of the soul during misfortune ... its shuddering when it looks at great devastation, its inventiveness and courage in carrying its burdens, enduring, interpreting, exploiting misfortune; and whatever has been has been given to the soul — depth, mystery, mask, spiritedness, trickery and greatness — has it not been bestowed through suffering and through the discipline of great suffering.[21]

His philosophy "reveals his inner contradictions: exultation, mingling pain and bliss."[22] It was the power of these two extreme states that thrust him into creative output.

> The immersion in bliss and agony, enthusiasm and suffering, always led Nietzsche towards a spiritual rebirth.... [T]he wounding of self and its uprooting from any sense of "home," were conditions within which his spirit luxuriated before they discharged themselves in new creations.[23]

Lou approaches Nietzsche as a preacher without God, "fundamentally a religious personality, a genius confronted with the death of God."[24] Lou writes,

> Nietzsche's story involves the "continuing effect of the religious drive within the thinker," which remains powerful after the God to whom he had related was smashed. There is an afterglow. "The sun has already set but the heaven of our life still glows and shines as if reflected from something we no longer see."[25]

In what Lou calls Nietzsche's "final creative period" — from Zarathustra onward — Lou believes Nietzsche's inner world took precedence over the external one. And the more he became entrenched in his inner world, the more he saw it as a pronouncement for all mankind: "*All gods are dead,*" she quotes him, "*now we want a superior man.*"[26] His "judgment turned into a universal imperative, a command to all humankind," Lou says.

She makes clear that it is the ingredients of psychosis, prefiguring Freud in leaps and bounds: the domination of the subconscious over the conscious world, the belief that one's inner world is the only reality and the delusion that one can rescue mankind. The loss of faith drives the thinker beyond God and he is left with only himself. There lies the danger in the philosophy of *Thus Spake Zarathustra*. In the creation of the Übermensch Nietzsche creates a god in his own image, which according to Lou was his downfall:

> His various philosophies are for him just so many surrogates for God, which were intended to help him compensate for a mystical God-ideal outside himself.... At first he fashioned the mystical superior-human ideal through self-intoxicate fantasy, dreams and rapture-like visions; and then, in order to save himself from himself, he sought to identify himself with them through one tremendous leap. Finally he became a dual figure, half-sick and suffering; half-saved: a laughing superior being.[27]

It is an astounding psychological analysis by one who had never studied psychoanalysis; in fact, she could not have read much if any on the subject. What she learned of psychology up to this point was from Nietzsche himself.

"[O]nly disaster could come of substituting an idolatrous version of one's self for the lost image of God,"[28] the modern translator of Lou's book on Nietzsche, Siegfried Mandel, wrote in the introduction. According to Mandel, Lou astutely portrays in her book "what she thought would ultimately be the consequence of Nietzsche's daring and perilous experimentation with 'self' in his quest for knowledge: a laughing Dionysus-Zarathustra mask which he would no longer be able to remove."[29] She quotes from *Beyond Good and Evil* when she relates that Nietzsche identified with "the sacrificial animal as God."[30]

In *Nietzsche*, Lou sums him up as a tragic hero. Nietzsche's efforts to express the loss of God for a whole civilization, to write with such beauty while enduring illness and madness: these were the traits that made him a heroic figure; this is what is so moving about his philosophy. Lou's book is in awe of his genius and sacrifice. Livingstone comments:

> Laudations recur throughout the book. She speaks of Nietzsche's unequalled ability to find the finest formulations for the finest nuances of thought, of the living force of his ideas, which can be contradicted but not killed, of his "delicate and expert hand," of his infallible instinct for discovering lacunae

in knowledge, his scrupulous honesty, his genius. "Even his errors open an infinity of new perspectives"; and "no other writer has been able to transform thought so completely into lived experience."[31]

After reading Lou's work, a close friend of Nietzsche wrote, "It is clear to me now (although Lou veils this) that with Zarathustra the madness begins, but *what* a madness, and what a fire it throws in shining flames over the world."[32]

Clear from her book is the great admiration Lou had for Nietzsche; clear, too, is the influence he had on her. But she was also dealing with public perception. In quoting Nietzsche's letters she often includes a few personal lines that demonstrate his affection and esteem for her. She may have predicted that Elizabeth Nietzsche would attack her credibility — and Lisbeth did mount a campaign against the book. However, the personal lines from his letters seem out of place in a scholarly work, for it is a work of analysis, not a personal account. The emotional distance with which Lou wrote her book on Nietzsche, mixed with her intimate knowledge and involvement, led many to believe she was a cold and calculating machine. It was as if she loved with her brain and analyzed with her heart. As when reviewing Hauptmann's play, she doesn't acknowledge her personal feelings in the drama openly, although at the same time she makes the reader acutely aware that she *was* emotionally involved. Her book on Nietzsche was as close as she would come to proclaiming her worshipful admiration of him and her strong identification with his inner struggle.

11

L'Homme Eternal

Sex is difficult, yes. But there are difficult things with which we've been charged; almost everything serious is difficult, and everything is serious.[1]
— Rainer Maria Rilke

After the failed romance with Ledebour, finishing her Gillot-inspired novel *Ruth* and her study of Nietzsche, Lou began her new lifestyle. Throughout the rest of the 1890s she traveled to the cultural capitals — Berlin, Munich, Paris, and Vienna — where she was easily accepted into the best literary circles. She carried with her the caché of being both a well-known author and the former romantic interest and intellectual companion of Nietzsche. Returning home from her adventures, inspired by her rich experiences, she would write in a feverish state. She wrote a continuous stream of articles on religion, women's issues and literary reviews. She continued her flow of novels and short stories. And while her memoir, written when she was in her seventies, paradoxically gives little in the way of insight, her fiction of the 1890s gives us a rare and surprisingly open look into her experiences in the cities of Europe as well as her deep inner struggles.

Lou had every intention of having a lifestyle of complete freedom. Again as demanded by her inner voice, she knew she must travel and follow her heart wherever it led her. Perhaps to lighten the tension in their marriage, she even encouraged Andreas to take a mistress. *What man wouldn't be happy with that?* she asked a friend. As for herself, she would always return to him from her adventures.

After her completion of *Nietzsche* she sojourned to Paris, one of the first among many of her continental excursions. There she made numerous friends, among them playwright Frank Wedekind. Wedekind had come from Germany to Paris in 1891, just after completing his first major play, *Spring's Awakening* (Frühlings Erwachen), a work that deals frankly with adolescent sexuality and the effect of the repressive sexual morality of the *fin-de-siècle* Europeans. The play's depiction of sexuality between two teenagers, along with a mixture of violence and grotesque comedy, was a bit too much for a 19th century audience. With characters like Hänschen Rilow, who takes pornographic pictures of women into the bathroom then flushes them down the toilet when he's finished with them, the century would have to turn before Wedekind's work made it to the stage, and even then it was heavily censored.

Years earlier, in 1886, he had befriended Germany's leading Naturalist, Lou's friend Gerhart Hauptmann. But Wedekind's approach to drama was in contrast with the Naturalists. He saw Naturalism as the *least* truthful art form. Art is not natural but reflective of nature and human nature, he believed. In the play *Children and Fools* (Kinder und Narren), written in 1890, Wedekind "lampoons the naturalist's obsession with impartial observation" when in the play, the naturalist playwright "kisses his wife and makes notes for a play over her shoulder at the same time."[2] While Naturalists were concerned about social injustice, Wedekind "was attracted personally and intellectually to artists, circus performers, pickpockets, prostitutes, and other inhabitants on the fringe of bourgeois culture. He was not interested in realistic depiction of society's ills, nor did he claim insight into the souls of his characters"; rather, "Wedekind explored the ambiguous moral world that lies beneath social appearances...."[3]

Lou in middle age (© Sigmund Freud Privatstiftung).

Like Freud, Wedekind believed that sexual instinct rules human behavior, and that the repression of it was the cause of neuroses. He fantasized about a world free of all sexual restraint. However extreme Wedekind's thinking, it demonstrates how an individual is affected by a repressed society — by a strict social-sexual code with which Lou, too, would soon find herself in conflict.

Like Lou, Wedekind believed that the artist's greatest inspiration comes from experience. And Paris was the mother of artistic experience, drawing writers and artists from around the world for decades to come. In the street cafes of certain areas one could mingle with dancers, writers, painters, titled aristocrats, and prostitutes. Wedekind wasn't interested in the well-educated but in those who lived and experienced life directly. He settled in Paris and established relationships with people in all classes of Parisian society. The year Wedekind met Lou, he had been living a bohemian life in Paris and working on his "LuLu" plays, which would become his most famous and influential work.

In the "LuLu" plays, *The Earth-Spirit* (Der Erdgeist) and *Pandora's Box* (translated as Die Büchse der Pandora), LuLu is the quintessential *femme fatale*. She is glamorous, sexy and dangerous. She uses her greatest weapon — her sexual appeal — to get what she wants.

Some biographers have suggested Lou was in part an inspiration for the LuLu character — or rather revenge for what would happen between them. But Wedekind had been working on the play for several years before he met her. And the Wedekindian *femme fatale* has little in common with Lou Andreas-Salomé. LuLu is a glamorous seductress, a lower class girl who uses her sexuality to entice upper class men. Wedekind found "Frau Lou" austere and ascetic. She still wore black dresses that rose to her chin and dragged the ground at her feet, which was considered a sort of uniform for women students from Zurich, a uniform that caused men like Wedekind to label her *sexless*.

The incident between Wedekind and Lou *would* result in fictional inspiration — but this time only for Lou. It would be the basis of Lou's novella *Fenitschka*. The novella is an interesting exploration of a man unable to comprehend the entirety of a woman, a man who uses simplistic sexual categories to define a complex being.

Late one evening Lou along with a group of friends went to a café, Les Halles. Wedekind was a friend of one of them and joined the group for conversation and coffee. Lou and Wedekind got into a frank discussion about the society and sexuality — Wedekind's theme in much of his work — that lasted to the early morning hours. Wedekind invited her to his room to continue the conversation. When she got there, Wedekind locked the door of his room behind her and put the key in his pocket. She realized he had mistaken her frankness for a seduction. From her reaction, he realized he had misjudged her behavior, was profoundly embarrassed and sought her forgiveness. They became friends after that and as she wrote in her memoir, "I spent more time in Paris with Frank Wedekind than anyone else."[4] He could usually be found sitting "at one of those sticky marble tables in front of some café in the Latin Quarter, scribbling poems."[5] She went to the Latin Quarter frequently with Wedekind and others. She was delighted by the French prostitutes, whom she found fascinating with their mixture of blunt openness about their sexual trade and their refined French manners.

Transforming life into fiction, Lou tells the story from the point of view of Max Werner. Werner is a Wedekind-type who is at once a brilliant and decadent man, who is well-versed in academic psychology, but with a blind spot when it comes to understanding real live women. Fenitschka, a Russian girl student, and Werner met among a group of late night theater-goers who have congregated at a café in the Latin Quarter.

Werner has no sexual interest in her at first, but observes her because "all women evoked a certain interest in him." He notes: "Her inconspicuous figure of medium build was enveloped entirely by black garb supposedly the favorite dress of many of the women students from Zurich."[6] Her prim student attire gives Fenitschka a "slightly droll and non–Parisian look — almost like a nun."[7] His interest in her came from "a burning desire to learn some practical psychology."[8]

The description of Fenitschka (he shortens to the long Russian name to Fenia) is in spirit very close to Lou:

> What struck him in Fenia above all were her intelligent brown eyes, which looked at every object — and every person as if it were an object — with a peculiar openness and clarity, and also the Slavic cut of her face with the short little nose, Max Werner's favorite type of nose, one which leaves sensible room for a kiss.... But this face was pale from hard work and showing the effect of a lot of mental strain and stress did not seem eager to be kissed at all.[9]

The group of theater-goers, sitting in a Parisian street café, under gas lights and drifting clouds of cigarette smoke, are distracted by a raucous group of working class men and women inside the restaurant. Lou calls the young women *grisettes* (a term used in nineteenth century Paris for working class girls who wore rough gray cloth dresses). One girl in particular was being teased by the group and what starts as drunken frivolity, turns into a shower of "foul and ugly language."[10] Even the young woman's companion joins in the "brutal laughter."[11]

As the vulgar language and laughter spill out towards the sidewalk table where Fenitschka and Werner sit with their friends, everyone grows silent, embarrassed by the display. One of the women anxiously tightens her veil over her face. Werner notices that Fenitschka is engrossed in the interior scene; then she rises to her feet spontaneously. She catches the eye of the humiliated girl who now has tears rolling over her rouged cheeks. Something in Fenitschka's eyes offer the girl unspoken support. Drawing on Fenitschka's unspoken kindness, the *grisette's* tears stop flowing; she picks up her "threadbare little silk jacket"[12] and leaves her companion behind and it is he now who is the object of the crowd's jeers and taunts.

As the outside group discusses the incident, Fenitschka comments that the girl "must have been dying for a little human kindness."[13] Max comments that he too has had similar occasions to offer a rare glimpse of kindness to "those girls."[14] Fenitschka tells him bluntly she would imagine "those girls" would rightly be suspicious of a strange man offering "kindness." Max is taken aback by the candidness of her comment, hardly what he would expect from the androgynous girl student. He marvels to himself at the lucid directness of the young Russian woman whom he had only just met, and with whom he was now discussing working class sexual mores as if they were "a rare species of exotic animal."[15]

Max tells her — with even greater bluntness — it would hurt the pride and self-esteem of such women if a man didn't at least notice "what she had to offer as a woman."[16] He leans in closer and tells her their class is not so different. We use "language that is abstract about subjects which are not abstract at all,"[17] he says pointedly. A young girl of their class may think that all "she wants from her companion is a sharing of intellectual interests and a communion of souls," when in reality all she really wants is to "love and possess him."[18]

As the conversation continues he begins to wonder if Fenia's sexless garb is only a cover for a "free and easy lifestyle."[19] The group takes a walk through the streets of Paris as night turns to dawn. As they move among the Parisians who flock to the open air markets in the early morning, Fenitschka begins to remind him of one of the women in the pre–Raphaelite paintings, "meant to personify intellect" and purity, "while the blossoms that adorn them in flaming colors evoke passion and intoxicate the senses."[20]

Lou Andreas-Salomé, the author, shows how Max's mind vacillates from one extreme to the other in his assessment of women — *either* a nun *or* a free and easy girl student; *either* a lady *or* a *grisette*. Is she a nice *bourgeoisie* or a wild bohemian? When he does detect something beyond her nun-like demeanor, he suspects that the outer appearance is merely a ruse for a "free and easy lifestyle." In judging her purely from his own needs and desires, he fails to see her as she really is — a young woman with healthy sex drives but a mind that attempts to analyze such powerful and unacceptable feelings out of existence. A multifaceted approach to her never seems to dawn on him.

When he steers their walk towards his hotel, he invites her for coffee. When she accepts he is "almost irritated at her obligingness," and "his confusion about this young woman plagued him."[21] Why would she trust him, someone she had only met hours before? When they go to his room, he starts to kiss her but she turns away. Ruthlessly and quickly, he locks the door and puts the key in his pocket, as Wedekind had done to Lou. Fenitschka turns and looks at him at first with "wide open, frightened and wondering"[22] eyes. But then her look turns to shock and disgust. Ashamedly, he retrieves the key from his pocket almost involuntarily and unlocks the door. Max immediately casts her back into her nun role. When she flees from the room, he runs after her, begging her forgiveness. There is nothing to forgive, she tells him. It was her own stupidity and lack of caution that put her in the situation. She had never been around an "indecent man"[23] before. However, she says, "Both of us should be excused because we didn't know any better."[24] This sentence sums up Lou's feelings about the gender issues of her day. She doesn't hold it against men that they misunderstand women. Women misunderstand men as well. There is nothing to forgive because we *don't know any better*. Nonetheless, Andreas-Salomé is fighting for a new level of understanding.

Max and Fenitschka run into each other a year later at a Russian estate where his sister is getting married. She has changed. No longer the unusual girl student who confused him, she now has something "soft and gentle about her that had not been there before."[25] She looks "like a flower in full bloom."[26] An earlier suggestion that she has a secret lover prompts them to get into a frank, philosophical discussion of sexual love. She describes sexual love as something at once essential and marvelous, both common and sacred "like the daily bread that is blessed and stills our hunger, like the stream of air which comes into our homes and refreshes us."²⁷ It is "the most important, most beautiful, and most natural"²⁸ of all human experiences. But society makes it seem like a crime, particularly for women. She tells him it is "disgusting" that women are "forced into secrecy":

> [I]t is the most denigrating thing I have ever known. Why should you have to deny and hide something from the bottom of your heart; why be ashamed when you should be jubilant!²⁹

Max argues that public opinion is only half of it. He says that sexual love is an intimate, private experience, and public revelation would cause one to feel violated. "Yes, that is the way men look at it,"³⁰ she replies. For women, the secrecy creates an aura of personal shame to which the man is less vulnerable. It creates a false cowardliness and a false hypocrisy in women, because they are forced to be constantly aware of public perceptions and to lie about that which brings the greatest of joy.

When she admits openly to him that she is having a sexual affair, Max admires her courage, and tells her that he and his fiancée are also sexually involved. She explains that she had shared numerous friendships with men at the university, but it was nothing like the present relationship. She came to realize that it's "a colossal mistake we make, to believe that 'mind' and 'soul'" are "deeper and nobler"³¹ than sexual love. The intellect is "certainly not nobler, but rather the grossest and most vulgar part of our being. With cold calculation it attaches itself like a leech indiscriminately to all sorts of people, only to drop them when it has extracted from them whatever fascination they held." In this startlingly frank passage, Lou seems to be reflecting on her youthful experience with Gillot and Nietzsche.

And yet her stance hasn't really changed, for Fenitschka tells Max she is unwilling to marry her lover. Max doesn't understand and she tells him flatly: "Love and marriage are simply not the same thing."³² Max is shocked to hear such a statement coming from a woman; he tells her it is only natural that a woman should seek a lasting union. After all, look at his fiancée, he tells her: "if she didn't want to share her whole life with me, then it would not be real love, it would be just sensual." She corrects his phrase: "—*purely* sensual"³³ (italics added). Fenitschka is suggesting something that no man of his era was willing to face: that he too could be used as a sex object, that women may convince themselves to do what society expects them to do—to desire marriage when in fact they too are sometimes drawn to the "purely sensual" experience. "Oh, nonsense,"³⁴ is his quick reply. And yet it had been Max himself who had suggested that women had the same animal instincts as men, that they merely feigned innocence, even to themselves.

In her stories Lou manages to air a number of different possibilities in the problems between men and women. The outer conflict in the discussions between Max and Fenitschka addresses Lou's inner conflicts. It gives her work a multitude of voices and a greater depth than much of the writings on the so-called "woman question," the major debate of her era. *Fenitschka* shows woman as the *mysterious other*, a European literary concept utilized by male writers. But Lou is offering a new understanding: when it comes to love, men and women aren't all that different. But men like Max Werner might not want to accept such a concept. *Fin-de-siècle* mores forced women to feel ashamed of their sexual needs and to repress such feelings, dressing them in a more acceptable form of desire: marriage. Such mental deceptions, whether conscious or unconscious, create what seems to men neurotic and irrational thinking. It is a Freudian-like statement that Freud himself never made.

Comparatively, Wedekind's *LuLu* remains a caricature of female sexuality. Fenitschka is the counterbalance of LuLu, and of the *femme fatale* image. Though she lacks the seductive glamour of Wedekind's character, Fenitschka is every bit as enigmatic, and certainly more true-to-life. *Fenitschka* suggests growth instead of destruction, understanding rather than condemnation, in the relationship between men and women. When Fenitschka tells Max that she had a dream in which she is sitting at the table among the *grisettes*— that she is one of the *grisettes*— Max is offended by her self-deprecation. In a reversal of attitudes, social pressures have caused Fenitschka to see herself as lowly, while Max has begun to see her in her the fullness of her humanity, despite the revelation of her sexual affair.

At the end of story Fenitschka decides she can no longer live with her private shame and secrecy no matter how falsely imposed. But neither can she marry her lover because her bonds to him are passionate and sensual. She rejects the idea of marrying not because she demeans the sensual but because marriage, under these circumstances, would also be a socially forced arrangement that would place her in yet another one-dimensional role. She breaks off the engagement in what becomes an Andreas-Salomé signature scene — two amorous men and one self-contained woman. While Max is visiting with Fenitschka in her room her lover arrives. Fenitschka conceals Max in her bedroom, where he is cast into a voyeuristic position as he overhears her breaking up with the unseen lover.

II. L'Homme Eternal 95

While Lou's weeks in Paris seem almost idle, the experiences became rich fodder for her work. She also met a group of Russians in Paris, and struck up a friendship with Russian physician named Savély. When August came, they traveled to the mountains above Zurich together. Although their closeness didn't go beyond friendship, they spent the hot summer months together in a rustic farmhouse. There they worked together on a play, lived on goat's milk and wild berries, and endured the rigors and the beauty of country life. In between her adventures she struggled to write a number of essays on religion.

At this time in her life Lou uncharacteristically began developing strong friendships with women, most notably Frieda von Bülow. Von Bülow, a writer and African explorer, was born of an old aristocratic German family and had spent over five years in East Africa with Dr. Carl Peters helping him to found hospitals there. The work was grueling and life in the jungle areas was full of hardships. She worked selflessly until the early 1890s when her health gave out and she returned to Berlin. She met Lou there in 1892. The two women were very much alike — intelligent, strong-willed and hard-working. Frieda's writing career was mostly founded on her writings about Africa. But Lou was the stronger of the two, and over the years of their friendship she endured Frieda's fluctuating mood swings.

In the latter part of the nineteenth century, the splendid city of Vienna erupted into an intellectual and cultural movement, rising like the cultural cream of Europe. In Stephan Zweig's memoir of *fin-de-siècle* Vienna, he depicts a city that is unified in its love of art, beauty and great music. It spanned across classes and ethnicities. "[O]ne was not a real Viennese without this love of culture, without this sense, aesthetic and critical at once, of the holiest exhurence of life."[35] The lingering musical spirits of Mozart and Beethoven were omnipresent in the city while Brahms, Strauss, and Mahler were alive and composing there. And while Vienna was well known for its love of grand music, rich coffee and divine pastries, the Viennese were lovers of theater as well. Theater embodied all that Vienna offered — culture and pleasure-seeking to the highest degree. Like their city's namesake waltz, the Viennese seemed made for stylized movements and costumes of seduction.

The growing power of the educated middle class had broken through the stuffy realm of aristocracy. Novelists, dramatists, composers, artists and other cultured *bourgeois* all gathered at the famed coffee houses where one could engage in intellectual conversation or read the daily newspapers from around the world while enjoying the coffee with fresh whipped cream, and perhaps a touch of liquor. "A Platonic Academy" and "the democratic club" were just a few of the names applied to the coffee houses of that era, which required only "the small price of a cup of coffee"[36] to enter.

The Café Griensteidl, set in the center of Vienna, was an elegant *kaffehaus* with high-arched ceilings. The small tables grouped throughout the large room took on the look of little altars beneath the vaulted architecture. Here a group of Austrian literati, known as *Jung Wien*— Young Vienna — met regularly. Many of the men of this group would become famous for their novels and theater dramas that captured that uniquely rich mixture of the cultural and the erotic that characterized *fin-de-siècle* Vienna. The group included dramatist and novelist Arthur Schnitzler, one of the most prolific writers of his age; poet-dramatist Hugo von Hofmannsthal, considered a poetic genius at a young age; Felix Salten, then a theater critic who was later noted for being the author of the popular children's novel *Bambi*; and Richard Beer-Hofmann, who was one of the first writers to use the stream-of-consciousness style. This talented group of young men met daily to drink coffee, to read their latest work to one another, to discuss the latest concert, their latest play, or even their latest sexual conquest. It was a lively scene in a lively city, fueled by exquisite coffee, erotic passion and the intense ambition of the upwardly mobile middle class.

In March of 1895, after a long visit with her mother and brother in St. Petersburg, Lou traveled to Vienna, with her friend Frieda von Bülow. Lou had been exchanging letters with one of the "Young Vienna" group Arthur Schnitzler, whose work she admired. They arranged to meet. When Schnitzler arrived at her charming rooms at St. Steven's Cathedral hotel, Lou had one of her frequent colds, being nursed by Frieda. She arranged for another meeting the next day, promising to be better company. They met the following day and quickly became friends. Schnitzler had a gallant air about him, even though his journals and dramas reveal him to be an unrepentant seducer of women. His usually ruffled brown hair was parted on the side — as if it had been combed neatly in the morning then tousled by an afternoon bedroom romp. This combined with his neatly trimmed beard and moustache gave him the look of both an impish boy and a worldly scholar. The son of a prominent Jewish Viennese physician, Schnitzler had also studied and practiced medicine until his drama *Anatol* (1893), a cycle of one-act plays that follows the exploits of a Viennese Don Juan, gained critical success.

Schnitzler introduced Lou to his brilliant circle of friends: Hofmannsthal (called Loris among the group), Salten, and Richard Beer-Hofmann among them. It was a vibrant, immensely talented, and mostly Jewish circle. Lou was immediately infatuated with the Young Vienna group and began meeting with them daily at the Café Griensteidl. She felt comfortable among the group of men whom she admired so greatly.

"[Lou] calls us 'happy people,'" Schnitzler wrote to Loris (Hofmannsthal), because "we love the city we were born in, and have one another."[37] No doubt, she saw them as her family of brothers, as much attached to the Vienna scene as her real brothers were attached to the St. Petersburg of her childhood. To Lou, they were not only the Young Vienna, they were the best of Vienna. She breathed them in like a wonderful bouquet. She quickly took center stage in the group. They attended the theater, hiked in the Vienna Woods and drank "white stearin" in coffeehouses, all the while excitedly discussing literature, life and love. She particularly enjoyed the Austrian countryside — "The environs of Vienna are so beautiful" that "friends and society constantly met there." She adds, "I always needed forests, broad fields and sun around me to fill the cup of experience to the brim." [38]

The Vienna experience not only excited her intellectually, but sexual feelings began to stir behind her nun-like façade. Vienna was a "confluence of the intellectual and the erotic life," she wrote. That she was in desperate need of confluence in her own life — a union of body and mind which she had so willfully drove apart — was woefully obvious. She began to succumb to the erotic drive of life, and her iron will suddenly began to melt from the heat.

Among the group of young men vying for Lou's attention, she liked Richard Beer-Hofmann best. Beer-Hofmann, a darker, more pensive-looking man than Schnitzler, was an Austrian novelist, playwright, and poet who would later be considered the most influential member of the *fin-de-siècle* Viennese circle. Two years before meeting Lou, Beer-Hofmann had begun a novel titled *Der Tod Georgs*, his third and most skillfully rendered stream-of-consciousness work, which would serve as an inspiration to the European community of young writers. Beer-Hofmann was twenty-nine. He had an air of "blithely sauntering"[39] through life that she found charming. It was an air she longed to breath.

In May of 1895, less than a month after meeting Lou, Schnitzler noted in his diary an obvious attraction between her and Beer-Hofmann. "Lou's turning a bit female,"[40] Schnitzler wrote after dining with the two. He was puzzled at Lou's apparent "need to be desired"[41] by Beer-Hofmann.

At the same time Schnitzler wrote his observations, Beer-Hofmann wrote a friend that Lou's "eyes and smile are so young...."[42]

Both Beer-Hofmann and Schnitzler fully embraced the stark double standard of the day: as men they sought as many "conquests" of women as possible, seemingly anywhere and anytime. Ideally, they preferred virgins, or "sweet young things" as they called them — young, innocent, non-intellectual girls. "Good breeding," wrote Zweig, "for a young girl of that time, was identical with ignorance of life."[43] Virginity was what gave a woman her greatest value and yet, ironically, it was the prize which they most wanted to take away. Schnitzler documented his many sexual adventures with minute detail.

Through her brothers, Lou had developed an acute awareness of how men of her era thought and felt about women. In a twisted attempt to please both her own needs and the double standard under which she lived, she had tried to swim in the erotic pool without getting wet — to be at once virgin and lover to various men. Her fictional writings became an outlet for the intense fears and desires that men evoked in her.

As the end of Lou's stay in Vienna drew near, the group arranged to meet in Copenhagen at the end of the summer. Before leaving she told Beer-Hofmann she was grateful to the group and that they signified "something positive, even beautiful to her." Her outward seeking for happiness in others seemed to sustain her and she returned home, freshly inspired by her adventures, to write.

However, back home, she suffered a short period of "melancholia" and an inability to concentrate on her work. After a number of notes about her inability to write, on June 26 she wrote excitedly, "Work frenzy comes at last!!"[44] Her private struggles were quickly to be worked into a new novel, *Out of an Alien Soul* (Aus fremder Seele). This novel is a fusing of the religious theme in *Struggling for God* and the erotic love story in *Ruth*. Once again Lou attempts to work out Gillot's power over her, as if to exorcise it through her fiction.

The story tells of a pastor who has lost his faith, a young woman who has lost her faith as well but loves the pastor, and the pastor's son who loses faith in his father. She demonstrates the tragedy of losing God as well as the attempt to reconstruct something or someone to replace that ideal, an attempt which is forever doomed. If, at this point in her life, Lou sensed tragedy in the quest for a god-substitute, she was also still haunted by the overwhelming power of sexual love and subservience she had felt for Gillot and her equally overwhelming resistance to it.

In August she sat her novel aside in order to write two book reviews and revise her essay "Jesus der Jude." Before the month ended she met some of the Viennese circle—Beer-Hofmann, Schnitzler and others—in Salzberg as a prelude to their planned Copenhagen vacation. The group went their separate ways for several weeks; then Lou, Beer-Hofmann and Schnitzler regrouped in Munich until Schnitzler returned to Vienna for the rehearsal of his play *Liebelei*, leaving Beer-Hofmann alone with Lou. She notes in September that the group plan to go to Copenhagen fell through, and that she and Beer-Hofmann decided to go together. They traveled to a mountain inn in Schönberg: "Glorious up there. The first night in the farmhouse on the slope, arrival in the dark over the meadows."[45] But the same day Beer-Hofmann wrote to Schnitzler that he had decided not to go to Copenhagen—"I discovered I just did not want to go and simply begged off."[46] Lou records that they quarreled. Had Beer-Hofmann, in an attempt to seduce her away from the group and perhaps engender admiration from his comrades, found that his prize was not so willing? Like the trip to Wedekind's room, traveling with Beer-Hofmann exposed Lou's inner conflict. Traveling alone with him and yet refusing to fulfill his expectations, she may have made Beer-Hofmann angry because she was not playing the Viennese stylized game of seduction properly. Lou seems to have been heartbroken by Beer-Hofmann's refusal to travel with her. "Tell me," Schnitzler wrote him, "how did Lou take to having to go alone?"[47] "Too hard to be put into words,"[48] Beer-Hofmann replied. He then rejoiced in the thought of leaving her behind: "[I]t is best to travel *alone*."[49]

After a brief trip to Munich, Lou returned home to write a short novel titled *Jutta* in what she described as "work fever"[50]—her wounds still fresh from her encounter with Beer-Hofmann. *Jutta* is a tale of seduction and the trauma it produces in the Victorian mindset of a woman. But it also exposes the psychological, the sexual and the social in a way never portrayed in the so-called "women's fiction" of her era.

It is written as a diary entry and at the top of the first page of the diary reads: "Jutta. A Pentecostal Diary." The narrator is an older Jutta who, plagued by shame, feels compelled to confess about an incident in her youth. She tells the reader that she is confessing this story in a diary because she can't imagine talking to a friend about it. She puts her name at the beginning, she tells us, so as to identify herself with the young, naive girl she is about to write about, suggesting she had dissociated herself from her youthful self, because it doesn't fit in with her *bourgeoisie* self-image.

There is a sense of distancing from the young Jutta in the beginning paragraphs — she is a little older now, she tells us, wants to marry and have a dozen children (echoing Lou's mother desire to have an "even half-dozen boys"). She wants to tell her story as a precautionary tale, in that, as she puts it, she isn't the kind of person who would do such a thing. In a Freudian sense, the older Jutta is playing super ego to the instinctual, impulsive Jutta. In Nietzschean sense, the older Jutta attempts to re-establish Apollonian order to the Dionysian indiscretion.

The older Jutta tells her story, giving us psychological clues as to why she was so vulnerable and naïve in her youth. Like Lou, she is the youngest child in a family of three brothers. The middle brother, Herbert, is a law student, and Jutta is also studying law. Jutta's brothers seem to dictate to her what they want her to do with her life, and she accepts this as her fate. She is submissive to the will of her brothers out of love and admiration for them. Herbert and Jutta had planned a vacation in a mountain village with Herbert's friends during Pentecostal vacation. When Jutta arrives, the six friends tell her that Herbert has injured his foot in a bicycling accident and will be delayed by several days in meeting them. Because her brother thinks so highly of his scholarly friends, Jutta agrees to spend time with them. Because she has grown up with brothers, she feels comfortable being the only female among them, but feels somewhat insecure because her intelligence and education don't rise to their level. As with her brothers, she admires the men and considers them her superiors. The men are boisterous and engage in witty conversation. She finds herself listening attentively, rather than joining in the repartee.

The group takes a hike on a nearby mountain, and the young men begin rowdily jousting for her attention along the way. At the top of the mountain the hikers are blessed with a splendid panorama of trees in blossom. As Jutta stands below a tree blooming in its full burst of springtime glory, several of the men shake it until she is covered in a veil of blossoms. One calls it "the Pentecostal veil," and they all jovially participate in removing the delicate pink petals from her hair. She is thrilled by the attention, but also imagines her brother's eyes watching her and feels she must be pleasing to these young men. While the older Jutta writing in her diary realizes the game that the men are playing, the youthful Jutta — not realizing the full implication of it — goes along with it, both out of an erotic impulse and a desire to please her brother's friends.

The symbolic marriage ceremony is a communal act and they playfully christen her *Fräulein Pentecoste*, a maiden-goddess of Spring. But when another complains that *fräulein* is too old-fashioned, they rename her *Pfingstfrau*—a title that suggests she is the Pentecostal bride to them all—a "common good," as one calls her. The communal game turns to a playful rivalry when a flower lady shows up and the men compete to purchase flowers for Jutta. One of the group, Florian, is more competitive than the others and takes the entire basket and pours out all the flowers onto his lap. Another among the group—Abel—finds one violet stuck in the bottom of the basket and wittily presents it to her as being from the remaining five friends. Florian is angered when he is outclassed by the subtle gesture and tosses the profusion of flowers aside. His friends tease him about his attempt to court Jutta individually, rather than as a team. When he becomes upset and embarrassed, each of them shares an embarrassing situation they have experienced, in an attempt to ease his discomfort. Jutta is impressed by the group dynamic, by the manly mixture of friendship and competition in which they energetically partake. But in her admiration of the camaraderie of men, she fails to see the danger for herself.

When Jutta is later sitting under a wicker arbor in the garden, sewing, Florian approaches her and says he came to say goodbye. When she reacts with dismay, he retorts, "Even though you are the cause of it?" He explains he feels rejected, that he made a fool out of himself in front of the group. "They say I chase after you and you ignore me." She is shocked by his words and is fearful she has offended one of her brother's dear friends. Sensing that she is eager to make amends, and playing on her naiveté, he tells her she could make it up to him by touring the mountain villages with him. When his friends join them, he informs them that they are going on the tour by themselves, before she had even had a chance to answer. Jutta, eager to please and out of fear of embarrassing her brother's friend, has compliantly accepted his offer through her non-response, not realizing that she is entangled in a game.

The remaining five men see them to the train station. Treating them like newlyweds, they place a canopy of flowers over their seats and see them off with what the older Jutta imagines as knowing glances. But on the train ride Jutta and Florian become quiet and do not speak to one another. Florian has a tinge of conscience and Jutta, confusion. When they arrive at the end, Florian asks if she wants one room or two. One is all she needs, she replies, thinking he meant for herself. Florian takes it as a signal that beneath her *bourgeoisie* persona is another kind of woman. The seduction begins. As the days pass, they begin to talk personally with one another—Jutta tells him about her three brothers, including her twin brother and another who had died. Florian tells Jutta what he is looking for in a wife: the Young Vienna version of the "sweet young thing," a nature child, someone unspoiled and innocent. He and his friends, he tells her, aren't interested in intelligent women. They want sweet, virginal girls.

When the seduction is completed, Florian is more emotionally involved then he had planned. Jutta, in shame, pulls away from him and flees the mountain hide-away. On the train as she is leaving she thinks she hears someone say, "Watch that she doesn't fall!" But when she turns, no one is speaking. Among the sleeping farm women she sees only someone "who suffers between life and death, suffers like a strangled animal and somebody who watches over that animal."

Rather than giving us the facts and allowing us to make a judgment, in the first few paragraphs, Andreas-Salomé, the writer, has Jutta attempt to speak directly to the audience as if pleading her own case. Her audience, Jutta supposes, is patriarchal and reproachful, as can be gathered from her defensive statement that she only studied law in imitation of her brothers, and what she really wanted to do was marry and have lots of children.

In Muriel Cormican's analysis of the story, she notes that the narrating Jutta and the young naive Jutta represent "how internalized social and moral edicts breed a psychic split in woman that makes her complicit in her own sexual repression and obstructs the sincere and truthful discussion of her sexuality, *even to herself*"[51] (italics added). Cormican believes that the older Jutta offers a vision of the people-pleasing naïveté of her youthful self as a "defense mechanism against public and moral outrage."[52]

The actual sexual encounter between Jutta and Florian — despite being *framed* as a sin and almost a crime — is presented in glowing terms by the narrator. According to Cormican, Jutta presents, for that magical moment in time, "a pre-cultural, natural, wholesome world full of drives and desires"[53] that cannot be written off as an offense. Jutta sees them as Adam and Eve — the only man and woman on Earth — living in a pre-conscious world of oneness with nature, a world in which good and evil do not yet exist. "Jutta's depiction of the sexual encounter as an overpowering physical ... experience emphasizes a natural, pre-cultural element."[54] The human experience — overpowering and non-cerebral — blows off any social models of classification. Cormican calls it the virgin/vamp dichotomy: Jutta sees herself as either *Burgertöchter* (a respectable middle class daughter) or *Studentin* (a liberated female student). The sexual experience itself supersedes all classification, labels, and even words. In this epiphany and in the recounting of it, Jutta breaks through the unconscious repression for a moment and comes face to face with the full force of life.

Cormican's reading of *Jutta* points out the depth in the story. The construction of *Jutta* and the use of her experience with the Young Vienna group is Andreas-Salomé's imaginative scenario of the seduction of a "sweet young thing" and the psychological effect that the men's sexual competition has on this type of woman. Lou most likely knew nothing of Schnitzler's diary of sexual conquests, yet she saw clearly the social dynamic among him and his friends, who often competed for and even exchanged mistresses as if they were possessions.

Lou explores through her imagination what she saw as the result had she given in to Beer-Hofmann's seduction. The split within the psyche of Jutta is not unlike the split within Lou. She has found herself living a double life — a sort of social infidelity — but without the sexual release infidelity provides. At the end of the story, Jutta hears the sound of someone suffering, "like a wounded animal," and sees someone watching over that suffering person. It is the moment when Lou Andreas-Salomé's true voice comes through, for she is both the one suffering and the one who silently watches over the sufferer.

Despite the struggle between her and Andreas, the loss of her friendship with Paul Rée, the turbulence of an almost consummated love affair with Lederbour, Nietzsche's collapse, the never-ending attacks by Lisbeth Nietzsche, Lou's adventures and misadventures with the literary elite in the cultural capitals of Europe — despite all these attractions and distractions, Lou never stopped writing. It was perhaps her most prolific period, even though she was highly productive throughout her life.

Lou's travels during this period left her with a specific "impressive memory." She witnessed "three springs in rapid sequence as I traveled from Italy, northward through Germany."[55] Her life too began to show the signs of rebirth and change.

As the century neared its end, monumental transformations were brewing in all of Europe. Nietzsche had begun to permeate the intellectual realm to such an extent that there was no art or science that did not show his influences. He formed links among writers, poets, composers, academics and activists in the German-speaking lands and Russia. Through Lou's essays and the dramas of the Naturalists, Nietzsche pervaded *Freie Bühne*, both journal and stage. And Lou's book on Nietzsche sparked intense interest and debate among those who admired his genius. Lou understood that those who struggled to understand Nietzsche's *Thus Spoke Zarathustra* in a literal or symbolic sense failed to simply *experience* Nietzsche. "His work was aphoristic, not systematic," writes Roy Pascal in a study of German literature and society, "ever-startling and paradoxical, gay and abusive, full of subtle subliminal argumentation, and always, no matter what the cost, witty and enlivening."[56] Lou for her part saw his philosophy as an attempt to transform his intellectual creation into a new god, which led him to madness. Lou's own need to cast another in the role of her lost god had let her down as well. The time for transformation had come.

In 1897, when Lou traveled to Munich with her friend Frieda, her achievements as an adventurer and writer were like a rare and intoxicating fragrance that hovered around her. She had about her the aura of having known and attracted many brilliant men of her time. The self-actualization of her girlhood goals was now in full force. She had lived and breathed the greatness of her age, stood at the very center of the flame of genius. And even though her inner struggles were unrelenting, her external charm was omnipresent. Her intellect, fame and magnetic appeal were, and had been for several years, at a climax. There were also signs that she was moving towards the resolution of the greatest barrier to her fulfillment, the one obstacle she had yet to overcome — sexual love.

12

The Inspiration of a Young Poet

> *And I take this beautiful gift,*
> *Want to mold it quietly,*
> *Unfold all its colors*
> *And hold it, full of shyness*
> *Up towards You.*[1]
> — Rainer Maria Rilke

This is how the relationship began, a relationship which would give birth to one of the world's greatest poets inspired by one of the world's greatest muses:

"Someone had been sending me anonymous poems for some time,"[2] Lou wrote in her memoir. Lou had received the anonymous poems at the house she was renting with her friend Frieda von Bülow in Munich. When she accepted an invitation to high tea at the home of novelist and friend Jakob Wasserman, she didn't know she was on her way to meeting the man to whom she would give more of herself than she had given to any other. The small group, which included Wasserman, Lou, Frieda and the young poet from Prague named René Maria Rilke, met on May 12, 1897. They shared fine tea and rich conversation as the sun's last rays lowered through the wide windows of Wasserman's drawing room. The intense and sensitive young man with large, sunken blue eyes and a wispy goatee made a slight impression on her. Lou noted in her diary that Rilke had "huge soulful eyes" and the brooding air of a "sickly aristocrat."[3] Within the delicate sophistication of the tea ceremony in which the four partook, Rilke barely restrained his passion for and admiration of the Russian-born writer who wrote so boldly on the topics of religion and sexuality, the woman who was known to have enticed and bewitched Nietzsche — the subversive hero of Rilke's generation.

For Lou, it was a pleasant way to spend the afternoon, with a fervent young poet, so full of youthful admiration. For Rilke it was the accretion of a dream. That evening "was not the first twilight hour that I was allowed to spend with you," he wrote her the next day. "There was another such dusk, imprinted in my memory, which made me very much want to look into your eyes."[4] Rilke felt he had first "met" her through her essay "Jesus the Jew," which was a substantiation of his own revelation of Christ in a cycle of poems he was working on, titled *Visions of Christ*. In Lou's essay she portrayed Jesus, not as a god, but as a man whose religious genius was the full flowering of Jewish thought, and, like Nietzsche, a tragic hero-genius. Lou's essay was sent to Rilke by a friend, who after having read Rilke's *Visions of Christ*, thought he might find interesting. But interest was hardly the word for it, he told her; it was an epiphany. He had wanted desperately to meet with the woman who seemed to magically voice his feelings, who seemed to understand his underlying fears and joys about God. "Your essay was to my poems as reality is to dreams," he wrote her, as "fulfillment is to desire."[5] *Fulfillment is to desire*. It was already the language of a lover. He had learned from an early age to gain the love of women through the beauty of his words. "Do you understand how much I was longing for yesterday?" he continued. "My heart overflows with gratitude for your sanction."[6]

The day after meeting her he wandered the Munich streets with a handful of roses, unable to summon the courage to go to her door. He hoped she would appear magically, and mother his poor orphaned roses.

Rilke wrote his mother soon after the May 12 meeting, that he had met "two splendid women!"[7] He named them as the famous writer Lou Salomé, and African explorer Frieda von Bülow. He knew his mother would be pleased by the two notable names. Sophia Rilke, nicknamed Phia, was a relentless social climber. Rilke described her as "a very nervous, slender dark woman who wanted something indefinite from life."[8] He was to later report that Phia poured cheap wine into expensive bottles to give the impression of refinement. She dressed him in the finest of clothes despite the fact that they lived in a gloomy rented apartment in Prague. Even though her influences on Rilke's childhood had been terribly damaging, he still sought to impress her with his latest literary connections. Early on he had made a secret decision to make poetry a career. Although he had published a number of poems by the time he met Lou, financial freedom from his family (and freedom from their conventional plans for his career) was not yet achieved.

Rilke's relationship to his mother was ambivalent at best. He was born René Karl Wilhelm Johann Josef Maria Rilke — settling for René Maria Rilke — on December 4, 1875, in Prague to Josef and Phia Rilke. One year earlier Phia had given birth to a daughter, who died within a week. This event negatively imprinted on Rilke's psyche in various ways. First, his sister's early death became the ghostly remnant that haunted him with unspeakable fears when he was ill. Even more significantly, Phia attempted to resurrect her dead daughter through his male person. Up until the time he went to school she dressed him in girl's clothing and "played with me as if I were a big doll."[9] She even called him Sophie. The sensitive child seemed to be willing to go to any length to win his mother's approval.

Phia taught him to recite poetry and affect all the airs of an aristocrat. His intelligence became apparent as she had him copying and reciting Schilller's lengthy ballads before he could even read. While Phia's intent may have had more to do with pretension than true love of poetry, the recitals bore more than just words into his young mind — they stirred his creative comprehension, as if to circuit poetry into his brain. Along with literary appreciation, Phia instilled what Rilke biographer Freedman calls "romantic religiosity, an adoration of saints and saints' lives, holy relics and fervent devotions, which enriched his repertoire of images for the rest of his life."[10] But like her aristocratic values, her passionate piety seemed to come from a shallow place, longing to *appear* deep. Rilke complained she often made him kiss the wounds of a crucified Christ figure. And although it enriched his mind with the symbols and images he would later work with in his poetry, the maudlin gesture also left a bad taste in his mouth.

Rilke's father, Josef Rilke, was a railroad official who dreamed of being a heroic military man. But it was a dream he never fulfilled. Naturally, Josef Rilke objected to Phia trying to turn René into a ghostly daughter. It was unmanly treatment, his father complained. Moreover, Josef had unfulfilled dreams of his own he wanted Rilke to fulfill. Hopeful that his son would take up the military mantle, he gave Rilke toy soldiers — as if this would balance out the ponderous weight of his life as his mother's baby doll. René, seeking to please his mother and father as well as his own boyish imagination, idolized a cultured manhood — the courtly image of the medieval knight. He drew numerous pictures of knights in armor on horseback, "bearing banners with crosses."[11] Bearing the banner with a cross became part of his adolescent self-image, at once manly and Christ-like, strong and sensitive — a warrior for God.

Having had enough of Phia's attempt to make a toy out of their son, his father sent him off to a junior military boarding school at St. Pölten. René went into the new surroundings with dreams of being a shining warrior-knight of Christendom. But after a lonely, sickly life at home, the reality of military school was an extreme shock. It would become one of the many tormented memories of his childhood — being institutionalized with "fifty antagonistic boys."[12] He decided to bear the ordeal with a Christ-like humility and saw himself as a martyr. Having played the role of his dead sister at home, at the boarding school he would play the tragic, poetic saint. Rilke's mother, seemingly approving of his new role, captioned a picture of the school with the words, "The prison of my poor sick child."[13]

As he had been at home, Rilke was often ill at boarding school and missed two quarters in his second year. Yet he had high grades in all subjects except athletic ones, and he was reported to be quiet, polite, studious and serious by his commandeering officers. In pictures he appears as a slim, self-conscious adolescent, anxious to play the role of the military costume he wears. But he was not and never would be a military man. Driven by the sense of isolation he felt from being with boys with different sensibilities than his own, he began writing poetry and prose to express his anguish.

While he was away at school Rilke's parents divorced. His mother was said to be having an affair with a man in Berlin and she traveled there frequently. Rilke, feeling abandoned by his mother, wrote her letters focusing on his poor health. The power of his words was effective and brought his mother to his side, like a "saving angel."[14] He'd learned an important lesson early on: women were moved by his beautiful words and found them irresistible. With this in mind, he knew two assured ways to win his mother's love — poetic language and illness. These would be the two methods he would later use on Lou to win her love. While Lou responded spontaneously and affirmatively to the first, the latter she found more distressing.

After spending the 1890–91 school year at a senior military academy in Mährisch-Weisskirchen, Rilke felt he could endure no more of the callous, indifferent military system — a system built on the premise of denying one's individuality. With the financial help of his successful uncle, he was able to leave the military school, and begin studies at a business school in Linz. Of course, business school suited him no more than military school — and he had already decided to make poetry his career. Still Rilke completed his degree through private studies and then enrolled at Charles University in Prague. Even though his uncle wanted to make a successful business man out of him, Rilke studied art, philosophy and literature with his uncle's financing.

In 1893, when Rilke was not yet eighteen, he fell in love. Valerie von David-Rhonfeld was an attractive, artistic young lady, slightly older than Rilke. He fell in love — as he would continue to do throughout his life — instantly. The next day he sent a poem extolling her clear eyes, rose-like mouth, and lovely hair. It wasn't long before they were discussing marriage. Like Lou, Rilke dreamed of a marriage that would be a working partnership, two comrades devoted to art and studies. Vally, as Rilke called her, became a sort of patron to her young poet, and she helped finance his first book of poems, *Life and Songs* (Leben und Lieder). The poems were somewhat awkward and they did little to reveal the genius that would emerge under Lou's watch. Rilke would later regret being published too early.

While on vacation at a Baltic resort in the summer of 1895 Rilke met the daughter of a physician from Prague. Again falling in love at first sight, Rilke wrote a coldly gracious letter to Vally, thanking her for "the gift of freedom."[15] "Farewell," he added. "And should you ever need a friend, then call on me."[16] Vally carried understandable bitterness towards him for the rest of her life.

Shortly before meeting Lou, Rilke had enrolled at the University of Munich where he was studying art history. He was by then fully devoted to becoming a major poet. It was a devotion he took seriously, and once he committed himself to it he gave it everything he had. Lou wrote in her memoirs Rilke "felt drawn to poetry as his inevitable calling, and never lost his sense of mission."[17] She went on to explain that a vital ingredient of his great success was his openness to improvement: "precisely because of his dreamlike certainty, he did not overestimate what he had done up to that point; it simply spurred him on to renewed attempts."[18] There was a remarkable optimistic quality in this hypersensitive youth, who drew on a well of feelings about his agonizing childhood for his poems. To humbly offer up the products of his bruised psyche for criticism has a heroic feat, a trait which Lou encouraged in him.

On May 14, 1897, Lou invited Rilke to join her and her friends at the theater. After the performance, the group went to Schleich's restaurant, where they enjoyed food and stimulating conversation until 1:30 in the morning.

Lou was physically quite a different woman in 1897 than the one who had encountered Nietzsche in 1882. Gone was the Russian girl with a whip — the coltishly tall, slim, tightly-corseted philosopher with the piercing stare. Rilke biographer Wolfgang Leppmann writes eloquently of her aura when he describes her as "a full blown blonde of thirty-six who could look back on an adventurous youth and was already considered one of the most fascinating characters of her time."[19] She had grown into a very maternal-looking woman but still with the face of a girl. Her new-found love of the outdoors had lightened the strands of her hair into flaxen blonde. She no longer wore it pulled back tightly, but loosely bound with escaping wisps, making her look at once disheveled and dreamy. The hard penetrating stare from her youth was replaced by maternal gentleness in her expression, a softness in her facial features. Her now fuller figure was covered by simple peasant-style dresses worn loosely, and sometimes decked with Russian fur stoles. Lou's style was closer to that of the Russian peasant than the wife of a German scholar.

While Nietzsche's biographers have a tendency to depict her as a *femme fatale*, Rilke's biographers see her as the all-powerful muse. These differing descriptions reflect both the impression left on each man and the significant change in Lou. One of Rilke's biographers describes Lou at this time as "highly intelligent, beautiful, emancipated, experienced in the ways of the world, with social and literary connections everywhere...."[20] Biographer Ralph Freedman writes, "Rilke was overwhelmed by her presence," but she was more than a "literary encounter" to the shy young poet: she was "his revelation."[21] While she had changed physically, her character remained every bit as enigmatic and as enticing as it ever was. She was still admired for her boldness of thought, her openness of spirit, her unique genius and her gentle, caring personality. Despite some biographers' insistence on her siren-like qualities, at thirty-six Lou didn't look like a seductress at all. She could be a tender and giving woman who had a genuinely vulnerable and sensitive air about her as well as fresh, unaffected directness that might remind us of the natural Nordic beauty personified by 20th century actresses Ingrid Bergman or Liv Ulmann. She was as unconcerned about her physical self as she was concerned about intellectual and spiritual life. Her sensuality was not vamp-like, but beguiling in its honesty and vulnerability. She retained an eternal childlike earnestness in her eagerness to experience the world with wide eyes and a whole heart.

From his work, the image of Rilke as the frail sensitive poet is prominent, but it's not a complete image. Lou tells us that despite his poetic nature, he had his own "type of manliness: his own style of gentle but inviolable control and dominance."[22] He had "manly grace to high degree."[23] Along with his intense sensitivities that burst forth in his poetry, he exhibited control and mastery of his personal strength. And even though Lou was may still have been a virgin at this time, Rilke was, at his young age, already skilled at seduction. Despite his perpetual insecurities, he had already been engaged to and abandoned one woman. Throughout his life story, there were always girls and women hovering near him, hungering for the sound of his beautiful, seductive personal love poems — the art that travels with the greatest velocity to a woman's heart.

By May 26 Rilke began writing his first of over a hundred love poems inspired by Lou. She wrote in her memoir that she was not impressed with the early poems — and critics agree Rilke's early work was overly romantic and gushy — but she must have seen something in him, some potential that she could alchemically turn to gold. For the first time in a love relationship Lou didn't play the role of the worshipful schoolgirl, but that of the inspiring teacher. It was in this reversed role that she felt safe enough to let down her guard. She was more than ten years his senior and a woman with a highly respectable position in the literary world of Europe. Now she could be the gardener, as Gillot had been for her. It was as if someone had entrusted her with a tiny sprout that she would nurture into a beautiful thriving plant.

On May 31, less than a month after meeting, Lou and Rilke took a two-day trip to Wolfratshausen searching for a summer retreat. There they became lovers. Judging from both her and Rilke's writing, it may have been Lou's first sexual encounter. It was, as she described it, her first *full* love. In the novella *Fenitschka*, which was published a year after meeting Rilke, she breathlessly describes the power and splendor of sexual love:

> There comes this new something and it overtakes you and you yield yourself completely — you do not reason any more and you keep nothing back — you give and receive without accounting, without a second thought — almost without consciousness — you laugh in the face of danger, you forget your own self — your soul becomes wide open —[24]

Why be ashamed, when we "want to be jubilant?"[25] Always true to her own instinctual needs, she now was open to this new way of being. She reacted to spiritual and sexual love with the whole-hearted optimism she brought to everything and seemed to lament the years lost to rigorous study.

"You come toward me in everything that's beautiful," Rilke wrote after their consummation of love, "you are my spring wind, and summer rain, my June night, upon a thousand paths, where no blessed one has ever walked before me..."[26]

Though some believe Rilke to be Lou's first lover, biographer Rudolph Binion believes that Lou may have first become sexual active earlier with Friedrich Pineles, an "internalist specializing in nerves and glands who was then serving an internship at Vienna's public hospital and taking Sigmund Freud's seminar on neuroses."[27] Known as Zemek, he had met Lou through his sister Bronica who was painting Lou's portrait, around Christmas time 1896, only a few months after Lou was abandoned by Beer-Hofmann in the mountains. Zemek was "Beer-Hofmann's virtual twin,"[28] writes Binion. He sees Zemek as surrogate for her lost would-be lover: "Beer-Hofmann was the stimulus, Zemek the fulfillment."[29] Lou spent that Christmas Eve with Zemek, visiting the hospital where he worked. Binion believes they began an affair, that Lou became pregnant by Zemek sometime that spring, and that the child was lost, either by miscarriage or abortion.

But there is much to indicate that Rilke believed theirs to be her first sexual encounter. Lou concurs that he was the first man that she loved *wholly*, when she later wrote:

> If I was your wife for years, it was because you were the first *truly real* person in my life, body and mind indivisibly one, unquestionably a fact of life itself. I could have confessed to you word for word what you said in declaring your love: "You alone are real." Thus, we were a couple before we became friends, and becoming friends wasn't so much a choice as it was the fulfillment of that underlying marriage. We were not two halves seeking the other: we were a whole which confronted that inconceivable wholeness with a shiver of recognition.[30]

In *Genealogy of Morals*, Nietzsche wrote, "[B]etween chastity and sensuality there is no inherent contradiction, every good marriage, every true love affair has overcome this conflict." With Rilke, the "inherent contradiction" vanished. *Now* she chose her rightful wholeness. Only now, she wrote, she could become her full self. If she had in fact had her first sexual affair with Zemek, then her words suggest she did not love him the way she loved Rilke.

Lou's lifestyle, by this point in her life, was as free as any single person's. She traveled, vacationed and worked with whomever and wherever she chose. That summer she set up house in a rustic cottage at Lake Starn-

12. The Inspiration of a Young Poet

burg, Wolfratshausen, to spend the summer with her friend Frieda von Bülow. There they planned to work on their separate projects. Much as Rée had once played the role of home to her wandering snail, Andreas chose to spend his summers at home with his own intensely demanding studies, sometimes joining her on brief visits.

Rilke had been called for military service and in June he happily received news that his poor health precluded him from duty. He readily joined the summer retreat with Lou and Frieda by taking a room nearby. He anticipated a summer of bliss. But the bliss had barely begun when Lou invited another man into the mix. Akim Volynsky, a writer and critic, had come to help her translate some of her works into Russian. Lou had no romantic interest in Volynsky — in fact, she later confessed to disliking him. Still Rilke was jealous. He glowered and became irate when her full attention wasn't on him.

In July, Lou began writing a short story called "Amor" but later published as "En Route" (Unterwegs). The short story has a very Russian feel. The images are crisp and clear, the characters complex and intense.

A Russian woman traveling alone and two Russian men in the next train car are the only characters. The attractive blonde Russian woman, Anna Iwanwna, is leaving behind her fiancé. Because she is a young widow, she has told her fiancé they must wait four years before they can marry, a length of time he found unbearable. As she sits replaying their last scene in her mind, she sees him in her mind's eye, receding in the distance. As she watches the opalescent dust dancing in the ray of sunlight that falls into her car, she cannot help overhearing the two men talking in the next car. The men are conversing about a woman who had murdered a man in a crime of passion. The topic leads to a philosophical discussion of love to which Anna listens intently, making facial expressions as if she were in the conversation — agreeing with this, disagreeing with that. She agrees with the man who seems more romantic about love, calling it "a naked, delicate thing." The romantic man also makes an inquiry about the pretty blonde passenger in the next compartment. His companion tells him he has heard she is a widow.

At one of the stops, the two men arrange to be introduced to the pretty blonde. Their names are Sergei and Michael, she is told. She invites them to join her in her compartment. Realizing that Sergei is the "romantic" whom she had heard inquiring about her, Anna tells him frankly that she overheard their discussion and she agreed with his comments on the nature of love and disagreed with Michael's.

As Sergei and Anna talk, Michael listens. Both he and Anna are smoking and though he doesn't join in the conversation, she notices that he blows the plume of smoke towards hers. The "bluish smoke swirls of the two cigarettes joined together and intertwined" in "almost rhythmical movements" as Michael watches her in unabashed admiration. One man, working on the cerebral level, blushingly talks about love; the other was working on the sensual plane, in the sensuous curl of smoke, intertwining with hers. When a porter comes to light the lamp, Sergei leaves the compartment to discard his cigarette. The young woman feels awkward being alone with the man who stares at her but doesn't speak. When she gets up to retrieve a blanket from the overhead compartment, Michael stands and braces her — in fact, *embraces* her — as if to shield her from the jogging movement of the train. She allows this protective gesture, telling herself it is acceptable in such a situation. The duel erotic input from both men, in contrast to the fading memory of her fiancé, whips ups an excitement in young Anna and when she sits down again her heart is pounding wildly. When Sergei returns the two passengers sit face-to-face in silence, in the twilight. He attempts to revive the conservation, but Anna is withdrawn. The two men arrange to meet her for breakfast the next morning and say goodnight.

The next morning when she promised to met them for breakfast, she instead walks right past them, lost in thought, leaving the two amorous men not knowing what hit them.

In "En Route," the young Russian woman is the mysterious other, the attracting force that both fascinates and baffles men. But, from her point of view, she is a woman with healthy sexual drives, who withdraws in order to regain herself, to sift through the experience in order to understand herself. She is, in a sense, the mysterious other even to herself. Like Lou, she seems to experience life in a two-step process. She is spontaneously drawn into an experience, pulsing with life and sensuality. But then she withdraws to absorb the experience, allowing it to transform her. Meanwhile the two men who provide the source of the transformation are left like a child's once beloved, now forgotten, toy. It is perhaps the rarest vision of personal experience written by a woman in her time.

13

Love and Other Difficulties

...artistic experience lies so incredibly close to that of sex, to its pain and ecstasy...[1]
— Rainer Maria Rilke

Though Lou and Rilke were seldom alone, that summer in Wolfratshausen was their honeymoon. They spent many romantic moments together, walking through the woods at dawn, observing animals and flowers. Years later, she still fondly remembered that when he closed the shutters in his rented room a small star-shaped hole allowed a single spot of star-shaped sunlight to shine over the bodies of the two lovers.

But, to Rilke's irritation, the honeymoon was ruptured from time to time by Lou's dedication to her work and visits with friends. But these ruptures caused Rilke to become quite prolific as well. Painstakingly, Lou guided his work, and brought him to a greater level of understanding about art. As they spent time together she took note of his intense mood swings, and helped him work through the despair. She acted as his mentor, teacher, lover, muse, and even psychoanalyst, as she helped him transform his childhood traumas into art. And to make the transformation complete she advised him to change his first name *René* to the German, more masculine, version of his name: *Rainer*. He not only changed his name, but he championed her vision — he struggled to find a true poetic voice free of sentiment. He became Rainer Maria Rilke, who would one day stand among the greatest poets of the modern world.

Halfway through the summer idyll, in late July, Andreas wrote that he was coming with Lou's dog Lotte to join Lou for a short stay. Rilke sulkily traveled to Munich for a week, but then returned to his rented room to be near Lou. He became just one of the numerous friends who orbited around her. Although some hypothesize that there was an agreement between Lou and her husband about her young lover, it is more likely that Andreas didn't think Rilke's presence at all unusual in the summer salon. His wife had many close friendships — both male and female. And while Lou was 14 years older than her lover, Andreas was old enough to be Rilke's father, and indeed saw him as a boy, perhaps failing to recognize the oedipal elements of the situation.

When alone in his room, the make-believe honeymoon disrupted, Rilke rewrote some of his novellas. Lou continued to guide him, helping with editorial decisions. Lou and he also took on a project of studying the Italian Renaissance with great intensity. Rilke was particularly struck by Botticelli's Madonna, with her mixture of chaste and sensual beauty.

It was a typical summer for Lou: people came and went all summer long. Along with Volynsky, architect August Endell was a frequent visitor. Frieda left for Holland in July and at the end of the summer Lou left for a week to visit a friend in Bad Hallein. She was followed by daily letters from Rilke, which she would later describe as excessively emotional.

In September Lou returned to the Berlin suburban apartment that she and Andreas shared. Rilke followed. He took an apartment nearby, in order — outwardly — to continue their studies of the Renaissance and — inwardly — to be as near to Lou as possible. She had become the center of his life, and if he had to live on the periphery of her life, then he was willing to do that.

Andreas was getting used to the young man being around and even became fond of him. Rilke felt differently. Though he liked Andreas — and most people were charmed by this kindly, eccentric scholar — he was intensely jealous of him. Still, by all accounts, on the surface the threesome seemed to get along well. Most certainly, it was the familiar triangle in which Lou felt most comfortable.

Rilke visited Lou daily. After hours of intensive studies, they performed domestic chores — Rilke chopped wood and helped Lou with cooking and cleaning. In the evenings they attended literary functions and Lou introduced Rilke to all the important literary figures in Berlin. While Lou never gave up her freedom of movement, and continued to frequently visit friends in other towns, she was endlessly patient and consoling with the young poet. She encouraged him to make poetry, rather than another human being, the central focus of his life. As she had commented on her marriage, her vision of their relationship was of two kneeling together, rather than one kneeling before the other.

Lou continued an intense writing schedule as usual. In October she began a short novel titled *Deviations*. In it she visits the Gillot story once again, but now with a deep psychological insight.

Adine is a young woman attempting to understand the two conflicting desires within her — the first being total subservience to the man she loves (even beyond what he expected of her) and the second, the desire for autonomy. Addressing the Gillot-like character, Benno, Adine tells him, "Of all the men I've known, you are closest to me, an integral and intimate part of everything that concerns me as an artist."[2] And, once more, Lou tries to clarify to herself: why are these two opposing desires, freedom and subservience, so strong in her psyche? It is the most psychoanalytic of her attempts to understand herself.

Lou gives Adine one of her own her childhood memories, one that has indelibly stained her susceptible young mind. On a hot summer day, Adine tells us, her Russian nurse was holding her in her arms as her brutal husband struck her nanny on the back of the neck. When the little girl saw the large red welts he caused she began to cry at the "shocking sight."[3] Yet the nanny responds to the child's tears with a "serene, happy laugh. My poor little girl's heart must have got the impression that undoubtedly such a blow was one of the particular blessings of her life."[4] The description is of a similar incident Lou herself had witnessed, after which Lou was perplexed and moved by the "dog-like loyalty common to Slavic women."[5]

Adine tells us that many of her other childhood memories "have vanished without a trace," but something about "that soft, sensuous devotion in the expression of my nurse's eyes and gestures has often surfaced in my memory later."[6] And in a profoundly psychoanalytical statement Andreas-Salomé says that such upsetting scenes strike the innermost core of a young child and leave "the hidden imprint of an early, very early tremor with which they touched our nerves and our dreams."[7]

Another thing that has an impact on Adine's psychology is her parents' marriage. While her father was neither violent nor abusive, her mother always deferred to her husband's authority, just as Lou's mother had to General von Salomé's. Because of this arrangement, Adine's childhood, like Lou's, was "a harmonious environment without upsetting experiences."[8] But "the facts behind the harmony were these: my dear little mother did everything as my father wanted it, and he in turn did everything I wanted."[9] This fascinating and familiar dynamic set up two conflicting facts in the mind of the child: men are the absolute rulers over women (augmented by the violence her nanny endured with seeming pleasure) but she had a unique power of her own, granted her by her father. The first fact both attracts and repels her. The second one seems to be her natural birthright. Adine's father, while fully accepting of patriarchal rule, encouraged his daughter to fulfill her dream of becoming an artist.

After explaining these strange psychological factors, Adine tells the story of her love for a Benno, a distant family relative who took care of her and her mother after her father died. A young man of great self-mastery, Benno was orphaned as a child but worked his way through high school and went on to study medicine. While his accomplishments vaguely impressed her, it was his looks that affected her most. "Benno was very good-looking,"[10] she divulges. He was "a striking young man with his serious expression and his blond head of hair and his tall, youthful figure."[11] Because of Benno, she fell into an "erotic and aesthetic trance and my womanhood was awakened."[12] In a state of "intoxication" she ardently pursued him and "in a short while we were engaged."[13]

When Adine's father dies, Benno takes care of her and her mother, "two spoiled women, severely lacking in independence."[14] He moves them into a boarding house across from the mental institution where he is interning. On the other side of the building is the state penitentiary. Both mother and daughter are aghast at the depressing environment. At fixed times in the early morning the prisoners are shuffled across the courtyard to work in the prison yard. "[J]ust look at the way they walk past," Adine tells Benno. "They never raise their eyes."[15] Benno tells her she's dwelling too much on the depressing sight. He encourages her to spend her time in a healthier manner — to cook, sew and do other domestic chores.

To please him, she takes on the new role as a "*petit-bourgeois* housewife."[16] Unlike her neighbor and friend Gabriele who hates housework, Adine is "patiently intent on being submissive, whether my own self broke into a thousand pieces in the process or not."[17] The image of being broken or shattered by her forced passivity and obedience to another — which was obviously alien to her character — is often utilized in Andreas-Salomé's fiction. It is the behavior she witnessed by the two most important female figures of her childhood: her mother and her Russian nanny. For Lou, however, a second knowledge existed, one also imprinted on her early mental configurations: the father figure who covertly obeys *her* commands. As well, there was the image of her Aunt Caro, who lived an independent life without the bond of marriage.

Adine, like Lou with Gillot, finds herself working so hard to please the man she loves that she sacrifices her health: "I grew pale and thin; I developed morbid feelings of insecurity.... In this forced submission to him my most delightful feelings of passion become mixed with the most painful, even horror."[18] Her strange feelings left her in a state of excitement and terror, taking away "her balance of mind."[19]

But Benno finds his fiancée's behavior strange and unhealthy. He takes no pleasure in the sacrifice and martyrdom of this manic Adine. He breaks off the engagement with her. When he tells her, she falls to her knees and cries out in pain. "I felt he had stamped on me and crushed me into miserable fragments."[20] The coldness of his action leaves Adine with a "exaggerated and falsified picture of Benno in my mind and made him appear cruel and violent and larger than life."[21] She is overwrought and emotionally shattered, and her mother takes her Western Europe to recuperate. There Adine finds the strength to engage the plans she and her father had devised when he was alive — to study art.

She studies art in Paris and the pain of her first love is healed through her profession: "I began to live for my art. This happiness finally became stronger than the passion of my youth. Like a dream which escapes as one awakens, it receded into the shadows."[22] She lives alone in a Parisian studio apartment, next door to a famous artist, with whom she becomes close.

Around Christmas time, at an art reception in her studio, Adine receives a letter from Benno. The letter admonishes her for her Parisian artist's life. "On the basis of some rumors that have been circulating about my 'all-too-free' life style, as he called it, he felt obliged to warn me against gossip, or maybe against myself."[23] Like Gillot's letter, Benno's letter contains "many bourgeois thoughts and worries that made me smile."[24] Standing among a group of her artist friends after reading the letter, Adine now sees him as a provincial doctor who knows nothing about "life in a metropolis and among artists."[25] The patronizing letter deflates him in her eyes and he is no longer the god-like man whom she had once loved. She couldn't believe he had dared to write her in such a fashion — he "who had not loved but rejected me."[26] But then, she catches a glimpse of an etching by an artist named Klinger, depicting an armored young man disdainfully looking down on a prostrate woman. As she looks at the "armed youth, with his brazen look ... a long, long forgotten sensation from my own existence started to stir in me darkly—."[27] Was it the memory of Benno "arousing in me the first ecstasy of love and the first horror of the dependence it creates?"[28] Or, she wonders, was something farther back in her childhood, "when I was held in my nurse's arms" and after a blow from her husband, "she humbly bowed down to him?"[29]

Adine suddenly becomes anxious to see Benno and travels home.

After having a conversation with him, she comes to realize from his expression that he has not stopped loving her, and the admonishment in his letter had not come from his pedantic nature but his possessiveness. He tries to kiss her, but she tells him it's too late. He leaves the room and she remains in the chair, feeling a "violent emotion" that "did not spring from memories. This was a living force, a real force that threatened me."[30] It was not love that held her — "not love, something darker, some instinct, something eerie." Like lightning, she says "the etching of by Klinger appeared in my inner eye."[31]

When Adine visits with her friend Gabriele they have a discussion about men and women. Gabriele sees the men in their small town as "[a]rrogant ... conceited and backward in their opinions."[32] But she believes that Benno is one of the few with the capacity for enlightenment on the subject of women. But Adine tells her she's wrong: "The magic of his influence on me came from his tyranny."[33] Gabriele tells her bluntly that she's talking like someone from her great-grandmother's generation, adding, "I hate old junk! It doesn't fit in with the demands of a practical life."[34] Adine agrees but tells her that sometimes old things offer something beautiful, if not practical. Clearly in this conversation Lou understands and identifies with both positions to some extent.

When Benno and Adine meet again, Benno admits that he had too much confidence and too little insight when they were engaged. He didn't realize what was "strong and healthy" in Adine.[35] He didn't realize until she went off into an independent life how much her art meant to her. She, too, had to share the blame, he told her. She put him up high on a pedestal. But now he realized she was far above him, the kind of woman who "rescues us from the wasteland of the soul."[36] But his confessions of love leave her cold. He is no longer the dictatorial man as she liked to envision him. Now he was bowing to her — and her love for him had vanished. Just as Adine's love fantasy of Benno had made him "appear cruel and violent and larger than life," now he had the illusion that she was his life-affirming martyr. In the final scene, she lies to Benno and tells him that rumors about her free and easy lifestyle were correct. It is a lie made to cover the truth of her love loss for him.

Adine's mother later tells her, "It seems difficult for a woman of today to subordinate herself to a man; but believe me, it is still the best way....

[I]n the long run we only love the man who keeps the upper hand."[37] Though the elderly mother doesn't know what happened between Adine and Benno, she has defined the problem from which Adine suffers. "Oh, Mama, I totally agree,"[38] she replies.

Lou treats Adine's desire to subjugate herself as a psychological problem (as symbolized by the nearby prison and mental institution). In the pre-civilized world, when *might* made *right*, subjugation to the stronger would in a sense be the practical, even the sane, thing to do. But as Gabriele implies, the time has come to throw away old, useless things. In this Andreas-Salomé realizes that to carry on old ways when they no longer apply is in itself a psychological problem. When an ex-inmate of the mental institution takes a job as a servant in their household, Adine is surprised to see the girl carrying the lamp with the ceremoniousness of "the torch bearer in a religious procession."[39] Her mother tells her the girl lives in a fantasy world, where she is the servant of a Chinese emperor. Adine replies, "I think I would like a little madness for Christmas."[40] So while suggesting that Adine's behavior is a form of madness, Lou also recognizes that neurosis (for reasons implanted in our childhood) seems like the right and proper thing to the psyche. It is the psyche's attempt to bring happiness through past behavior, despite the fact that such behavior is no longer rational.

Adine's story is not the story of awakening and emancipation. While female independence is a feature of the novella, Adine comes to independence through the auspices of her father's encouragement and her fiancé's rejection of her. Adine would have happily stayed with Benno, despite the mental imbalance her erotic impulses caused. *Deviations* is not a feminist novel, but a deeply personal and psychological one. And Adine is not a champion protagonist, but the subject of a human experience which the author struggles to understand. Adine fantasized Benno into a tyrant, and he fantasized her into a saint. Both were creating fantasy images and projecting them onto the beloved.

The exploration of Adine's masochistic tendencies is a sharp psychological study, which utilizes some of Lou's personal experiences in its content as well as using the "archeological" approach to understanding herself—by digging into the past—even though at this point, surprisingly, she knew nothing of Freud.

Lou had many German characteristics, but her interest and insight regarding psychological states are very much distinguishing traits among Russian writers. Russian novelists, such as Dostoevsky (who lived in St.

Petersburg around the same time as Lou), show a rare, unflinching look into the secret inner life of their characters. Dostoevsky believed the Russian mind was closer to the unconscious than the western European's. His characters suffer from pathological illness and struggle for answers to the deep, burning questions of their lives. Andreas-Salomé certainly shared with the Russian writers the startling self-exposure in a need to comprehend the mystery of the self.

By the end of 1897 Lou and Rilke planned to take a trip to Florence together, to fulfill their studies of the Renaissance. In the first week of April 1898, Rainer Maria Rilke arrived in Florence, Italy. Lou was scheduled to join him after a brief visit of her family in St. Petersburg, but the plan to join him never materialized because her brother Jenia was seriously ill.

Rilke kept a diary written to Lou during his stay. It was later published as "The Florence Diary," one of three in the volume *Diaries of a Young Poet*. It begins with a poem to her:

> From our winter-shaped terrain
> I've been cast far out, into spring;
> As I hesitate at its edge
> The new land lays itself lustrously
> Into my wavering hands
>
> And I take this beautiful gift,
> Want to mold it quietly,
> Unfold all its colors
> And hold it, full of shyness
> Up towards You.
> — April 15, 1898[41]

As the spring days in Florence passed, Rilke draws more from the Renaissance art, and makes frequent references to the paintings of Mary.

Upon seeing the ubiquitous Madonnas, Rilke was struck by the triumph of the Renaissance artists. He saw the Madonnas of Botticelli and Michelangelo as a point of transcendence. Surely, in this he thought of Lou who was at once the virgin-wife, the lover and mother to him — defying all labels while living them all at once. Women are living art, he concluded.

Rilke's artistic epiphany through Botticelli's Madonna refers not only to his reverence for Lou, but also the fertile ground she cultivated in him in order to facilitate his artistic awakening. Lou's inspiration is the fertilizing seed to his soul, and within him it is nurtured and brought into the

On the balcony of the summer house, 1897, left to right: Professor Andreas, August Endell, Rilke and Lou (akg-images).

light. He wrote, "I thought, 'Lou, how splendid you are, what space you've opened in me.' For if the Italian days showered me with treasures, it was you who created room for them in my soul."[42]

Clearly Lou had influenced Rilke's view of women and their relationship to creativity. In his Florence diary, he espoused the view that the creative act is a model of the procreative act — the union (between artist and inspiration) as the height of pleasure; followed by incubation in the subconscious and a surrender of the artist's work as a gift to the world. The muse and poet roles are a reversal of the traditional gender roles — the poet, receptive and emotional; the muse, active and forceful.

While Rilke was writing about Botticelli Madonnas and the creative force in women, Lou was writing about fulfillment and wholeness as a woman, a state of being unknown to her before her love affair with Rilke. In her essay "Religion and Culture," she connects religion, art and sexual love as motivational drives that spring from the same source. Each of the three drives is capable of inspiring us creatively and creating the greatest ecstasy within the human psyche. In the hierarchy of the church, religious experience was at the highest level and human sexual experience at the base level. Andreas-Salomé gives them equal weight and value when she describes them both as "too intimate, intense, or precious to go by a human name."[43] Lou believed that intimate experiences are impossible to put into words, but we should not devalue or underestimate their importance because we do not speak of them.

The author of *Three Women*, Walter Sorell, writes of the formation of Lou's ideas on creativity and the artistic life:

> She envisioned a wonderful interrelationship between the exaltation of the spirit and that of the body ... the stronger the physical love the more meaningful the physical union. She believed that sexual love, the creative urge, and religious zeal were parts of one and the same life force. They are the realization of primary needs and the loftiest dreams of the human species.[44]

But Lou felt that a woman need not make creative work the center of her life. Lou made her life a creative act. She believed that competing in the masculine world would rob women of their innate feminine qualities. Rather, her natural instinct was to act as an alchemist and nurturer of ideas — it was the only thing to which she remained committed, rather than committing herself to the poet or writer whom she inspired.

An early feminist and friend of Lou's wrote an essay voicing her disagreement on Lou's essay on women. What might be right for some women is hardly right for all of them, her friend argued. Some women thrive in the masculine competitive world while others prefer the nurturing warmth of relationships to children, husbands or lovers. She goes on to say that beautiful writing — referring to Lou's essay — does not make the idea right. (Lou took her friend's criticism in stride.) It was true: Lou was not a typical woman of her era, and in her attempt to discover herself and what fulfilled her, she often generalized about *all* women. Nonetheless, her unique views and lifestyle make her voice all the more important. Her striving for individual autonomy within the feminine psyche is her most impressive legacy and continues to allow women to look at life and love in a new way.

In March Lou had traveled to see her family in St. Petersburg, only to discover her brother Jenia had contracted tuberculosis. On May 4, 1898, he died. On May 11 Rilke traveled to Viareggio, near Pisa. He was anxious to reunite with Lou. After several delays, they met finally in Zoppot, a seaside resort on the Baltic Sea. What Rilke expected to be a reunion with his muse (inspired diary in hand) turned out to be fraught with tension. While Lou had her own stresses and worries, apparently Rilke hoped to bring her "much festiveness, unspoiled and holy and surround You like the dark niche receives its statue."[45] But he became disheartened when she seemed less than festive. Rilke seemed unable to give Lou the mourning period for her favorite brother that she needed. Instead, he felt their reunion should be a celebration and when she didn't fulfill his fantasy, he became agitated and frantic. Lou tried to be soothing.

After his fit of distress had subsided he felt ashamed. He was dismayed that he had not grown from their separation, and that he continued to thrust her into the role of a caretaker. "I only know that You patiently listened to my innumerable small complaints, and suddenly I noticed that I was complaining again and You were listening again just as before. That made me so ashamed...."[46]

Once again he saw himself as "the smallest beggar at the outermost threshold of Your being."[47] While he felt she gave him so much — courage, inspiration, insight and life-affirmation — he felt he could give her nothing at all in the face of her personal loss. He had envisioned their reunion as her coming to him, to be "guided by *my* care and *my* love" (italics added). But instead he found himself playing the poor child and when she reacted by consoling him, he hated her as someone too magnanimous, as something "too great."[48]

Rilke had won her heart, her body and soul with his outpourings of love. But now, Lou became fearful of his overdependence on her, as well as his severe mood swings. They began to refer to his drastic change in character as *the other*. While attempting to help Rilke with his neurotic dependency and his growth as an artist, Lou was always insistent on having the freedom to come and go as she pleased. Several times she interrupted their reunion to visit with friends and family. Her absences only made Rilke cling to her all the more. She and Rilke traveled to Danzig together in July, but in August she spent several weeks in Munich.

In September Lou returned home to Schmargendorf. Rilke took an apartment even closer than before and again frequented the Andreas household daily.

It was in this phase of their relationship that Lou took on the role of a venerable teacher. Like a Zen master, she encouraged him to share in her simple lifestyle of humble living and hard work. When he first met her, it was typical of Rilke to complain about not having enough money and enough luxury — very much his mother's son in this way. But with Lou a major change had come over him. Like Lou and her husband, he became a vegetarian and began taking barefoot walks to enjoy the feel of the grass and be in touch with nature. Like Lou and her husband, he didn't drink alcohol. He chopped wood and helped Lou cook and wash dishes after she served him vegetarian meals.

Lou put Rilke and herself through rigorous lessons, as she had with their joint studies on Italy, but now studying the art, language, and literature of a far more vast and mysterious land — Russia. After the revelation of wholeness, of mind and body reunion, that her relationship with Rilke had brought her, Lou was ready to re-embrace her motherland. She wanted to experience true Russia, to see the land that she felt was deep inside her soul, yet had never come to truly know because of her isolated childhood in the cosmopolitan capital of St. Petersburg. Instinctively she knew that Russia and Russian people would also help Rilke to define his own vision — his poetic image of God. In addition to their Russian studies, Rilke wrote poems, essays, and a play called *The White Princess*. In it, we see a rare view of Lou's sexless marriage.

In *The White Princess*, with its intensely poetic dialogue, Rilke tells the story of a beautiful princess who has been in a sexless and loveless marriage for eleven years — the same number of years that Lou and Andreas had been married. Like Andreas, the Prince has an "excessive, savage temper which no one can control when he's enraged."[49] (Andreas' temper outbursts have only been recorded as harmful to himself, such as stabbing himself in the chest on the eve of his engagement to Lou.) The White Princess — who is still a virgin — awaits a lover who is coming by boat when her husband is away. She explains the situation to her younger sister. She had met the man years before, and in her heart she became "engaged"[50] to him. "Even my husband saved me for him," she tells her sister. So you've never lain with your husband, the sister asks, astonished at the revelation. Lain, but *only* lain, the Princess tells her. She describes how she restlessly she watched her husband sleep, and knew "he dreamt of other women ... but dreamt not of me. Then I was free."[51] Then in a lyrical description she describes her erotic longing, which she projected across the sea to a man she met once. For hours she looked through the high-arched windows past her sleeping husband:

> And I was free, awake, with no one there to watch me,
> And like a dream, drifted through space.
> I stretched and as my body moved,
> a fragrance seemed to spread from me and touch it all.
> Just as flowers give themselves to space,
> so every breath of air is laden with their scent — I drifted willingly into the dream toward my lover.[52]

The fantasies of her imaginary lover melt into the vision of nature: sea, sky, and setting moon merging with the flower-like fragrance of desire. But as her husband awakens, the images of nature and ecstasy change to bleak images of death.

> When I would awake within and *he* stood there outside,
> perhaps in readiness to break in the through the door —
> I was a tomb then: stone beneath my back,
> And I myself as hard as sculptured stone

And,

> ... thus the seconds passed: year after year.
> And underneath me in the same position
> Lay my decomposing corpse.[53]

Her sister embraces her to ease her pain. Thus, "there is death in life,"[54] the White Princess continues. "Birth and death occur in us daily."[55] And in passage that would have been shocking to the turn-of-the-century reader, she describes the anguish of being in a sexless marriage: "Many times I cried so loud, I woke myself, found myself crying...," and "One such night as this — I remember still — Christ melted from his ebony cross; so monstrous was my passion. His arms outstretched, Christ lay upon me."[56]

These passages connect closely to Lou — Lou as the virginal bride wed to a man whose emotional outbursts seem threatening to her. But there is a twist. Was the marriage sexless by *mutual* consent, as the play suggests? Certainly, Rilke is indulging in a bit of romantic fantasy when he depicts the Princess saving herself for this dream lover, and having her husband unknowingly collaborate in the preservation of her virginity. "I saved up all the fires of each year," she says, "for my belated wedding day."[57] Perhaps Lou had suggested as much to Rilke. The Princess says her husband "dreamt of other women ... but dreamt not of me. Then I was free."[58] In this we can hear Lou's cry for unrestrained freedom, but we also recognize an unspeakable loneliness.

Before the Princess's lover-to-be arrives by ship, a black robed figure brings the message of death — the plague has struck. In contrast to the darkness of death, the Princess continues to dream of life-affirming sexual love.

A chaste marriage, the saving grace of infidelity, and the ever-looming image of death are the themes of this courtly love-style drama. The ominous and tomblike atmosphere of the play reflects Rilke's perception of the relationship with Lou, even though it greatly nurtured his artistic life.

Meanwhile, Lou put together a collection of ten short stories and titled it *Children of Man*. One story in the collection, "The Return to the All," seems to be an attempt to discover a somewhat eastern concept of the cosmos. The All is somewhat like the Tao in that it is the vast and incomprehensible source of existence. Through the characters of Irene and her cousin Undine, she shows two sides of her own character and the two options she feels she had. Irene is a cold, indifferent woman who is warm only when she is enjoying nature and animals. She disdains human relationships and looks down on human displays of emotions — particularly sexual desire — and enjoys the impersonal embrace of nature over the entanglement of human relations. Conversely, Undine prefers the warmth of male companionship, motherhood and family. Each takes her own path — Irene ventures out into nature and her cousin takes the estate. Livingstone calls "The Return to the All" an "idiosyncratic answer to the question of women's emancipation, suggesting a female possibility that does not overlap either with wife-and-mother or with career-woman."[59] That is, Andreas-Salomé offers a new alternative — a Buddhist-like retreat from human emotion. Lou stresses a new way at looking at womanhood, not only through social relationships (wife, mother, career woman) but through its transpersonal unity with nature. As Livingstone points out, feminist writers of that era stressed the idea of protest through their writing: "society must be changed, it is unjust that woman is helpless and forced to succumb in a man-made world."[60] But Andreas-Salomé's female characters do not succumb. Through the intensity of their relationships with men, they move beyond them and "discover their freer self."[61] They nurture the men they love, but they also use their relationships with men to inspire *them* to something greater — so that the freedom and inspiration are mutual.

According to Lou, women were by nature more holistic and undifferentiated in their endeavors. This, she says, is not a negative quality, because the finest writings by women are merely a hint of the finer person that lies behind them. She mentions German writer Marie von Ebner-Eschenbach, whom she had met during her days with the Young Vienna crowd, as an example. And though she never hints at it, it surely describes her as well. A man's art can be greater than the man himself, she might have said, but the experience of being a woman far exceeds any art. Lou formulates woman and man not as two halves of a whole but as two positive values that can unite and create a third positive value: love, a child, art.

In Andreas-Salomé's work no concept exists without its opposite. She relates in her essay "The Problems of Love" that both being in love and creative inspiration show this paradox. The lover, as well as the artist, is at once giving and receiving, selfless and selfish; the ephemeral moment is experienced as eternity. It was a key paradox in Lou's personality: to give so much of herself to another that she could empty out herself in order to come back as whole.

There doesn't seem to be any record of Andreas being bothered, or even concerned, by Rilke's constant presence. The apartment had nothing that could be called a living room, so Andreas worked in his library while Rilke and Lou worked in the kitchen. They must have seemed to Andreas like two schoolchildren doing their homework while he was absorbed in the knowledge of the ancient world. One can imagine the apartment with dignified quietness of a library — the only interruptions being the sound of a turning page, the scribbling of notes, an occasional cough and an infrequent exchange of words and smiles, as each of them went into their own separate worlds of intellect.

Within a year, Andreas and Rilke — congenial friends and covert rivals — arranged to escort the most important woman in both their lives to Russia.

For Lou, it was coming home to herself.

14

To Russia, with Love

Lou—how splendid you are, what space you have opened up in me![1]
— Rainer Maria Rilke

On April 25, Andreas, Rilke and Lou boarded a train to Russia. To Andreas, Rilke was just one of the many men who sought his wife's company. Their relationship may have appeared platonic from his point of view. To Rilke, it was a secret rivalry, of which his rival seemed unaware. Andreas' presence made it clear to Rilke that his bond to Lou was in no way exclusive. But oddly enough, Andreas and Rilke became friendly and when Lou stayed in the hotel in Moscow with a bad cold, the two men went sightseeing together. That Lou brought together two men — one on the threshold of manhood and the other in middle age — into a three-way relationship that functioned almost like a family unit is yet another example of her extraordinary personal power over others. It's hard to believe that Andreas wouldn't suspect something. And perhaps he did. But there is no record of any animosity in the relationship. Perhaps it suffices to conclude that *being* with Lou was more important than the guarantee of exclusivity for both men. Of course, Rilke knew everything — that Lou's marriage, over a decade long, was sexless. And even though he pouted when she was not with him and became nasty when she wasn't giving him her attention, he seemed quite happy with the arrangement, as long as he felt close, physical and emotionally, to her.

They arrived in Moscow two days after boarding the train in Berlin and checked into a hotel near the Kremlin. The Kremlin is a medieval fortress from the ancient state of Kievan Rus. Like a Russian doll, it nests within the great city of Moscow, a city within a city. There is Cathedral Square, the heart of Russia and the seat of the Russian Orthodox Church, with the magnificent Cathedral of the Assumption. The Kremlin abounds in medieval palaces, cathedrals and museums. That same evening the tired but excited travelers browsed through the open air market and climbed the Ivan the Great Bell Tower, the tallest structure in all of Russia, dominating the entire Kremlin with its gleaming gilt dome. Later they visited the romantic-styled Alexander Gardens, along the west wall of the Kremlin.

The next morning Lou spent some time settling into her new nest and writing.

Rilke spent the morning actively seeking an introduction to Tolstoy through his connections. With a touch of serendipity, he was introduced to Leonid Pasternak, Tolstoy's portraitist. Pasternak wrote to Tolstoy on their behalf. For both Rilke and Lou, Leo Tolstoy was Russia's greatest living novelist and the embodiment of all that was great about the Russian spirit.

The meeting with Count Tolstoy came on Good Friday, as the Russian Orthodox Church prepared for Easter. He invited them for tea and the three of them sat in his study and discussed Russia. Biographer H.F. Peters described the discussion:

> Lou noted that Tolstoy was not in sympathy with the efforts made by the Russian intelligentsia to enlighten the people. He felt the Russian people did not need enlightenment as much as they needed love. All that was needed was to tap the vast reservoir of their inner resources.[2]

Lou disagreed. She thought that the Russian people, in their "childlike naiveté, their piety and warmth of heart,"[3] had to enter the modern world where science replaced faith. Tolstoy felt Lou was mistaking superstition for piety. Tolstoy took a greater interest in Andreas' Persian studies and spent most of the meeting questioning him, not bothering to include Lou and her protégé in the conversation. The language barrier only increased Rilke's awe and anxiety. When they left Rilke gave Tolstoy a copy of his *Two Tales from Prague*. Tolstoy thanked him absent-mindedly.

Despite Tolstoy's admonishments against Russian piety, the three travelers were thrilled to witness the Russian Easter festivities that were taking place that weekend. As Easter arrived in the early morning hours, from Cathedral Square of the Kremlin, they heard the cries of joy, "Christ has risen! Christ has risen!" along with a cascading waterfall of ringing bells. Gogol in his time had also been struck by the Russian Easter bells, "the booming sounds of all-ringing bells that rejoice and resonate over the entire earth."[4]

Rilke quickly understood what Lou loved so much about the Russians — the simplicity and spontaneity of their enjoyment in life. What Tolstoy saw as superstition, Rilke and Lou saw as a reflection of the depth of the Russian soul. As Lou watched the Easter Sunday celebration from a hotel room, she was reunited with the part of her personality that Gillot had encouraged her to repress. While Gillot had *de–Russified* her, Rilke had aided in her *re–Russification*. With Rilke by her side, she felt open and ready to embrace her more human, mystical, and passionate side, what she regarded as the eastern side of her personality. On this Easter, looking down from the balcony of her hotel room, visually embracing the throng of Russian worshippers, Lou experienced true Russia for the first time.

For Rilke, the Russian motherland was the earthly manifestation of Lou's spirit. Her imperial and magical essence resonated through the vast snow-covered land. Like Lou, the people had a reverence for humanity, a big-heartedness that gave the Russian character both passion and innocence. Rilke would, throughout his life, call Russia his spiritual homeland. And yet he would only travel there twice, both times with Lou. Perhaps it was his only way of comprehending Lou herself. She was his true homeland: as vast and cold as the mysterious winter land, as passionate and spontaneous as the people. Like Russia, the vastness of Lou's soul was both enveloping and overwhelming to him.

The following week the three tourists visited monasteries, churches, art galleries, and museums. They visited the Tretyakov Gallery with its collection of traditional Russian art and the finest assortment of Christian icons. Rilke marveled at the Russian peasants, whom he observed spontaneously uttering profound insights about art. Lou later wrote that Rilke was deeply affected by these people who "had a primitive sense of the internal connection of poetry and life."[5] Here, art was not separate from everyday life. Here, human life *is* poetry. These impressions of the Russian people "rejuvenated him," she tells us, "and made him more childlike."[6]

On May 3, in the early hours of the morning, Lou, Andreas and Rilke arrived at St. Petersburg. Lou's relatives were awaiting them in a gentle falling snow at the train station.

Rilke took some time to visit Elena, the young woman he had met during his Italian sojourn. Several times in May Lou noted succinctly in her diary that Rilke was at Elena's. Lou took a daytrip to the family's summer home in Peterof with her aunt Caro while Andreas and Rilke toured the Hermitage Museum.

Lou and her husband returned to Schmargendorf at the end of June. After visiting a friend, Rilke followed them home. Within days Lou and Rilke joined Frieda in an old country house atop a mountain in Bibersberg. They spent their second summer together — in some ways their second honeymoon — by living off fresh milk and eggs, picking berries and working exhaustively on their studies of Russian art, literature and history. "Work and oats. The days are too short for us,"[7] Lou noted in her diary. Frieda complained that she only saw them at dinnertime, and by then they were too exhausted to provide stimulating conversation. But Rilke later wrote her a glowing letter about how wonderful it was to stay in her home there — even though the real reason of his exuberance was that staying at Frieda's country house allowed him to be alone with Lou.

On September 11, Lou began a new novel titled *Ma*. This novel is marked by its more mature themes — widowhood, motherhood and self-sacrifice — but it is also marked by the lack of sexual tension that gave her early novels their drive. The title character called Ma, short for Marie, is a young widow with two daughters on the verge of adulthood. She identifies so strongly with her motherhood that when a doctor falls in love with her, she declines his marriage offer and chooses to send her love out towards her two daughters who have both left home in pursuit of independent lives. The daughters see their mother's self-sacrifice as intrusive — just as Lou of Zurich had resented her own mother's. But the message seems to be that a woman can guide her capacity for love and self-sacrifice into a number of outlets.

Livingstone sums up the story smartly:

> The book is all about love, and the statement it makes, I should say, is this: without love, a woman does not live, but she does not have to love a man, she can love her children, and when they are gone, she can just *love*. As for the man, he is a necessary friend, and always has to be looked up to, but one should not bind oneself to him at the price of individuality.[8]

Ma may be Lou's attempt to understand her mother — her mother's sense of duty and sacrifice towards her family — as well as her own tendency towards self-sacrifice in her work. Lou chose not to focus her capacity to love on a husband and family, fearing her individuality would be destroyed in the process. She chose instead the abstract world of creativity, art, and intellect as her primary focus in life.

In *Ma* Lou moves into a territory that is more of a psychological treatise than compelling fiction. As Livingstone points out, the erotic drive that was so strong in her early novels is now barely evoked, making the reading of this novel far less stimulating.

The summer of all things Russian ended when Andreas sent word that Lou's dog Lotte was deathly ill. She and Rilke returned to Schmargendorf, and according to Lou's diary the three of them buried the little dog in its basket in the forest by moonlight.

Beginning in September and over the next 25 days Rilke wrote the first of his breakthrough poems, "The Book of a Monastic Life," which would be the first part of *The Book of Hours: Love Poems to God*. Gone was the rapturous excess of his early work, Lou commented proudly. His poetic voice and vision united. Just as Lou had turned her love of God onto Gillot as a point of transformation, Rilke turned his love for Lou onto the Russian-style God. It is "possible to read into their creation the sensuous awakening of Rilke's relationship with Lou,"[9] wrote Rilke translators Anita Barrows and Joanna Macy. "The God of these poems is the God Rilke seeks to love and be possessed by with the same passion he had for Lou."[10] The intellectual concept of poet as seer breaks through: "My looking ripens things/and they come toward me to meet and be met."[11] The work that Rilke produced during this period shows a burst of creative energy which is every bit as passionate and spontaneous as it is masterfully skilled and controlled. Lou had successfully helped Rilke transform his muse from the personal (herself) to the transpersonal (the Russian concept of God). It was an alchemical act she performed with great skill. Rilke's *Book of Hours* is a reflection on Russia and "a redemption for him,"[12] Lou later wrote. It was conceived, she tells us, "from the most immediate experience of the hours, verse for verse, prayer for prayer, suspended through days and nights that are filled with inexhaustible devotion — as perhaps has never been revealed before in poetry or prayer."[13] Lou points out, "This Russian God does not reign as a strange abstract authority," but instead represents "closeness and intimacy."[14] And in a statement that shows how much of her own childhood vision of God she had instilled into Rilke's art, she writes, "This all-pervasive sense of security, this omnipresence, leads to a confidence in the surroundings" and a primal unity such as experienced "within the unity of the womb."[15] This is the vision of the Russian God she had experienced so powerfully as a child, the close and ever-present, invisible but absolute God. It is the God of rebirth, which unites one with the father principle of the world. If the mother image offers security through her body, the father image offers security in the outer world. This is the vision she presented to Rilke as a lover's gift. As he had written to her earlier in his "Florence Diary," he took the gift, molded and presented to her as an offering.

In November he wrote in his journal, "I have begun my life."[16]

We now see the full fruit of Lou's inspiration and influence. Russia becomes a spiritual portal to the emotional experience of God. The poet becomes the constructor of God: "Our hands shake as we try to construct you, block by block. But you, cathedral we dimly perceive — who can bring you to completion?"[17] God is something so unfathomable that we must construct him in our minds to comprehend — "it is my mind that will fashion and set the last piece in place."[18] This puts the poet, the artist, into the role of one who prays and through his prayer creates a vision of God for mankind. Prayer to the pre–Revolutionary Russian, Lou tells us, was a cumulative release of devotional feelings, "the discharge of the sense of devotion."[19] And this is the voice which echoes through Rilke's poetry, and carries him into the realm of great poets: a voice of intimate, devotional prayer.

In another burst of inspiration — in a single night alone — Rilke wrote the poetic story that would make him famous: "The Lay of the Love and Death of the Cornet Christoph Rilke," a poetic version of an historical ancestor.

Lou wrote a series of stories about Russia, as well as numerous articles. In her article called "The Human as Woman" ("Der Mensch als Weib") she clearly formulated her ideas on gender. Men and women were not two halves making a whole, but two distinct modes of being, the article says. Woman is not a complement to man but "a positive value in her own right."[20] Lou compares the procreative process to the creative one: the male element being active and mobile, the female, full and receptive. Masculine creations are the more objective, coming from a detachment of ego and self. Feminine creativity is subjective, coming from an innate sense of the union of masculine and feminine modes of being. A woman's way of creating is a natural and spontaneous giving, like fruit falling from a tree. Men and women create differently; one way is not superior to the other, only different.

While feminists of her era deeply respected her accomplishments, they hotly debated her theories. Hedwig Dohm, a feminist with whom Lou was an acquaintance, gave a fair criticism on Lou's essay "The Human as Woman." She says that in the essay, we get a feeling that Lou is giving us a seductive glance, "as if through long lashes, sideways." Lou

> elegantly grazes the most ticklish motifs in sex life. She envelops the starkly nude in shimmering haze.... There is something mystically seer-like about her, only unlike the spiritualist she does not materialize spirits but spiritual-

izes crude matter. Her psyche, rising above reality, easily soars out of sight.... [S]he leads us into a fairyland of pure minds and hearts ... where women glow, dew-hazy, resplendently youthful and beauteous.... I too should like to unfold like a flower, exhaling fragrance afar, to roll up soulfully with languorous smile, in intact harmony, like a shimmering droplet of water. Only ordinary things do not work out that way. Frau Lou's magical melodies half allured me, I half swooned.[21]

There are many kinds of women, Dohm points out, "Amazons and sacrificial lambs, Hypatias and simple housewives — all wanting to act out their own inclinations, and right in this, a thousand times right."[22]

But Lou's intention doesn't seem to be to make women behave in a manner contrary to their true desires, but to wake feminists up to the *masculinization* of women, to allow them to remain true to their feminine nature. Her wish was to preserve that which is feminine, to authenticate it and validate it. She felt the feminist movement of her time was led by women for whom the masculine aggressiveness came more naturally. Ironically, they, like the men they rebelled against, devalued femininity. Lou believed that there is strength in passivity, as long it is coming from one's true nature. There is honor in bowing down in reverence, if done with sincerity. When she discusses woman as a human being, it might be better put that she is talking about Woman as an archetypal concept — the yin of existence. She gives an oriental flare to her occidental philosophy. The *Tao Te Ching*, which she studied at Zurich, identifies the yin, the feminine, elements in nature as ironically as the stronger:

> [N]othing is more soft and yielding than water
> Yet for attacking the solid and strong, nothing is better
> It has no equal.
> The weak can overcome the strong;
> The supple can overcome the stiff.[23]

A trickle of water can, over time, wear through the hardest rocks and smooth out the sharpest shells into the softest sand. It is the eternal paradox of strength. And perhaps, it is the key to the forcefulness of Lou's complex personality.

15

Together, Alone

Every angel is terrifying.[1]
— Rainer Maria Rilke

Lou and Rilke both benefited from a year of intense inspiration. And the money they earned gave them a chance to return to Russia — but this time without Andreas. Whether they excluded him from their plans or he excluded himself is not known. But for certain, Lou and Rilke began their second trip to Russia on May 7, 1900, together and alone. Years later Lou wrote,

> It was an extraordinary trip for both of us; in his case it offered a breakthrough in his creative life, for which Russia offered appropriate images at a time when he was still studying the country and its language. For me it was simply the intoxication of being in Russia again, enveloped by the total Russian experience: this land of the people spread about me in all its vastness, its human suffering, its resigned and patient longing.... The most extraordinary thing about this double adventure, however, was that identical moments in time, and identical objects, gave each of us what we needed — Rainer finding creative inspiration, while I was put in touch with my most profound needs and memories, by living through them.[2]

While the second trip may have given Lou what she needed, she and Rilke were experiencing separate and highly individual experiences. Lou wanted the trip to help Rilke gain independence and inspiration. She also wanted to embrace the Russia within her, which had for years lived partly in exile.

Rilke simply wanted to be with her and to share her love of her homeland. He may have considered it somewhat of a triumph in wedging his friendly rival, Andreas, out of the picture. And if, in his mind, Lou became Russia and Russia became the homeland of his soul — then he could have her in a way which she approved. It was this very transfer of spiritual love — from Lou to Russia — that she encouraged, and which opened him to his life as a poet.

The first three weeks spent in Moscow were full of cultural nourishment. They met princes, artists, monks and workers. Their Russian friend Sofya Schill, a teacher and activist, was extremely helpful in getting the poet and the writer all the proper invitations. She even invited them to her political meeting for workers. She wrote of their attendance:

> The two of them were not interested in the Russian workers' first attempts to take an active part in politics, but in their everyday lives, the village element in them, the healthy roots....[3]

Seeing Russian life as living poetry rather than brute politics fit the twin attitude the two travelers had adopted. Lou's love for Russia and the Russian people — echoing back to her father who had such a strong reverence and compassion for them — reverberated in Rilke's poetry. Lou's Russian love of life and strength of intellect took poetic form in Rilke's psyche. She — and Russia as her surrogate — became the prime mover within him.

Sofya Schill found their attitude both naïve and charming:

> They saw in the people everything pure and bright and this was truth. But they did not want to see the other truth just as true — the fact that the people were perishing without rights, in poverty, in ignorance and that the vices of slaves were growing in them, laziness, filth, deception and drunkenness.[4]

Lou and Rilke traveled around Russia holding hands, absorbing both the beauty and the ugliness with equal acceptance. They visited museums, galleries and churches. "Everywhere they were looking for the true face of Russia,"[5] Schill wrote.

"[T]hroughout the vast stretches of land," Lou wrote, "...along its rivers, between the White and Black seas, from the transuralic to the European borders, it seemed we were constantly meeting the same man."[6] The population showed unity in their diversity, a common brotherhood so strong among the many different groups, in a cold land where cooperation and survival are so closely linked. It was the constant impression of the "openness and spirituality of the Russian face"[7] which had a strong affect on Rilke.

But still, for both Lou and Rilke, the heart of Russia was in the company of Leo Tolstoy. Although little came of their first meeting they both pinned high hopes of enlightenment on their second.

There are polite versions and more realistic versions of the second visit to Tolstoy. Rilke gave one of the more detailed ones in a letter to Sofya

Schill. According to Rilke, they telegraphed Tolstoy to inform him they were coming. Though they hadn't received a reply from Tolstoy, after telegraphing their visit, they decided they would go ahead assuming they would be welcome. They took a carriage to Yasnaia Poliana, passing under "a green valet foamy with treetops in which two little round towers on the left, topped with green cupolas, mark the entrance to the old, overgrown park in which lies hidden [Tolstoy's] simple house."[8] A servant took their cards. Tolstoy's eldest son opened a glass door, and the count appeared before them. "He seems to become smaller, more bent, whiter, and his shadowlessly clear eyes, as though independent of his aged body...."[9] The count recognized "Frau Lou"[10] at once and greeted her cordially. He excused himself and promised to return at 2:00.

They remained in the company of the count's son for awhile, strolling around the grounds. They returned to the house, to discover Countess Tolstoy in the front room putting away books:

> Reluctantly, with surprise, and inhospitably she turns to us for a moment and explains that the Count is unwell.... Now it is fortunate that we can say we've already seen him. That disarms the Countess somewhat. [She] throws the books about in the front room and shouts at someone in an angry voice: We have only just moved in![11]

It became clear that they had walked in on a family row when they heard a young lady crying and the count attempting to soothe her in the next room. When Tolstoy returned the visitors were distraught. He offered the choice of a walk in the park alone with him, or joining the family for dinner. They were more than pleased with the first offer. As they walked in the wind, the count's beard fluttered in the breeze, but his face remained "quiet, as though untouched by the storm."[12]

Lou, who gave a more flowery version of the second meeting, wrote that on the walk Tolstoy picked forget-me-nots, inhaled their scent then carelessly let them fall to the ground. Neither Rilke nor Lou attests to an epiphany, or moment of artistic transcendence. Like the forget-me-nots, they seemed to have been picked, inhaled, and then carelessly dropped.

To ritually free themselves from the awkward situation, they decided to return to the train station on foot, gathering in the beauty of the Russian countryside along the way, allowing the balmy spring breeze to erase their discomfort. Looking out over the plains, Lou felt as if Russia was borderless — a country ever moving outwards in all directions, "as if it can't stop anywhere, as if it must go on, surrounded by invasions and influences from every side throughout history, as if that were its destiny:

to confirm its vastness by a receptivity for even the most foreign elements, preparing itself for passage between right and left for a final synthesis."[13] It was the moment in which she sought her own synthesis — between East and West, between her nomadic drive and the desire to be a home unto herself.

They traveled through the countryside, staying at an Izbá — the Russian name for a peasant hut — drinking fresh cow's milk and eating fresh-picked berries for breakfast. Lou noted the strong, bare, birch logs of the Izbá, weathered and darkened. It offered the rustic simplicity they longed for.

But Lou began withdrawing into herself. The spiritual bond she was developing with her homeland was independent of Rilke, whereas his love for Russia was solely dependent on her. Russia was the landscape of his beloved's soul — he hoped that traveling there together, and apart from Andreas, would form an unbreakable bond between them. But for Lou the bond with Russia was a way of coming home to herself. She had escaped into the western world in her youth, the world of intellect and science, to help her live with her God-loss. Now she was ready to fully embrace the Russian side of her soul — the passion, the religiosity, the unfathomable spirit. The one-on-one relationship with Rilke began to unnerve her. Lou had always preferred the buffer of a *third person*. Despite the intoxication of being in Russia, the second trip was characterized by its underlying tensions.

Taking a steamboat along the river, they disembarked in the upper Volga region and made their way inland, where they found the peasant hut of a Russian poet named Spiridon Drozhzhin. They had been in touch with the poet before they left Germany through Sofya Schill. Schill had sent Rilke some of Drozhzhin's poems. Impressed with the Russian peasant's skill, Rilke had offered to translate his work into German, an offer which pleased Drozhzhin.

Born a serf, Drozhzhin had gained fame as a "peasant poet." His poetry dealt with simple natural observations — the beauty of nature, the beauty of love, working in the fields and other aspects of everyday life for the Russian peasant.

Lou was impressed with the people in the rural area and cheerfully noted that in conversation they "immediately reached the deepest things, the great problems, God, death...."[14] But in a picture taken at this time we see that Lou, sitting on a step beside the peasant poet, looks tired and drawn, perhaps a bit older than her age. Deep lines of stress enclose her expression. Rilke stands near her looking youthful and strong.

An ugly incident happened during the stay, causing them to cut their visit short. The nature of it is unknown because she and Rilke both would later tear out the diary pages of that day. The only possible clue we have as to what happened is in a short story Lou later wrote, depicting a rustic poet, admired by a Rilke-like character, who turns out to be an insensitive lout and makes a drunken pass at the woman visitor.

Despite this earthy realization, Lou's view of the Russian people remained constant. "Debauchery and licentiousness of all sorts can occur in Russia, just as anywhere else, perhaps in an even coarser cruder fashion," she wrote, "but the spiritual life remains innocent and childlike."[15]

After the incident with Drozhzhin, whatever it may have been, they moved to a nearby estate owned by a relative of Tolstoy's who welcomed them. Lou recorded her impressions of the people and their lives on the estate in her Russian novel *Rodinka*.

Despite the unpleasant incidents with their literary idols, they both thrived on the experiences. "Couldn't we fill whole books with everything we absorbed with such eager interest? Didn't we spend years that way?"[16] Lou wrote years later, after the unpleasant memories subsided.

On the eleventh week of traveling through Russia, they went to St. Petersburg. With Lou by his side Rilke wrote a lovely poem about the lovely city. But when Lou left him briefly to visit her family, who were vacationing in Finland, St. Petersburg suddenly turned cold and frightening in his eyes. Waiting nervously for her return, Rilke sent her an "ugly letter."[17] Lou must have responded with soothing, reassuring words, for he wrote back that her letter had touched him "like a wave, so strong and resounding."[18] Despair was something unknown to her, he wrote, "in the beauty in which you live."[19] He sensed the circle of her love was closing and he was on the outside. "Come soon!"[20] he entreated her.

In August she did return and together they went back to Berlin, having spent the whole of spring and summer of 1900 traveling. She had mothered his anguish for three years, loving him when he was himself and even when he was *the other*— the name they had given him when he flew into rage and despair. Now Lou realized she could no longer carry his burden. She was emotionally exhausted and felt she could do no more for him. She needed badly to mother herself.

The strain of her relationship with Rilke led Lou to seek out her old friend, lover, and doctor Zemek. He told her she was suffering from nervous exhaustion. Lou spent some time in the country with Zemek and his family, recuperating and regaining her strength. They had long talks about Rilke and his emotional problems. Zemek, who had attended some of Sigmund Freud's seminars in Vienna, told her about some of the techniques used to help one to overcome childhood traumas.

In September, Rilke traveled to Worpswede, where he stayed at an art colony. There he befriended two young women, Paula Becker and Clara Westhoff. His diary at this time shows a growing independence from Lou — at least on paper — as he makes future plans to go to Paris and study with Rodin. He referred to his "Russian journey with its daily losses"[21] while musing on his artistic development.

In the early days of October he left Worpswede and returned to Schmargendorf, where Lou was. In December he and Lou sat alone in the dark theater, watching the dress rehearsal of Gerhart Hauptmann's play *Michael Kramer*. The two lone figures, sitting side by side and alone among the empty theater seats, each feeling raw and vulnerable in their own way, made the poignant play all the more moving

On New Year's Eve of 1900, Lou confided to her diary, "What I expect from the coming year, what I need is almost only silence. I need to be more by myself," she continues, "as I was up until about four years ago."[22] Though unnamed, the reference to "about four years ago" makes it clear that she is talking about separating from Rilke. She wrote about the experience of her 1900 Russian pilgrimage: "All individual recollections run together in One Feeling...."[23] Something in her big Russian soul absorbs the vastness of individual experiences, like "little huts cuddled along the Volga somewhere in the midst of its boundlessness."[24] It seems Rilke was just one among a number of little huts.

Back home, during the cold month of January, Lou spent her days sitting in a little blue room, by a Christmas tree lit with candles, writing incessantly. Rilke visited daily but her mind was on her work. She became so preoccupied with the characters in a novella titled *Volga* she had difficulty giving it up even in her sleep, as if the story continued writing itself "on the sly."[25] She was relieved when she finished it: "Now I shall sleep —."[26] She deemed the work a "flop."[27] In sharp contrast, biographer Binion called it a "stylist tour de force, and a thoroughly lovely short story too: indeed, Lou's very finest."[28]

While *Volga* had been a much needed distraction, she experienced some guilt after Andreas stayed up until 3 A.M. correcting her proofs for her novel *Ma* and brought her coffee in bed the next morning. "And what

15. Together, Alone

a monster he does that for!" she lamented. "I was bad to Rainer too," she added, "but am never sorry about that."[29]

Once the novella was finished her mood turned festive. Despite her diary entry that attempted to reduce Rilke into a single droplet in the oceanic scheme of things, she seemed to rejoice in their walks in the mixture of frosty air and bright sunshine. She was refreshed by a two-hour walk alone with Rilke. When they returned, she read Dostoevsky's *Poor People* out loud in Russian for him, and they spent hours discussing Russian art and literature.

But at some point after their return from Russia she told Rilke that they could no longer be lovers. The relationship continued under the strain of Lou vacillating over the relationship and Rilke fearing it was over.

Clara Westoff, the sculptress Rilke had met at Worpswede, came to visit him. He then made an abrupt and decisive move, shocking in its finality and suddenness: He asked Westoff to marry him. In mid–February he made the announcement formal.

On February 26, Lou wrote him a letter she titled *Letzter Zuruf*— Last Appeal or Last Call. While the title of the letter suggested a plea on her part, the content read as a sort of threat. She had fulfilled all her responsibilities towards him, she wrote with some obvious anger. And she warned, "If you drift into an uncertain area, you are responsible for yourself."[30] If he married Clara, she wrote, she would no longer be available to him — only in time of "direst need."[31] They could never commit themselves to one another, she went on, because it would cause him to "revert back to ill health,"[32] referring to the severe mood swings he suffered. It was "what we called the 'other' in you, who would be by turns depressed then excited, all too fearful, then all too frenzied."[33] Ominously, she told him that Zemek had warned her that Rilke could become suicidal. But it only caused her "tragic guilt"[34] because of her inability to lessen his anguish. "Gradually I too grew warped, tormented, overwrought, went on beside you automatically, mechanically, could no longer put any full warmth into it, depleted my own nervous strength."[35]

But his love had a healing quality for her as well. "Despite our difference in ages," she notes reflectively, "...and as strange as it may sound, I had to grow into my youth because now I am young and for the first time what others could be at eighteen — true to myself."[36]

The letter is a strange mixture of pushing him away and an underlying jealousy. Having learned nothing from her loss of Rée, she still seemed to attempt to keep Rilke for herself alone while giving only a slender part of herself to him. A harem of men seemed to be something she considered her birthright, and indeed, she came close to accomplishing that.

But regardless of her veiled demand, on April 29, 1901, Rilke married Clara Westoff. The newlyweds moved to Westerwede, and before the year ended they would give birth to a daughter. The child would be named Ruth, after the literary offspring of Lou.

In May Lou turned to Zemek, whom she hadn't seen for two years and who seemed ever ready to be an oasis of peace for her. On May 8 she wrote in her diary that each relationship was like the perennial blossoming of spring, a "Maytide ever again at each reunion."[37]

When she returned home, "Oldster," as she called Andreas, pampered her like a beloved child.

16

The Land in Between

...I have no notion where I'm heading, yet it is always homeward.[1]
— Lou Andreas-Salomé

Adolescence and middle age are like platforms we stand on, waiting to leap into the next inevitable phase of life. At 16, we may leap unthinking, eager to begin our adulthood. In the middle years we long to hold back that final jump, not wanting to connect with its inevitable result — old age and death. Lou had turned 40 in February 1901, and she began to mentally prepare for that final leap. She began to reflect on the severe intellectual training she had submitted herself to in her youth, which had been swept away during her love affair with Rilke. She no longer saw Gillot's teaching as a positive force, but as a sort of violation against her natural self. While Gillot had given her a way out of Russia and her fairy tale existence, Rilke had given her a way back in. She returned stronger, wiser and wholly herself.

After returning home that spring, Lou returned began writing a series of essays called "Old Age and Eternity" in which she surmised, "[K]nowing how to live and knowing how to die go together."[2] In 1902, she published a series of stories which she called *A Land in Between* (Im Zwuschenland). It included stories inspired by her Russian trip as well the usual parade of adolescent girls unwilling to leave their world of fantasy for a world of adulthood and its shocking ally, sex. Middle aged Lou returned to that childhood fantasy world through her fiction, but now she had new wisdom and a positive view of sexuality on her side.

In mid-summer she and Andreas vacationed together in Denmark. Some biographers have concluded she had become pregnant by Zemek in May, and that Andreas may have found out about it. Rudolph Binion cites the novel *The House* (Das Haus) in which the Lou-like character and her husband discover her pregnancy when she faints while bathing. Binion believes that she may have miscarried during the Denmark vacation.[3] In his biography, H.F. Peters likewise claims she was pregnant and tells an elaborate story in which Zemek plans to confront Andreas and demands a divorce. Yet neither biographer cites a source confirming such an occurrence, which seems to be more of a conjecture than a documented fact. Perhaps the only certainty is that Lou was *not* pregnant when she returned home in September.

Not long after her return to her home in Schmargendorf, Lou received word that Paul Rée was dead. He had fallen during a mountain climb. In a letters to various friends she expressed feeling of guilt over him. His untimely death made the loss of his friendship even more poignant. She went through his letters and memories. She called it a "principal event"[4] and dwelled on it for weeks. She concluded that Rée's death was not an accident. His Jewish self-hatred was the cause, she deduced. When they were together "he found refuge from his self-hatred in her love only to feel mortally rejected and despised when she married."[5] Rée's relationship to Lou was a fatal paradox — she gave him emotionally uninhibited love, along with a total inhibition of any physical expression. Whether his death was intentional or accidental, it was likely that self-hatred and hatred of Lou were strong. Rather than holding herself responsible for his early death, she would have been more realistic to accept that she created a great deal of pain in his life. But she could not fully grasp her early fear of sexuality and the destructive impact it had

Lou Andreas-Salomé in the 1890s (akg-images).

on others. It could not yet be named a neurosis, for the man who was about to open the vault of repressed sexuality for the civilized world stood almost a decade ahead on the timeline of her extraordinary life.

During the next two years of her life Lou's traveling was less frenzied. Her main excursion was spending the summer of 1902 with Zemek, who treated her with fresh air and loving kindness. Her writing, which she had performed at a manic pace after returning from Russia, now dwindled down to nothing. She languished in her land in-between, not yet ready to make the final step: "Simply incapable of anything."[6]

The spring of 1903 brought a roller coaster of emotions. During a short visit to St. Petersburg, Lou learned that Gillot — who was over 60 and widowed — had married a young girl. She heard much about Gillot "going to the dogs"[7] amongst her relatives. For the first time she recorded negative comments about her first love and mentor. She berated him in her diary, accusing him of "manly, ideal posturing with green girls" — which would have included her — "for unmanly and un-ideal motives."[8] Had it merely been the lechery of an older pastor and not the ideal love she'd fantasized? Certainly the effect on her life remained the same — she had loved him ideally and he had inspired her onto an extraordinary life course. But the romanticized love affair of her youth now made her queasy. Her idealized vision of Gillot could no longer withstand the rigors of reality.

But also that spring she received news that delighted her: Andreas was offered a professorship of Iranian and West-Asiatic culture at the University in Göttingen, a cultured German burg which lies in the southern part of Lower Saxony between Bonn and Berlin. In June they cheerfully began house hunting in their new location.

That July Lou received word from Rilke. He wanted to see her, for "who knows whether in the direst hour I shall be able to come."[9] She agreed heartily, suggesting they first resume letter writing. Rilke wrote her long letters every three or four days throughout the summer pouring out his struggles and anguish. Her letters to him radiate a special gentle kindness, an earth-motherly tone, as if he could fall into the safety and radiant warmth of her being and she would nurture him there. When he wrote of the terrible depression he suffered while living in Paris in poverty, she wrote back reassuring him: do not be afraid, it was merely caused by the flu from which he had recently recuperated. When he wrote of his desire to make art out of his enormous fears and sensitivities, she told him his letters themselves were like works of living art which they shared. And most prophetically she told him together they *shared the vision* of the great artist he would become. She encouraged him to write more letters because writing was both a therapeutic and artistic exercise. Write to friends in far away places, she advised, send your words out into the world. Despite his depression, Lou assured him, he had never been healthier. Her reassurance inspired him to write a powerful and moving novel titled *The Notebooks of Malte Laurids Brigge*.

The novel begins with a description of life in the French capital for the Rilke-like protagonist. At night in his room at the *Hôtel Dieu*, the unnatural noises of urban life pour in through the open window:

> Automobiles run their way over me. A door slams. Somewhere a window pane falls clattering; I hear its big splinters laugh, its little ones snicker. Then suddenly a dull, muffled noise, from the other side. Someone is climbing the stairs.... Coming, coming incessantly.... And again the street. A girl screams, *Ah tais-toi, je ne veux plus*! And car races up excitedly, then away, running over everything. Someone calls. People are running, overtaking each other. A dog barks. What a relief: a dog. Towards morning a cock even crows, and that is boundless comfort. Then suddenly I fall asleep.[10]

"I'm learning to see, I don't know why it is, but everything penetrates more deeply into me...."[11]

These images had come, almost word for word, from his lengthy letters to Lou and emerged as the portrait of the hypersensitive artist confronting the nerve shattering mechanization of the modern world. The sound of a dog bark and a rooster crowing are the only assurance that the rhythm of nature still exists, and it brings him the island of peace that allows for sleep.

That summer he also sent her a copy of a small book he had written on Rodin. The first week of August she wrote back that she liked it the best of all his published works, a validation which pleased him enormously. "To learn that my little Rodin book means a lot to you, Lou, was an unspeakable joy to me."[12] He now felt inspired, and a quote from Rodin became his motto: *toujours, travailler — toujours*. Always work — always.

In October, Lou and Andreas moved into a house they named Loufried on the outskirts of Göttingen. The house, in the middle of a long-forgotten orchard, was perched on a slope. The university town was sprawled out in the valley below. Lou was thrilled by the fairy tale half-timber structure. The location "fulfilled our longing for a truly rustic life,"[13] with more woods and gardening space than in the Berlin suburbs.

16. The Land in Between

Lou was an interesting specimen to those in the academic community who had heard about her association with Nietzsche, as well as her large oeuvre of prose and essays. But neither she nor Andreas associated with the community. Their lives here separate and apart not only from the immediate community, but also from one another. They took different levels of the house as their own spaces. Fittingly, Lou was loftily upstairs and humbly Andreas was placed downstairs. Lou began gardening with zeal and her garden seemed to become a symbol of her center, her wholeness. (When visiting, Rilke too would come to see her garden as an Eden-like spot which brought him inner peace.)

Lou saw Andreas' new position as a financial and emotional turning point in their lives.

In addition to her domesticity, Lou began working on a novel for "only through work did I really settle into Loufried as a home."[14] But her interest in that novel lost momentum and by the first few weeks in 1904, she had begun another titled *Marriage* (Ehe), an odd area of expertise for a woman who had never fulfilled her own. She was so preoccupied with nesting that she had to set a sheet of paper alongside her working novel on which to jot down decorating ideas that intruded on her concentration.

During the nesting period in Göttingen, she began to suffer from heart trouble, an ailment for which Zemek prescribed bed rest, a prescription she heeded from time to time. Rilke wrote her in January 1904, while traveling in Rome, worrying about her health and eager to hear from her. "Lou, dear Lou, I am writing the date of your last letter over mine only because I want to know that nothing you have written has been lost."[15] Airing his doubts about the Italian postal system, he was also, not so subtly, pointing out her last correspondence had been almost three months ago. He describes in detail a fragment of a mural he had seen in Naples, in which a man — a youthful traveler — sits telling a tale to a "quiet, stately woman ... a tall, home-filled woman" and as the man in the picture seemed to be revealing, "the past, as it returned took on the aspect of the eternal, resembling the those events that comprised and transfigured the life of the woman."[16] Rilke draws a parallel to Lou when he says, "Then the courage to write you, dear Lou, came into being; for it seems that every path, even the most confused, could acquire sense through such a final return to a woman, to the one woman dwelling in maturity and quiet, who is big, and like a summer night, knows how to hear everything...."[17] With these words, Rilke builds an image of her as the looming archetypal muse. She sees the divine within the ordinary. She chooses, as she did when looking into mirrors as a child, the infinite rather than the finite. It was in this way she nurtured his poetic vision. Rilke's vision inspired Lou as well. Lou incorporated this image of the traveling man speaking in the language of eternity to the "home-filled woman" into her novel then called *Marriage*. In it, a young man traveling in Rome "poetized the live woman into a legendary one."[18]

In February 1904, Russia entered a war with Japan. Lou reported that she spent months worrying about the fate of the Russian people. Russia's military inferiority became clear as it suffered a relentless series of humiliating military defeats on land and sea. The immense Russian pride in the defeat of Napoleon that had been woven into the country's psyche by Tolstoy's *War and Peace* was now a distant memory. Throughout the year-long string of battles, Lou was distraught by the continuous bad news. In a March letter Rainer hopes that "the Russian war has not brought terror and danger to your family...."[19] He wishes he had been a doctor so he could help in the Russian war effort. Soon after she sent the words *Christos voskres*! in Russian at the top of her letter. It evoked the memory of their Russian Easter together where they experienced rebirth in the fresh waterfall of tolling bells and the call "Christ has risen!" Together they struggled to evoke the Russia of their vision, knowing that the Russia they'd toured was forever gone.

Requesting a manuscript of his Russia-inspired poems (*A Monk's Songs*) he had left with Lou, Rainer incorporated them into the *Book of Hours: Love Poems to God* and when it was published, it bore a dedication to Lou. It read: "Laid in Lou's hands."

"Dear Lou," Rilke wrote in May, "if it were possible to meet you this summer, do, do let it be possible."[20] She then invited him to her new home. After he stayed for over week — and Lou records nothing about his stay — they traveled to the Harz Mountains together to visit with their mutual friends, the Klingenbergs. If he imagined an inspiring reunion with Lou, it did not eventuate. He wrote his wife — from whom he was separated, but on friendly terms — that he could not imagine any reason to stick around.

Next, Rilke went to Sweden, having arranged a long stay there with the help of Ellen Kay, who was actively promoting his work in her home country. Rilke suggested to Lou that they meet during the summer while she was touring the same region with Zemek. Binion notes that while in

Copenhagen Lou sent a postcard with her hotel in the picture, an enticing X marking where she was staying, but no text. Rilke grabbed the first train he could, only to find that she and Zemek had just left. She later lamented the prank and apologized to him.

In August Lou's diary indicated that their maid, Marie, was pregnant by Andreas. Although she had encouraged him to take a mistress, she was distressed by his lack of discretion. She refers to the situation as something "not to have happened in this house."[21] Apparently she would have preferred the ignorance provided by distance between wife and mistress. She then left Andreas and his mistress at home while she took a month's tour of Scandinavia. But when she and Andreas went to Berlin on New Year's Eve of 1905, Lou returned to Göttingen alone to watch over the expecting mother, because "I did not like leaving her alone"[22] in that condition.

As the New Year began, with Lou approaching 44, Marie's child was born. She was called little Marie—*Mariechen*—and became a lively addition to the Andreas household. At first Lou was cold towards the child and made the little girl nervous. But she would soon come to love her like her own daughter.

Lou's heart ailment worsened and she spent months at a time barracked in the upstairs level of Loufried. She was still writing, but gone was her desire to explore passion for God and philosophy, and the erotic self-suppression of her youth. Rilke, and perhaps Zemek as well, had helped her to bring a satisfactory conclusion to that phase of her life. But her fiction suffered somewhat. Still the brilliant flashes of her mind came through here and there, illuminating human behavior in its unique fashion. But the brightly burning fire of her mind, as Peter Gast had called it, was now dampened by the domestic contentedness of her characters. The fear and excitement of being close to a man without giving in to the desire to be conquered and subjugated had mellowed, if not disappeared entirely.

The novel that she began with the move to Göttingen, *Marriage*, wasn't published until 1919, under the title *The House* (Das Haus). Neither title is very intriguing. Angela Livingstone says that the book explicitly tells us that the perfect marriage "has a brother-and-sister quality and, it implies, consists of a strong thinking male and a devoted, emotional female."[23] Livingstone sees the book as being "built up on a system of contrast, of polarities and affinities"[24] amongst the characters. The story proceeds, writes Livingstone, "through intensification and variation of these attractions and clashes, but with little incident."[25] Lou's drive to explore her life and her soul through fiction was deteriorating. Yet, dutiful worker that she was, she continued to push herself until some new and greater driving force came along to take its place.

The next few years of Lou's life were spent partly in bed for months at a time, with her heart ailment. She was visited by friends, mostly female. She discouraged Rilke from moving to Göttingen when he suggested taking up studies there. She attended theater productions in Berlin with her husband when she was well enough to do so. She even tried her hand at writing a play. Titled *The Magic Cap* (Die Tarnkappe), it is a strange and surreal story. The three acts of the play correlate to three states of consciousness — moonlight, the unconscious, daylight, the conscious and twilight, the state in between. Ernst Pfeiffer writes that three themes she intended were childhood imagination, the psychological nature of the artist, and psychological wisdom of the human being.

At midnight a dwarf enters the room of a fantasy-obsessed little girl who was hoping a fairy would come instead. The dwarf shows the girl and her family what he says is his magic cap. But after he becomes closer to the girl and her brother, he tells them he lied about the cap being magical. The grandfather and mother, however, believing it to be true, live out their secret dreams when wearing the cap.

In the third act — the twilight hour between conscious and the unconscious — the little girl helps the dwarf find an art through which he can express himself. But the play seems to be more a psychological investigation than a drama.

It is clear that Lou's desire to explore her psychological insights had begun to overtake her desire to write fiction.

Years passed by and still Lou remained in the limbo of middle age, the transition. In 1908, Lou traveled to the Balkans with Zemek, where she found the Slavic women so angelically beautiful that she wished she were a man. When they returned to Vienna she viewed the works of Gustuv Klimt in a museum. Klimt was one of the numerous artists and musicians who were inspired by the other great European muse, Alma Schindler, who after her marriage to composer Gustav Mahler became famous as Alma Mahler. Almost as an intuitive salute to a fellow muse, Lou said that Klimt clearly understood "the soul in sex and the flower in woman."[26]

Lou's longtime friend Frieda became deathly ill in 1909. Lou wrote the suffering Frieda reassuring letters that, despite the agnosticism they shared, she believed that the soul would not die and that we are not our bodies, but merely have our bodies for a while.

Frieda's lengthy suffering and subsequent death in March, along with a break with Zemek, must have caused a brief but dark depression in Lou, for she queried Ellen Kay about "a painless poison that leaves no traces"[27] in case she might have a lingering illness such as Frieda had suffered. But the darkness passed and Ellen assured her that the letter with the solemn request was torn to pieces and tossed into the sea.

Literarily Lou seemed to be at sea, as well. She had produced hardly anything of any value in the last five years, with one exception. She had pulled together her ideas on erotic love in an essay titled "The Erotic" (Die Erotik). It was greatly praised by Martin Buber, now considered one of the major religious and philosophical thinkers of the 20th century. She and Buber had met and become friends several years earlier. He wrote that her work on the psychology of the erotic was a "fundamental, pure powerful piece of work!"[28] He encouraged her to expand it into book length. It was published in 1910 and edited by Buber.

In August of 1911, Lou traveled to Sweden to visit Ellen Kay. There, she relaxed and sunbathed in the nude. She wrote that she was "naked and happy in the sun."[29] It was in Sweden that she would serendipitously (and wasn't all her life serendipity?) step into the final and most significant phase of her life.

III
FATHER FREUD

I have never met anyone with so deep and subtle understanding of psychoanalysis.
— Karl Abraham, letter to Freud
about Lou Andreas-Salomé, in
Lisa Appignanesi and John Forrester,
Freud's Women, p. 241

Freud had a special admiration for Lou Andreas-Salomé, her distinguished personality and ethical ideas, which he felt far transcended his own.
— Ernest Jones, in Angela Livingstone,
Salomé: Her Life and Work, p. 152

17

Oedipus Rex

> *I missed you at the lecture yesterday.... I stared spellbound at the space that had been left for you.*[1]
> — Sigmund Freud to Lou Andreas-Salomé

Today, in Hampstead section of North London, stands a beautiful red brick building in which all artifacts of Sigmund Freud have been preserved. Freud and his family had fled his Berggasse Street no. 19 apartment in Vienna in 1938 when the Nazis annexed Austria. His personal possessions were transferred to London in the 1930s and there he reassembled his famous office and practice. His patient receiving room in London, as it had been in Vienna, is not at all like the modern utilitarian office, but an exotic museum-like room with warm, dark colors and glowing, rich textures. Here the famous couch still sets, on which patients had laid reciting dreams and fantasies. The couch is covered with an intricately designed woven Persian velvety blanket. It has a particular maternal voluptuousness that must have allowed the patient to feel safe and protected. Oriental rugs, intricate and elaborate in design, cover the floor and walls. Scattered throughout the room on tables and shelves there is an extensive collection of ancient antiquities, copious rows of statuettes and vases, gathered from archeological sites throughout the world—Egyptian, Greek, Indian, Chinese, Roman. The archaic pieces, excavated from deep within the earth, were both a fascination to him, and symbolic of his role as an *archeologist of the mind*, exploring the depths of the mind for buried and archaic drives that dictate human behavior.

His enormous collection included a small statue of the Sphinx found in Thebes. In this depiction of the mythical creature, the Sphinx was lion from the waist down, with the head and bust of a woman and the wings of a bird—this is the she-creature who destroys those who cannot solve her riddle. Freud's favorite statuette was of Athena, the armed warrior goddess, which he placed in the center of his desk. And to the right of center, adhered to the bookcase, is a framed picture of Lou Andreas-Salomé, preserved exactly as he had left it. He kept it on his desk, he told her, for inspiration. Below it is yet another depiction of the Sphinx, the symbol of what Freud considered nature's greatest riddle: woman. Athena, the Sphinx and Lou — it seems wholly appropriate that they have been enshrined together by Freud.

The bookshelf behind Freud's desk prominently displays the works of Goethe, Shakespeare, Gogol, Balzac, Anatole France, Darwin, numerous religious texts on Moses, and, of course, Nietzsche. Freud greatly admired Nietzsche's mind and acknowledged that no matter where he went in his exploration of the unconscious, Nietzsche had always preceded him.

Freud began his career as a medical neurologist and became an internationally-recognized expert. He and noted physician Josef Breuer broke new ground when they collaborated in research on hysteria. Breuer recognized the nervous disorder as a psychological rather than a physical problem, and he and Freud had some success treating patients with hypnosis. Freud's work with Breuer led him to insights that would be the foundation of psychoanalysis — that neurotic behavior is motivated by repressed, unconscious desires.

As his work developed, Freud theorized that the repressed sexual drive was behind many of the anxieties of the age, a view that nineteenth-century European society considered repugnant and indecent. Isolated from the mainstream of scientific development, he began working with a succession of psychologically disturbed patients in the 1890s. Through this process Freud pioneered the talk therapy method, which sought to reveal unconscious conflicts and desires relating to one's childhood.

In 1911, Hugo Heller presented a paper to Freud's circle on Lou Andreas-Salomé's fiction. Two weeks later, Lou came to Vienna to attend the psychoanalytic congress with Poul Bjerre.

By this time in her life Lou Andreas-Salomé was a legend, an intellectual celebrity. A glowing article about her published a year later in a German scholarly journal shows to what extent her personality had captivated the German intellectual community. Frau Lou, wrote Helene Klingenberg, had the "seriousness of a man combined with the carefree nature of a child and the devotion and lovingness of a woman," and "an immense readiness towards life."² She was "devoted and courageously candid."³ An intense mixture of intellect and instinct, she reflected a deep glowing aura. She rejected anything that bound or hindered her, Klingenberg wrote, such as labels and social limitations. The secret to her youthful essence was the perpetual rebirth of her mind — ever curious, ever burning for new experience. Constant intellectual activity, astonishment and growing curiosity gave her the "power to create new blossoms"⁴ from the dying withered ones. Growing old was "to be active and grow richer during your whole life...."⁵ Her soul collected "treasures" and she spoke of them with "a burning heart." Her thinking was "a passionate event, not something cool, pale and life-negating."⁶

With intriguing publicity like this, Freud was surely flattered to admit Lou to his assemblage.

"Two very different experiences in life made me particularly receptive to Freud's depth psychology," Lou wrote in her memoir, "sharing the extraordinary and rare spiritual destiny of another person and growing among a people who were naturally oriented towards the inner life."⁷ The latter reference is to Russia, she tells us. "I won't refer here to the first of these,"⁸ she wrote guardedly of Rilke. In her relationship to Rilke, she often played the analyst. She did not seek to rid Rilke of his sensitive nature, but rather, helped him develop it to its fullest. In her ability to entice the artist to fulfill his potential she surpassed even Freud in her psychological insight. But is the first experience she refers to really Rilke — or a veiled reference to herself with Rilke as superficial candidate? For whose life would need more of a psychological explanation than her own?

In her chapter of her memoir titled "The Freud Experience," Lou shows a deep reverence for this man, who led her search for meaning and fulfillment to its climax. Freud considered her a genius, a valuable member of his inner circle, as well as a remarkable human being. His role in her life was fatherly, and unlike Gillot and others he never crossed that invisible boundary that made him fall from grace in her eyes — despite an incident in their future that would cause Lou some private concern.

Poul Bjerre, who had first introduced her to the Freud school, was awed by Lou as so many others had been. "To young Bjerre," Peters wrote, "Lou was inspiration personified, mother of his unborn thoughts, the mistress of his youthful passion."⁹ Though she was fifty at that time, Bjerre described her as still having a mysterious magnetism:

> One noticed at once that Lou was an extraordinary woman. She had the gift of entering completely into the mind of the man she loved. Her enormous concentration fanned, as it were, her partner's intellectual fire. I have never met anyone else who understood me so quickly, so well, so completely as Lou did. [10]

He goes on to say that talks with Lou inspired his theories to grow and thrive. "Like a catalyst," he said, "she activated my thought processes. She may have destroyed lives and marriages but her presence was exciting. One felt the spark of her genius. One grew in her presence."[11]

As soon as she arrived in Vienna, she boldly approached Freud and told him she wanted to study with him. Instantly charmed by her childlike eagerness, he expressed surprise that a gracious woman would want to get involved with the washing of what he described as dirty linen. But she was far more fascinated by the so-called dirty linen than the perfectly neat and clean, she assured him. "Even after we've talked about the most terrible things," he told her, "you look like Christmas is coming."[12]

Christmas is a fitting metaphor for Lou's enthusiasm for psychoanalysis because it brought her not only a gift, but one with deep spiritual value. It reunited the cerebral, the emotional and the sexual forces that were torn apart by her social, religious and intellectual training. It also suited her abstract thinking about private issues, without revealing too much of herself. Her fiction had served this purpose only partly, for it was all too clear that she was writing about her personal experiences. And yet it is clear from her memoir that she preferred to conceal more than reveal, despite the strong desire to intellectually explore her psyche.

Five years older than Lou, Freud found her enthusiasm for psychotherapy childlike and charming. Lou was famous as both a writer and a thinker, and infamous for her liaison with Nietzsche. Freud had heard both the praise and gossip about her. But somehow he had not expected this joyful and wholehearted woman, so much in love with life. Had he expected her to be the Sphinx-like creature full of riddles and destruction? Or perhaps he found it difficult, even when squinting, to see the woman who was known as an intellectual *femme fatale*: the woman who excited Nietzsche's mind and broke his heart; the woman who had provoked the jealousy of Elizabeth Nietzsche, who continued to slander Lou at every chance; the woman who molded the anxiety-ridden Rilke into a world class artist. But, like everyone who came to know her, Freud came to see Lou as an extraordinary and brilliant human being who had an extremely positive effect on his work. No doubt he revered her like his prized Athena, the guardian goddess of heroes.

The Weimer Congress, headed by Freud, greatly excited Lou. Without hesitation she decided to devote her life to this new science. She wrote to Freud after the convention, "Since attending the Weimer Congress last autumn, the study of psycho-analysis has continued to preoccupy me, and the further I penetrate into it the more absorbed I become. And now my wish to spend some months in Vienna is about to be realized."[13] She came to realize that her drive to write was not fueled by artistry but by a need to discover and explore her own psyche. The repressed sexuality of the Victorian age was the core of Freud's work. In Lou's life, repressed sexuality had played a significant role.

Carl Jung, years after he had broken off from his mentor, Sigmund Freud, wrote that Freud was an historical necessity. Freud was an important safety valve for Victorian era, an era beset with intense sexual repression, resulting in deep-rooted neurosis. However, Jung believed that Freud overextended his theory by reducing *all* psychic products, such as art, philosophy and religion, to nothing more than expressions of repressed sexual instinct. With the benefit of Jung and others who refined many of Freud's seminal ideas, we now see many of Freud's theories as partially preserved antiques.

When Lou began her study of psychoanalysis, she focused not on the separation between the neurotic and healthy person, but on the connection between the two. Mental illnesses give us a rare glimpse of the inner workings and structure of the human mind. In the mentally ill person "one could decipher, as [if] under a microscope, things which remained almost invisible in the case of the normal person."[14] Freud, she writes, had carried out this "grandiose spadework," these "analytical excavations ... with infinite methodical care and caution, bringing to light, layer by layer, increasingly deeper levels of our primal being."[15]

After attending the Vienna Congress of psychoanalysts, Lou became enraptured with the study of psychoanalysis. When she returned home she devoted herself full time to it. From Göttingen, she wrote Freud requesting permission to attend the Third Congress in the autumn months of 1912. Freud replied that he considered her presence at his lectures a "favorable omen."[16]

She arrived in Vienna on October 25, 1912, for the Third Congress with her friend Ellen Dep. They checked into the Hotel Zita, which turned out to be only a few steps from the Alte Elster restaurant, where the Freudian group often met. "[A] promising beginning,"[17] she noted in her journal.

But the Third Congress was marked by ruptures in the movement, and once again with amazing accuracy Lou found herself in the center of a major historical event. It was a painful time for Freud, but it was also a period of growth and changes, just the sort of environment where Lou so often found herself in the center. She felt she was once again in the company of brothers, the familiar scenario she had sought all her life. The group took on the semblances of a family, with Freud as the fatherly head. There were rivalries among the "brothers," and Lou was quickly entangled in triangles of jealousy and contention between Freud and his followers, as they vied for power and approval. One of Lou's earliest notations upon arrival was that Freud looked older and more harassed than the year before. But the effect of being with people with whom she thought much alike was revitalizing to her spirit. "I feel altogether more at home and more comfortable every time I'm with these people around Freud," she wrote in her journal; "...it is good to be here."[18]

Unknowingly, her very first step took her into a rift between Freud and Alfred Adler. Adler was a Freud follower who had recently parted company with the master on the subject of infantile sexuality. Freud perceived human behavior as driven by sexuality and other basic biological needs; Adler characterized it as driven by ideas and values. Applying Nietzschean thought to psychology, Adler theorized that the will to power — not sexuality — was the major drive behind all human behavior.

Lou contacted Adler and informed Freud she wanted to attend Adler's seminars in addition to Freud's. Freud wrote to Lou politely but firmly that he considered Adler a traitor to the cause. "We found ourselves obliged to break off all contact with Adler's splinter group and our own," he wrote, adding, "and even our medical guests are asked to choose between one or the other."[19] But he made an exception for Lou. "I would never dream, dear lady, of imposing such a restriction on you."[20] But if she did decide to go, he asked that she not speak about it. These statements, though cloaked in civility, reveal the depth of devotion Freud expected from his followers. He seemed to want to create a group something like the Knights of the Round Table, bound to an oath of allegiance to him as sovereign. In his earlier years he gave out rings, with a special stamp, to his disciples.

Lou did as she pleased: she went to see Adler. "Freud the man has a critical attitude in me," Adler had warned her, adding defiantly, "I cannot regret it."[21] Lou gained interest in Adler's work after her first attendance to the psychoanalytic conference the year before and had been exchanging letters with him before her return to Vienna. He invited her to his Thursday night discussions. On their first meeting they talked until the early hours of the morning. After meeting with Adler, she discovered that she was as skeptical about Freud's emphasis on sexuality as Adler was.

Personally, Lou found Adler "charming and intelligent," but she made two observations: insightfully, that he took the rift with Freud too personally; and comically, that he looked "like a button."[22] Pictures show him with round and pleasant face. But perhaps she even saw his thinking as button-like: "As though he got stuck somewhere inside himself."[23] They got into a spirited dispute during supper. She did not like his use of assigning negative and positive qualities to the terminology of opposites — above and below, masculine and feminine, superior and inferior. With a mixture of Taoism, Nietzsche-ism and pre–Jungian insight, she insisted that a so-called negative trait could be positive in certain circumstances. Both knew their Nietzsche well, and she may have influenced Adler to understand that the human being needs to embrace both sides of the self— what Nietzsche termed the Apollonian (rational) and Dionysian (irrational) polarities. To refute or over-emphasize either one can lead to discord in the personality. Lou believed Freud, in contrast to Adler, saw inner compromise as essential, a mutual interweave of the polarizing impulses within the psyche. Adler's thinking, she believed, could cause an unhealthy response — the repressed polarity becomes masked and denied by the conscious mind, resulting in neuroses. That which we repress consciously can and will burst out unconsciously.

What, then, did Lou believe was the driving force behind neurotic behavior? Between Freud (repressed sexuality) and Adler (the will to power), she took the middle path: "To me every neurosis appears to be a mutual conflict between ego and sexuality." In an ideal healthy system, will and sexuality work in unity; in a neurotic one they "abuse one another."[24]

18

Ego and Eros

> *...I realized it was this very struggle in Tausk that most deeply moved me—the struggle of the human creature. Brother-animal.*[1]
> — Lou Andreas-Salomé

When Lou arrived early for Freud's Wednesday lecture, she met the handsome, young Dr. Victor Tausk, whom she described in her journal as blond and headstrong. Dressed in his white coat, he looked quite impressive. They got into a discussion about her friend and the editor of her book on the erotic, Martin Buber. Though she disagreed about something Tausk said, she demurely and uncharacteristically did not dispute his opinion.

Tausk was strikingly handsome with finely cut features, blond hair, expressive blue eyes and a trim mustache. Brilliant, neurotic, creative and talented, Tausk was a towering figure in the eyes of fellow analysts of that time. He was studying medicine at the University of Vienna, but already held a degree in law, and had been for a short time a journalist. Despite the fact that many women were attracted by his dashing good looks and vulnerable charm, Lou was touched by his beautiful mind and his poignant inner struggles. Unwittingly she had stepped into a monumental rivalry between Freud and Tausk that would become legendary.

When Freud arrived he seated her by his side and charmed her with flattery. The attention of both men must have certainly pleased her. The sign of her significance to Freud was already apparent to everyone. She became his fixation point during his lecture, and he relied on her receptive and perceptive expression to make him feel confident. When she missed one of his classes, Freud wrote flirtatiously that he was spellbound by her empty chair, almost unable to lecture without the reassurance of her face.

Lou was timid during the class, choosing to listen rather than talk.

But she actively had one-on-one discussions with her fellows after class. While chatting with Freud, she was surprised that he acquiesced to her view that neurosis was a conflict between ego and libido, rather than the libido alone. But his books read otherwise, she offered, giving the libido center stage. He told her humbly that it was his most current formulation at the time.

During an intermission, she got into a discussion with another psychoanalyst, Dr. Paul Federn, regarding one of Adler's theories. Adler believed, Federn argued, that a child made unreasonable demands as compensation for his feelings of inferiority. Lou's response was typical of her thinking: she looked more deeply and more optimistically into the matter. No, she said, it is the *strength* of the child, his feeling of superiority that makes him believe that his demands should be met. Whether they agreed with her or not, the psychoanalysts all found her thoughts fascinating and admirable — a fresh burst of air into the staleness of the all-male group.

During Freud's lecture on the unconscious, Lou noted that he brought up Carl Jung. Jung had become the most famous and influential of Freud's defectors, and Lou had arrived at the time that the rift between the two men had become the most explosive. Perhaps it is only the strength of Freud's ego that makes him considered the sole father of psychology. By modern standards, some of Freud's work is archaic, whereas Jung's is still vibrant and growing. Jung's system, while every bit as scientific, has a humanist side. Like Lou, Jung focused on the healthy lessons we can learn from the illnesses of the human mind. Lou and Jung came closest to one another in their holistic approach to the psyche. Jung, building on Freud's foundation, believed that "all was libido rising by phases above its crass instinctual beginnings through evolutionary time according to an inner perfecting principle."[2] But perhaps out of loyalty to Freud or simply because Jung's theories weren't fully formed yet, Lou commented that his "inner perfecting principle" was a theory that turned in on itself, seemingly eating itself alive. Neurosis, according to Jung, was an attempt for the psyche to make adjustments for unhealthy circumstances in the past. The behavior becomes neurotic when one continues to react to something that is no longer a threat. So, neurosis in a sense is *getting emotionally stuck* at the time when one suffered trauma. Perhaps she might have agreed with his later more developed theories as seeing the holistic nature of the psyche, and its desire or drive to put things right. Jung, for his part, found Lou's work both strange and profound.

At one meeting Freud made an analogy of Zeus and his wayward son, Dionysus, in reference to himself and Jung. Lou and Tausk exchanged glances, almost unable to repress their laughter. Like the children of a beloved and powerful father, they enjoyed mocking his grandiosity. But the analogy was apt in the sense that Freud as the self-proclaimed father of psychoanalysis had spawned many errant sons, including Tausk himself.

In a fascinating study of the relationship between Freud and Tausk, Paul Roazen writes that history has cheated Tausk of his rightful place in psychoanalytic history. Roazen's book *Brother Animal*—a phrase taken from one of Lou's letters—sheds light on the tragic relationship between the two brilliant and ambitious men. Roazen writes: "To the generation of psychoanalysts who came after the First World War, Tausk is known as the genius who failed."[3] Citing Lou's track record in attracting troubled geniuses, he sees it as a high estimate of Tausk's worth: "A woman like Lou would hardly waste her time on a nobody."[4] Among the elite of early psychoanalysis, Tausk "looms as a mythical figure from the past who died at the height of his powers."[5] Freud's jealousy of the younger, far more attractive and brilliant man is certainly understandable. But for Tausk the father-son rivalry would result in a mysterious tragedy.

Eighteen years younger than Lou, Tausk related to the opposite sex more or less as she did. A pattern of falling wildly in love, only to run away from the intensity of the overwhelming experience, may have made him appear a dashing Don Juan. But he was deeply troubled and neurotically feared the dependency love caused in him.

Tausk was born into a non-practicing Jewish family in Yugoslavia, to a tyrannical father and a traditional mother. Roazen describes Tausk's mother as self-sacrificing and devoted to the point of martyrdom. His father failed to provide for his family properly but was successful at charming and attracting other women, and often strayed away from home. Tausk's relationship to his father was "strained and antagonistic."[6] Tausk was the oldest of nine children and as such bore the pressure of a mother who had great ambitions for him.

Tausk wanted to go to medical school but his family couldn't afford it. Instead, he studied law at the University of Vienna. While there he had a love affair with a fellow student, Martha Frisch. Martha was madly in love with Tausk and when she became pregnant, they married in 1900. Tausk returned to Yugoslavia where he successfully practiced law. They had two sons.

Unable to withstand the dependency that marriage fosters, Tausk caused the marriage to quickly deteriorate. They separated in 1905. He moved to Berlin and his wife stayed in Vienna with their two young sons. "The way I live now is truly the best," he wrote, "independent because no one depends on me, not a slave because not a master."[7]

With his intelligence and persuasiveness, Tausk could have had a lucrative career in law. Instead, he went to Berlin and attempted to start a new career. Roazen pointed to Tausk's capacity for renaissance genius: "Employing his multiple gifts, he wrote poetry, practiced his violin, drew charcoal sketches and directed plays."[8] But it was only through journalism that he was able to make any money. He disliked the journalism trade, but wrote so that he could provide for his sons. He was an eloquent and talented writer, and yearned to be creative. But after the pursuit of another woman ended in frustration, Tausk collapsed. Suffering from a lung ailment and chronic fatigue, he went to a sanatorium where he was diagnosed with mental and physical exhaustion. While there he sank into a deep depression, and ominously was told that he had "a hereditary inclination towards the psychopathological side."[9] He poured out his suffering and attempts at regaining mastery over himself in moving letters to his estranged wife, with whom he remained extremely close. The letters reveal that "Tausk's inner world was troubled and he teetered on the edge of an abyss." [10] And yet he was profoundly analytical about his condition, as if some part of him remained separate and intact. "I've lost my feeling for nature," and "I am incurably ill in the soul. My whole past seems to be nothing but a preparation for this terrible collapse of my personality.... I'm groping in the dark.... One needs a guide."[11] He suffered immensely from grief over his inability to work and send money for his sons. "Obsessional ideas, heavy depressions, pressure in my head and tired, tired. Everything is ill and without guidance."[12] The guidance that he so often groped for was soon to come — psychoanalysis would become his Persephone, Queen of the Underworld, guiding with a torch of enlightenment.

After being in the sanatorium for over three weeks, Tausk had a sudden and spontaneous recovery. His remarkable record of his symptoms and feelings in his letters to Martha may have played a role in it. He had discovered the power of talk therapy. Freud, the academic, the man of science, arrived at his insights through the study of his patients; Tausk traveled through the uncharted territory of depression with the genius of a lost explorer, willfully pulling his way out of depression and bringing himself back.

Tausk seemed to thrive on new beginnings — another trait he shared with Lou. After his brief but intense depression, he decided to become a psychoanalyst. He returned to Vienna, where Martha — who was working in her father's firm to make ends meet — was living with their two sons. He and Martha finalized their divorce but his relationship to his sons greatly improved.

In 1909, he began the study of psychoanalysis. His remarkable talent and insight into the subject were immediately obvious to everyone. He specialized in the treatment of schizophrenia and manic-depression. His work would make a great and lasting impact on the Freudian psychoanalysts. But despite his numerous gifts, or more likely because of them, Freud felt threatened by his presence.

After Freud's lecture, Tausk and another student escorted Lou to her hotel. Tausk told her he was offering on a course on Freudian thought. She would be more than happy to attend, she replied.

In early November Tausk brought a trade journal that had one of Jung's latest essays — a work on the libido which marked Jung's sharpest departure from Freudian theory. Both Tausk and Lou were loyal to Freud in the face of Jung's defection. But Lou felt Tausk devalued Jung excessively. She, herself, felt Jung's ideas were premature and naïve. And to the extent his theories were not fully developed until years later, she was correct.

She notes that she and Tausk "frequently talked" and "always with pleasure."[13] The following week she began attending Tausk's introductory course on psychoanalysis. She preferred his lecturing style to Freud's and noted that his comments on a paper written on sadomasochism were so kindred to her own that she felt she could have "made them myself."[14] When Tausk lectured on sex and ego the following week, she began to differentiate her own thought from Freud's. She and Tausk agreed that Freud took a pedantic approach to mankind. "In most of Freud's writing, civilized man appears as a sadly domesticated savage, and sublimation by the aid of his repressed savagery assumes an essentially negative quality — drive and culture being contrasted...."[15] Whereas Freud saw the cultural and the natural in opposition, Lou formulated the cultural as part of what was natural in the human being. That is, it is human nature to be cultural.

Tausk and Lou began spending a great deal of time together. Though ever discreet, she noted numerous visits at her hotel room, where he brought her gifts of his past works. His translated versions of Slavic ballads pleased her greatly. She found them fascinating. His depiction of the

Nordic people was not Nietzsche's "blond beasts of prey" but Promethean hero-types whose sins against the gods are the boon of mankind.

We have no indication when an affair began or ended, but according to the folklore of the gossipy psychoanalytical circle, Lou actively set out to seduce Tausk. Roazen points out that Tausk, who was incredibly appealing to women, had the choice of any number of them — younger and more malleable than Lou. But it was most likely her penetrating way of understanding him, her unique capability for insight into his soul that made her so appealing: "[F]rom the very beginning I realized it was this very struggle in Tausk that most deeply moved me — the struggle of the human creature. Brother-animal. You."[16] Youthful beauty couldn't match Lou's empathetic understanding of his troubled soul.

She began spending time with Tausk at his clinic, where she spoke with and helped in analysis of his patients. Both were tireless, driven to work, and compassionate towards others. She records that they spent long evening hours together, going over their notes and theories.

One Sunday, when Lou was laid up in bed with a fever, Tausk brought his two sons to visit. She was deeply moved to see them together, Tausk trying to fit a lifetime into the Sunday visits with his sons.

Her relationship to Tausk had a playful schoolboy-and-girl nature, with Freud as the frowning schoolmaster. Lou recorded an incident when she and Tausk once ditched Freud's class, like a couple of teenagers, to go to a movie. The new form of entertainment must have been a joyful novelty to the budding psychoanalysts, for the images projected in the darkened room were much like dream images which are cast upon the inner screen of our subconscious minds. Despite the large of amount of work they both had, they began to go to the movies on a regular basis, sometimes taking his sons with them. "I always have to laugh at this activity in which we indulge,"[17] Lou wrote with rebellious pleasure.

When Freud noticed the budding relationship between Tausk and Lou, he told her in a fatherly fashion that he felt Tausk might exert a bad influence on her. But like Rilke, Tausk was a troubled genius she'd come to love. What Freud saw as rash and reckless in Tausk, Lou saw as primal struggle, channeling his deepest passions and fears into his intellectual work — a quality she had also encouraged in Rilke. It was, in fact, quite heroic to her. She too had long struggled to understand and guide her destructive emotions through intellectual work. She had great compassion for his personal turmoil, but at the same time she held him at distance, fearing the unhealthy effect on her.

Lou continually stood up for Tausk when Freud aired his doubts, and encouraged Freud to be patient with him. Freud admitted that he "would have dropped Tausk" had it not been for Lou's fondness for him, "because he considered him a threat to the future of psychoanalysis."[18] He was also a threat to Freud's relationship to Lou. Though Lou's relationship to Freud was non-sexual, it had all the markings of a marriage-like bond. He sent her flowers, she often had dinner with him in his home (presumably with the family) and it was common for them to stay up till two in the morning talking. While such behavior was constant in Lou's relationships, it is doubtful that Freud ever valued a woman's intellect as much as he did Lou's.

His own wife was a necessary and useful companion. Their sex life died of natural causes when Freud was only in his forties, and he didn't seem to mind it. Frau Professor Freud kept the family home spotlessly neat (constantly chasing after him to catch the ashes of his ubiquitous cigars) and laid his clothes out for him every day so that his mind could focus on loftier things. "She even put toothpaste on his toothbrush,"[19] Roazen reports. Freud was demanding of his wife, and by his own admission, had "a tendency towards tyranny."[20] The family and home life revolved around Freud's work, since his office was in their Viennese apartment. His wife accepted these terms, and strove to fulfill her duty, even when the work required her to call on the help of her sister.

But Lou was different. She not only excited his intellect with her understanding but she also saw him as a god-like father, a role he felt destined to play. Roazen writes of Freud's feelings for Lou:

> Many years later, Freud wrote that he had admired Lou immensely and had been very attached to her "without a trace of sexual attraction." Freud was always moved by the great charm of what he called narcissistic women. Through Lou Freud was in touch with spirit of Nietzsche and the best of German cultural life.... He took her into his confidence to an extraordinary degree.[21]

Throughout her life Lou had set up a three-way relationship with men wherein she was the centerpiece. But the triangular connection of Freud, Tausk and Lou was more about the two men. In a traditional oedipal scenario, the two men were vying for power. Lou as a mother figure to Tausk and an intellectual wife to Freud was merely a symbol of that power. This is not to say that the two men didn't truly value her — they did. But in the re-enactment of Freud's primary myth, competition between men was the primary focus. Women were the trophies. Freud was not threatened by Lou's intelligence because for "such an old-fashion man, women were simply not competitors."[22]

Lou and her friend Ellen spent that Christmas at the home of her old Vienna friend, Richard Beer-Hofmann. "In the past," she wrote, Beer-Hofmann was a "gay and easy-going wanderer through the world, now he is sedentary and melancholy and could not be further from the things that used to delight and cheer me in those serious days of mine."[23] For Lou *serious days* equaled her *sexually repressed* days. In her fifties, she was more open to her womanliness and seemed to grow into a second childhood—even more life-affirming than the first. For Beer-Hofmann and the former Young Vienna writers, the past was filled with sexual conquest, but they had missed out on the true joy of loving sexual relationships. Both Lou and Beer-Hofmann had lived in extremes—she in sexual repression and he in the promiscuity of the men known as Young Vienna—and as a consequence both had something vital missing from their lives. But Lou had now surpassed Beer-Hofmann in her new-found joy of life. She described him as looking old and weary; he looked at her, it seemed, the way a grown-up looks at a child. He seemed to be "awaiting the return of a neglected joy."[24] Perhaps there is a note of revenge in this observation—he had, after all, been one of the few men to turn away from her.

In January of 1913 she eagerly returned from Christmas vacation to her psychoanalytical circle—her true Christmas present. She attended a lecture on dreams and fairy tales and afterward continued discussions, ending up at the Alserhof. In a debate with Otto Rank and others, Lou was impressed with Tausk's lively and persuasive arguing and the beauty of his mind. But Freud had made it clear to her in private that he found Tausk's beautiful mind all too "clever and dangerous."[25]

The group broke up at two in the morning and she returned to her room to find a telegram waiting. Her mother had died.

The next day she went to class, half numb "living with my dead Muschka."[26] Despite her closeness to so many of the men there, she told no one of her mother's death because in this place "no one knew [her mother] and yet everyone would have to say something."[27]

19

The Beautiful Narcissist

> ... *transforming yourself endlessly, you will always imbue the strongest and most intrinsic potential in others...*[1]
> — Victor Emil Gebsattel, letter to Lou Andreas-Salomé

Mirrors: they played a significant role in Lou's life. In childhood they were her enemy. They showed her as a limited being, with outline and finite shape, while she *knew* herself to be limitless. She knew that the power of her own spirit had no limitations, and she proved it to herself and to the world.

Though Freud may have considered her a narcissistic woman — and he believed vanity in a woman was a sign of health, as in a cat that preens itself excessively — Lou was not at all vain about her appearance. Her focused energy poured into her intellectual relationships, study and reflective writings, leaving nothing left over for the most superficial aspects of life. Lou's life seems to, in every way, reject that limited mirror-image and travel to a realm beyond it. Limitations simply did not exist for her (as her father's long ago permission made school non-mandatory for her). In her work, she took on the myth of Narcissus, the Greek youth who fell in love with his own reflection, as a primary archetype. It is not surprising that she chose to view self-love as healthy and life-affirming, as opposed to Freud's negative interpretation of the fable.

Earlier in the year, during a *tête-à-tête* with Freud, Lou got a first hand construal of Freud's view of narcissism. He told her the story of a cat that frequented his office by climbing through an open window. He didn't particularly care for animals, but after some time he began to anticipate the creature's visits. The cat would walk with feline grace through his maze of ancient statuettes, purring with delight. He would give it a saucer of milk and the cat began a daily ritual of coming in the window, walking through the artifacts, then drinking its milk. But, despite Freud's increasing affection for it, the cat looked at him coldly with its "green eyes and slanting pupils toward him as toward any object."[2] Freud saw the cat as a "symbolic picture of all the peaceful and playful charm of egotism."[3] Freud clearly related felines to the feminine, and may well have seen this story as an analogy to Lou's relationship to him. Psychology was the warm milk he gave her with pleasure.

After listening to Freud's cat story, Lou countered with her childhood vision, which perhaps she was offering as a more positive view of feminine narcissism. As a little girl she imagined that women had precious stones within, like a mountain with buried gems. She remembered a fairy tale, in which jewels, in place of words, gushed forth from the mouth of a princess. This symbolic image of her womanhood is certainly richer, more affirmative than the one of Freud's indifferent, self-satisfied green-eyed cat. It also suggests that women's inner resources are so rich, valuable and beautiful that charming egotism is only natural.

Freud pioneered the use of the Narcissus myth as an example of neurotic self-love, whereas Lou theorized that self-love was an important foundation of the healthy human being. She depicted Narcissus' fate of falling into the water, into his own image, not as destructive but rather as *moving into nature*, including his own nature. Unlike Freud, who saw man as a poorly-tamed savage, she believed that human culture and nature were not opposing forces, but that "the cultural *was* the natural"[4] for human beings. "It is wrong to see nature and culture as opposed like sunlight and shadow in respect to our natural desire for happiness and the ego's fulfillment,"[5] she wrote. Biographer Livingstone explains Lou's unique genius for changing the interpretation of a suicidal Narcissus into a life-affirming hero:

> Narcissus [is] in love with himself, and therefore with the whole world he created; human culture conceived as a second reality which is equivalent to, and which intensifies and expresses, human nature...[6]

To Lou, Narcissus falling into the water is not symbolic of death but a merging with his whole self, "becoming fully himself; self-centeredness is identical with selflessness."[7] That is, selfishness and unselfishness become one in the same because we cannot differentiate between our innate drives. Thus, to give is to receive: "If we give ourselves, we possess ourselves entirely.... A seeming modesty!"[8]

While Freud concentrated on the unhealthy mind, Lou (like Jung) saw in the mind healthy drives, groping for a path to wholeness. Lou's interpretation of Narcissus is her defining intellectual moment. She defines a "beautiful narcissism," Narcissus as the one who merges with himself in an act of holistic self-love — Narcissus as "the discoverer of the self, the self-knower."[9] Livingstone calls this redefinition of narcissism "Andreas-Salomé at her best: Nietzschean, evolutionist, religious atheist, poetic psychoanalyst, eclectic and original at once, infusing the ideas she had inherited and developed with the profound *joie de vivre* that was wholly her own."[10] Freud welcomed her insights, telling her he saw them as stimuli rather than criticism.

Though she never strayed too far from Freud's graces, Lou sharply contrasted her view of psychology with Freud's. Lou seemed to be looking upward towards the light, rather than down into the dark abyss of psychosis.

After spending most of the spring and summer in Göttingen with side trips to Munich and Budapest, Lou eagerly returned to Vienna at the end of August.

> The arrival in Vienna was indescribably beautiful and so was the drive home, accompanied by Tausk, my old hotel room, No. 28, with many flowerpots in the window. Even the employees gave me a hearty welcome. Something inexpressible about the hot depopulated town. (Every day strictly devoted to work.)[11]

Perhaps not *only* work. She and Tausk seem to take up where they left off. She discussed with him what was developing into central theme of her work: narcissism. Their relationship was marked by a close spiritual connection, and most likely their sexual liaison was an expression of that. If a love affair was resumed, it was most certainly ephemeral in Lou's eyes: "Tausk is deceiving himself about me with his fantasies," she wrote in her journal. "In the long run no helpful relationship is possible."[12] At the same time, she intellectually defended her behavior in her journal. Infidelity was a necessity, she insisted. It was not a betrayal of one's spouse, but a way to be truly whole. Each time she returned to Andreas, she *strengthened* her bond to him, she concluded. The homecoming was done, not out of duty, but out of free choice. She voiced an opinion that could have only been shocking to the Victorian mindset:

> A woman has no other choice than to be unfaithful or to be only half herself. In her love she is like a tree awaiting lightning to sunder it, but also, like a tree she desires to put forth an abundance of blooms.[13]

In her view, love was the destructive but *desired* element in a woman's life. Only after a tree is split by lightning does it regenerate anew, fulfilling its unique potential for rebirth. Destruction is an essential element of creativity — destroying the old to make way for the new. In Lou's view, remaining with Tausk after the initial burst of desire would leave her reduced to nothing. "Let it not be taken as arrogance," she wrote, "that [a woman] requires a new beginning again and again."[14] For her, she concludes, it was a necessity.

Tausk had once commented to her that women "psychically wedded"[15] a multitude of interests as a sublimation of their repressed desire for many men. Tausk may have been hinting that the reversal was true for Lou — her fidelity to psychoanalysis, as opposed to her many lovers. For the Lou-with-many-husbands, there was little need of sublimation.

In May Lou returned to Göttingen and Andreas, where she worked diligently. During the summer, her relationship with Tausk was supplemented with a new relationship: Victor Emil Gebsattel, a medical doctor who practiced psychoanalysis. He was a friend of Rilke's and he and Lou had met years earlier. She stayed with him at Munich, where she recorded only a discussion on art — Rilke's art in particular. Even though Tausk accompanied her to Vienna at the end of August, Lou spent September with Gebsattel. In his thirties, and a baron by title, Gebsattel was overwhelmed by the flood of emotion and inspiration her presence triggered in him — "suddenly gushing forces of my suddenly liberated life,"[16] he confessed. Though their affair seems to have been brief, his letters show both the creative and destructive aspects of her powerful personality. He wrote of her "transforming yourself endlessly, you will always imbue the strongest and most intrinsic potential in others...."[17] And with Nietzschean glee he would later express the epiphany-like affect she had on him: "There is no sin; life lies beyond good and evil," and "Were you not a symbol to me signifying that original sin was a fiction?"[18] And with Rilkean humility, he told her he longed to approach her as though she were a king, "whereas I was a beggar."[19]

Lou's relationship with Gebsattel continued erratically. Despite his stature as a medical doctor and psychoanalyst, he became just another worshipper on the threshold of her being. He urged her to meet him in Munich the following July, "to see and talk to you."[20] When she came, they quarreled excessively. And when Germany declared war on Russia on August 1, 1914, she fled to Göttingen in despair. But Gebsattel took it personally — "you cannot cease being reality for me, Lou. Maybe that means nothing to you."[21] He confessed he was "[s]haken and thrown, utterly destroyed by our encounter...."[22] Within two months he suffered a nervous breakdown and was hospitalized. In the face of a world war and her taking leave of the brokenhearted Gebsattel, Lou wondered if she grown "soft on mankind" to make up for being "hard on her lovers."[23]

Mankind at large was taking a step towards destruction and she grieved over the mortal hate among her countrymen. She had been absorbed by the world of inner conflict in her studies with Freud; now the external world suddenly, painfully, surprisingly encroached on her reality. In a letter to her at Göttingen, Freud pondered, "Do you still believe that all the big brothers are so good?"[24] "They have all gone stark raving mad,"[25] she replied. Saddened that three of Freud's sons were in the military, she wrote, "I don't really believe that after this we will ever be really happy again."[26] Managing to pull back to the inner world, she analyzed mankind's need for war in a statement that shows a great deal of Nietzschean influence:

> We wage war because we are already at war with ourselves: one could hardly imagine any two forces more strongly opposed to each other, nor more fiercely struggling for space, than the two levels which inhabit our own nature. Mankind engages in ... a double life, emotional and rational....[27]

This statement expresses succinctly her own struggle in life. Her two beloved homelands — Russia, the rock-hard foundation of her soul, and Germany, the superstructure of her intellect — had long been at war within her.

She voiced a rare negative comment against mankind — and it echoed Freud's view of civilization. Because men repressed their feelings so intensely, only "war seemed real to so many men; it appeared to them a sanction for the exploding of an unbearable self-control."[28] But she cautioned against imagining that women would do any better: "[H]ow easy it is to think that things would be different in the world, if only women ran it."[29] But she believed that such a view ignores the fact that there are creative and destructive forces in men and women alike. "The maternal transmits its devotion and its brutality alike to every child."[30]

Her anxiety over the occurrences in Russia had been going on for some time. From Bloody Sunday in 1905 — the massacre occurring in Lou's former courtly playground in St. Petersburg Square — through to the Revolution, it seemed to Lou that Russian life had been one long conflict. She disapproved of the Bolsheviks and the violent tactics they used towards their idealistic goals.

19. The Beautiful Narcissist

Her brother Robert and his family suffered greatly from the revolutionary struggles. After fleeing briefly to Crimea, he returned to find his home and everything he owned had been seized. His former servants were living in his summer home, and he and the family had to rely on the good graces of their former employees to allow them to stay there. He was given cabbage soup if he worked in the fields, and his children and grandchildren picked wild mushrooms and berries to satisfy their hunger. Showing the typical Salomé family strength and compassion, Robert became close to his former servant and came to admire him. They were able to go beyond the roles of master and servant, Lou wrote, and into the realm of the merely human. "What altered both men was having been placed on the margin of a turning point in history."[31]

The war had a deeply personal effect on Lou. Her "internal experience of the war," she wrote a friend, was that of great suffering. "I have not suffered so intensely since my childhood."[32] Her lifestyle was altered. The years of travel throughout the culture capitals of Europe became restricted and she limited her transport to mostly Göttingen and Vienna from then on. Since 1914, she wrote, "I have become another person."[33]

20

That of Loss

> *I experienced my memories of you not merely as something past, but as something which at the same time was walking towards me.*[1]
> — Lou Andreas-Salomé writing about Rilke

Lou's memoir begins sharply with a chapter entitled "The God Experience." Its first lines read: "Our first experience, remarkably enough, is that of loss. A moment before [birth], we are everything, undifferentiated, indivisibly part of some kind of being—only to be pressed into birth."[2] We fall from a "universal fullness" to a "deprivating void."[3]

Though cloaked in a generalized discussion of birth, this quote also clearly defines her own experience of losing God. Falling from *universal fullness* into a *deprivating void*. But then Gillot offered a new universal fullness, the universe of intellect. It was the only glint of light in the void. He became Gillot the master, Gillot the lord. But then a second loss: he was merely a man, weak in the area where all men were weak—sexuality. She vowed never to succumb to such weakness and left Russia for good. But she carried with her a vision of love, a vision of Gillot that could remain intact only by leaving him. But this vision too would be shattered and she would be left with only the fiction she had created about him. When Gillot died in 1916, she hypothesized (in light of his near-pedophilia) that she unconsciously *needed* a pretext to make break-off with him. With this statement she came closer to the truth than she ever had. She would have left Russia one way or another. Her worshipful stance—in the form of her appreciation for his freeing her from her childhood fantasy life—never totally subsided. He taught her to "receive the world as a gift" she wrote a friend; the "way out of myself was like an entrance —."[4] Both 'lord and instrument," Gillot was a value and a valuable tool towards her unique life.

The pain of loss and disillusionment became a constant feature in

Lou's life. Still she always managed to look upon life as a series of gifts. Although she saw Freud's psychoanalysis as the greatest gift she had received, Gillot's death seemed to catch her in a revolving door of even greater personal loss, starting with the suicide of Victor Tausk and the implication of Freud. But this time she sent out a final refusal to accept disillusion.

Tausk

In 1919, Victor Tausk returned to Vienna to resume his psychoanalytic practice. He had, since the years he and Lou had shared, been called into service in 1915 to act as an army psychiatrist. Having suffered a great deal of anguish from his war experiences, he asked Freud personally to take him on as a patient. Freud refused flatly and the refusal made Tausk's self-deprecation increase. Freud recommended him to Dr. Helen Deutsch, a junior analyst who had only been practicing for six months. It seems to be an attempt to re-enact the triangular relationship with Lou. This mocking move backfired on Freud when Deutsch became so fascinated with Tausk that she would discuss him during her own analysis sessions with Freud. In March 1919, Freud cut off Tausk's sessions with Deutsch all together. Freud seemed totally indifferent to the effect that termination of his therapy would have on Tausk. Rather, Freud was more concerned with his own personal conflict.

Meanwhile Tausk had fallen in love again, this time with a musician named Hilde Loewi. Soon after being shunned by Freud, he proposed to Hilde and they became engaged. But his fear of love and the conflict with Freud overwhelmed him. In the early morning hours of July 3, Tausk wrote out a matter-of-fact and lengthy will. He then wrote two letters, one to his fiancée and the other to Freud, while sipping Yugoslavian brandy. He then tied a cord around his neck and put a pistol to his head and shot himself, strangling in the fall. The overkill of the suicide implies his commitment to dying. Roazen points out that the "double suicide" also echoes the double bind of failure in love and work. He suggests that suicide is desire to murder turned inward — all signs pointing to Freud. That Freud turned away from Tausk professionally and personally, some have suggested, may have taken away Tausk's last hope.

"Poor Tausk...," Freud coolly informed Lou by mail, "committed suicide on 3.7."[5] With inexplicable cruelty, he added that he didn't really miss Tausk, because he found him "a threat to the future."[6]

"Lou was taken aback by Freud's cold portrayal of Tausk's death," writes Roazen. "But her reply by letter is a masterpiece of diplomacy."[7] She simply echoed Freud's sentiments in her letter—"Poor Tausk. I was fond of him. Believed I knew him; yet would never, never would have thought suicide."[8] Despite his strong character, she thought, Tausk remained "powerless over the unbridled violence of his inner being" and a "beserker with a tender heart."[9] And she considered that both his charm and his danger.

But Lou may well have inserted her inner protest of Freud's cold eulogy into her fiction. Before the year ended, she began a story titled "Siblings." The protagonist is Jutta, the title character from an earlier short story. Just as the first "Jutta" story reflected the young writers of Vienna— Schnitzler, Beer-Hofmann and others—in "Siblings" some of the in-fighting, jealousies and treacheries of Freud's Viennese circle come to light. Like many of her earlier stories, it is the tale of a young woman, in a household of brothers, who worships an older man. On the surface it seems like the Gillot story again but now the older man that Jutta worships takes on shades of Freud. Trebor, a podiatrist, occupies quarters in a room above where the siblings live. Jutta, who is attracted to this intelligent older man, goes upstairs to visit him secretly. When her brother Stephan, who also admires Trebor, discovers her secret visits, he tells her to stop. She doesn't know men the way he does, he tells her. He demands her to break it off. When she later goes to Trebor's room to tell him she can no longer see him, Stephan sees her and thinks she has ignored his demand. Consumed with jealousy of both his sister and Trebor, he kills himself.

Biographer Binion connects Dr. Trebor the foot doctor to Freud the head doctor (Trebor as a foot doctor also connects to Oedipus, the Greek word meaning *swollen foot*), and the suicidal Stephan resembling the suicidal Tausk. With shades of Gillot, the near-pedophile, and Freud the near-murderous father, in the character of Trebor Lou attempts to come to grips with the immoral behavior of the men she worshipped. Following the death of Stephan, Trebor is arrested for unnamed *immoral* crimes. Jutta's shock over Stephan's suicide is superseded by a greater shock: Trebor, *the man upstairs*, the man who was like God to her, is actually an immoral wretch.

Binion points out that Freud's cold statement about Tausk in his letter to Lou is mirrored in Jutta's shock over Trebor's exposure for *moral crimes*—that is, the downfall of her "god" overshadows the suicide of her brother-friend momentarily. Binion sees "Siblings" as a psychological tool to deal with what seemed shameful to her about Freud's behavior in relationship to Tausk. It puts her in a role of the go-between, the emotional conduit, once again. As such she seems to be the receptacle of Freud's guilt, as if to feel that which he coldly refuses to feel, or at least express. Binion writes:

> [H]erein lay the first function of "Geschwister" [Siblings] for its author: it smuggled her preconscious response to Freud's post-mortem on Tausk into her consciousness — lodged the material threatening her peace of mind, bound the attendant affects, and so disposed of the issue. Or almost disposed of it: though she never wrote another word about Tausk, [in "Siblings"] she was nonetheless vindicating him....[10]

Whether Lou was fully conscious of her moral repugnance towards the Freud-Tausk issue is not known. She was only willing to express it covertly through her fiction. Linking Freud to the seamier version of Gillot, the *moral criminal*, signaled yet another major God-loss, another hour without God. But this time she was unwilling to let it destroy that which she worshipped. Had Freud been her lover, she might have more easily written him off. But his father-God position and his gift of psychoanalysis was far too important to her.

Poor Tausk.

Rilke

"The Lay of the Love and Death of the Cornet Christoph Rilke," which Rilke had written in a single night in between his trips to Russia with Lou, was published in its final form in 1906. It was a great success, and Rilke became famous. Like Lou after her first novel, he received numerous letters from adoring fans, and his thoughtful return letters have become as famous as his poems. But fame seemed strange to Rilke: the adoration difficult to accept, the invasion of privacy difficult to endure.

His imitation of Lou's way of life was clear — a series of travels and lovers to fuel his art. He made Don Juan appear pale in comparison, an acquaintance proclaimed. Not only Lou's lifestyle but her influences can be seen in his philosophy of life. In quotes from letters written in later years he shows clear signs of reading and absorbing Lou's essays on art and women: "...artistic experience lies so incredibly close to that of sex, to its pain and ecstasy, that the two manifestations are indeed but different forms of one and the same yearning and delight"[11]; and in women, he writes, "life lingers and dwells more immediately, more fruitfully and more confidently

... than easy going man...."¹² He even issues a Salomé-ism all his own: Some day girls and women will no longer be seen as only reflecting the masculine, "but something in itself, something that makes one think, not of any complement and limit, but only of life and existence: the feminine human being."¹³

Long after their romance had broken off, Rilke continued to write Lou in worshipful tones — depicting himself as her child she has sent out into the world, who wants come back to the doorway from time to time:

> ... your being is so truly the door by which I first came out into the open; now I keep coming from time to time and place myself straight against the doorpost on which we marked my growth. Allow me this dear habit and love me.¹⁴

After her first trip to Vienna, Lou was anxious to share with Rilke her new-found religion, psychoanalysis. She introduced him to Freud, and Rilke considered going into treatment with Gebsattel. But both Rilke and Lou feared psychoanalysis would cast out his angels along with his demons, resulting in loss of his artistic drive.

In 1912, Rilke wrote both to Lou from a castle in Austria (in a location that is now part of Italy) called Duino. Perched on a high cliff, Duino had a breathtaking view of the Mediterranean. Rilke's elderly patron, Princess Marie von Thurn und Taxis, had given him use of this medieval structure to write, and it is here, over the next ten years, he created his greatest cycle of poems.

He felt that the castle was a huge body without a soul. But nature abhors a vacuum, and Rilke became that soul. To Lou he wrote, "a soul has no alternative but to find its harmony in the immense exaggerations of art...."¹⁵

Not long after this correspondence with Lou, Rilke was one day preoccupied with a business letter he had to write. He had climbed down to the bastions that looked down from a steep cliff onto the wild blue sea. The north wind blew violently as a storm approached. The sun shone as brilliantly as glittering diamonds on the sea surface as the wind tossed the waves. He paced back and forth, lost in thought. Then, in the beating of the wind, he heard a voice: "And if I cried, who'd listen to me in those angelic orders?"¹⁶ It would be the first line of what would become his masterpiece. He took out his notepad and the words seemed to be dictated to him. By that evening he finished the First Elegy of the *Duino Elegies*, a work which would take him nine more elegies and ten more years to complete.

20. That of Loss

While Nietzsche envisioned the *Übermensch* to be the bridge between man and God, Rilke poetically saw mankind as dwelling in the land in between animal and angel, ever looking upward to that which is greater than us. In the beauty of angels we search for comfort, for an end to our suffering. While Nietzsche points upward, defiant in the face of suffering, in order to lead mankind, Rilke raises his eyes to behold the terrifying beauty in order to praise it. He defines religion as the human *need to praise*, to look up to something, someone greater than ourselves, even if the object of our praise is indifferent, or worse yet, non-existent.

For beauty is nothing but the beginning of terror which we are still able to endure. Surely, Lou had been a terrifying angel in his life as well: too beautiful to let go, too terrifying to cling to (*I hated you as something too big*). Yet it was in his creation of the angel—a being so radiant that it threatens to destroy us—that he would win her greatest admiration and pride in him.

Lou was greatly moved by Rilke's work, and felt he had finally fulfilled his genius. She showed a newfound respect for him—something he had long hungered for—and now it was her letters that urged a meeting.

In July 1913, during a reprieve from the emotional entanglements of her Viennese lovers, Tausk and Gebsattel, Lou sat in the twilight stillness of her garden at Göttingen. She looked up to see a figure at the gate: it was Rainer. They clasped hands over the fence. "The whole time he spent here made me so very happy!"[17] she wrote. It was a true union with him, she clarified, with no trace of the *other* who filled her with anxiety. She felt that through his poetry he had, in fact, reunited with his own soul, which had been sundered by his painful childhood: "the inner center of his personality no longer split in two."[18] But when he lamented that his body had now had become the problem—complaining of pain, swelling and discomfort with even simple activities—she reassured him that the body had long borne the burdens of his soul.

During his visit he gave her narrative of images gathered in his travels—from Egypt to Duino to her garden gate. She noted them cryptically in her diary: "The breathing sphinxes. Lotus flower. Cow. Potter's wheel...."[19] After his visit was complete, she sat thinking warmly of his poetic breakthrough, "as if I'd wandered into a great garden before autumn was yet to come."[20]

In October she met his mother, Phia. Despite the Slavic resemblance to Rilke, Lou found Phia "hollow" with her "empty exaltations," and "fancy phrases."[21] She admired Rilke's poetic depth all the more after meeting his frivolous mother.

There were several meetings after that and in 1916, Lou stayed in Munich for two months with Rilke and his live-in lover, artist Loulou Albert-Lasard (whose name was oddly similar to Lou's). Livingstone quotes Albert-Lasard in a wonderful depiction of life with the senior Lou, giving us a fascinating glimpse into her complex and perplexing appeal:

> Lou brought with her a veritable whirlwind of external events. "From the moment she got there, our days were filled with her programmes. In the morning, a spiritual séance, in the afternoon historians or astronomers, finally in the evening psychoanalysts, writers or doctors. Taken separately, each of these gatherings might have been interesting, but this mad potpourri made me dizzy. What was more, Lou took Rilke with her on numerous visits and long walks, which got him out of breath. Even the dog she brought filled the house with noise."[22]

Albert-Lasard also described Lou as a woman of "penetrating intelligence and powerful temperament."[23] Despite clear evidence of a "strong sensuality," Lou was "too exclusively cerebral."[24] Despite the elder woman's age and lack of interest in her appearance, Albert-Lasard marveled at Lou's ability to still attract passionate admirers: "I recall one of them getting tears in his eyes from a passing word of Lou's.... Her glance radiated great power."[25] Albert-Lasard observed that both Lou and Rilke had beautiful blue eyes, but with completely different effects. Rilke's gaze was a soulful blue-violet, whereas Lou's was a "magnificent tiger-gaze"[26] that seemed to devour the on-looker. It reverberated with Nietzsche's early description of Lou: *sharp as an eagle, brave as a lion*. But there are also descriptions of Lou as the quiet listener with wide open, expressive eyes, "which always looked full at the speaker."[27]

In 1922, Rilke completed the Tenth Elegy, the final of his *Duino Elegies*. After reading it, she wrote him, "[H]ow you have enriched me!"[28] And it was more than sheer joy, "but something more powerful, as if a curtain were divided, torn through, and everything at once became quiet and certain and present and good.... But where *is* there anything like this in poetry?"[29] But it was more than admiration she felt: it was the fruition of their cerebral union, their brainchild. She had laid the seeds and he had toiled.

He also composed another cycle of poetry called *Sonnets to Orpheus*, inspired this time by a beautiful young dancer who had died young. The two books of poetry were published in 1923 and represented his greatest works.

All during the time Rilke composed the *Elegies*, he had continued to write Lou with complaints of swelling and pain, accompanied by anxieties and unnamable fears. Lou as always sent words of encouragement. It was normal to feel drained after such a lengthy and laborious effort, she assured him.

He visited a sanatorium in Val-Mont several times in 1924. His fame continued to grow and he continued to travel a great deal, including a return to Paris. He had been an unknown poet, a secretary to Rodin, when he been there years before. He returned as one of the world's greatest poets. Now he was fêted and fawned over by the literary elite.

Soon after his fiftieth birthday he returned again to the Sanatorium Val-Mont. But after five months of treatment, he continued to have painful swellings in his mouth and throat. He left the sanatorium to stay in a number of hotels, where he was mostly confined to bed. Returning to Val-Mont for a final time, he was diagnosed with leukemia. On December 13, 1926, he wrote to Lou, telling her even though he had suffered physically and mentally his whole life, that this pain "is burying me completely."[30] He asked her, "Where will I find the courage?"[31] And although Rilke had his doctor include a letter detailing Rilke's morbid condition, Rilke himself requested not to hear his own prognosis.

On December 29, 1926, he died in the early morning hours. Lou would eulogize him by writing a book on his work, first published in 1927. "Mourning," she wrote, is not simply "a state of emotional preoccupation.... [I]t is more precisely, an incessant discourse with the departed one, in order to draw him nearer."[32] In an epilogue of her memoirs, she did not label Rilke an *experience* as she had labeled God, Gillot, Nietzsche and Russia. Rather she would address him directly in a discourse, a conversation that seemed ever alive to her.

Andreas

My love for my husband was an inner command. It was the destiny to which they both surrendered. But if Lou's oriental soul believed in divine destiny, her occidental mind refused to accept all the man-made rules that came with it. If marriage was a supernatural necessity, then her individual will became its divine adversary. It seemed that Andreas, the man who had her longest and most officially, had no real claim on her at all. Gillot was master of her intellect and soul; Rée, of her sisterly spirit; Nietzsche, of her devilish and cerebral spirit; Rilke, of her sensual and maternal spirit.

Beer-Hofmann, Ledebour and Gebsattal had her impulses; Tausk, her warm and cold heart; and Freud, her eternal father-worship. It seemed as if little was left for Andreas — other than the house they shared.

Yet on closer look, one can detect the depth of her need for Andreas. After all, *she* was unable to give *him* up as well. Despite her vow to spend her life with Rée, she married Andreas. From Ledebour and Zemek offers of marriage may have titillated her, but did not for a moment seriously tempt her. She merely held them at bay with exotic tales of Andreas' violence and tears, until they gave up out of frustration.

And yet, in her memoirs she speaks *most* cryptically about Andreas — and in her memoir she speaks cryptically about all the men in her life. From reading *only* her memoirs, one might conclude they had no real relationship at all, merely some unbreakable bond which held them together. And worse still it was torturous for both of them. "For how weak the bonds of sacrament or society seem in comparison with the indissoluble bond created by my husband's character and nature, which would not admit of the slightest of loosening."[33] Such quotes lean more towards *bondage* than *bonding*. She says Ledebour offered her "salvation from almost unbearable loneliness,"[34] a line that echoes Rilke's play *The White Princess*. And she suggests that Andreas was violent, just like the husband in Rilke's play. But she also points out the simple goodness of his nature and his genuine pleasure in other people's happiness. Rather than divorce, she tells us, she and Andreas had once thought about committing suicide together, to avoid *dying of one another*. But instead Lou worked out a life of independent travel and male companionship. Surely, the few pages devoted to Andreas in her memoir tell almost nothing of the complexity, depth and peculiarity of their relationship. It does nothing to clarify the relationship which was barely even understood by the principles involved.

The only thing she offers as any form of connectedness was their mutual love of intellectual pursuits. They were truly supportive of one another's efforts to work tirelessly. Once involved with psychoanalysis, she felt her intensity and devotion to it and her occasional short story writing must have made her "very hard to be around, and quite worthless," to which he replied, "with a shining face I'll never forget, 'You've been so happy!'"[35]

"I was always aware of his inner state," she tells us, and yet, "it never became a topic of conversation between us."[36] Oddly, she claims they never sat down face-to-face and had a *real* conversation until the last year of his life when he came to visit her during a stay in the hospital. The "visiting hours" continued when she returned home, she writes, "and not just between the hours of three and four."[37]

On October 4, 1930, at the age of 84, Andreas died quietly in his sleep. Lou was relieved that his death had been an easy one. But at his funeral she struggled to contemplate his assuredness that they belonged together — despite the suffering they brought one another. In spite of it all, she wondered, hadn't he "been right about the two of us?"[38] Had she been "overpowered" by his assuredness "because it arose from an ultimate truth?"[39] But she answers her own question ambiguously: "I don't know. I'm sorry, forgive me: I don't know."[40]

21

Return to the All

One finds nests everywhere, lays eggs everywhere, one becomes lighter and finally flies away.[1]
— Lou Andreas-Salomé

"Perhaps in our old age, we revert to a half dreamlike view such as belongs to childhood,"[2] Lou wrote when she was forty-one. This remark seems to emphasize her lifelong despair after losing the *unio mystica*, the pre-conscious state that she associated with her childhood love of her Russian God. For Lou, Tsarist Russia was a dreamy Oz-like country. Both God and his pastor turned out to be only a man behind a curtain operating an elaborate hoax, and Lou spent a lifetime ever anxious to return to that magical moment before she lost her rich and wonderful faith. Home was nowhere and everywhere. Home was the hour before she lost God, the moment before she lost Gillot. But that home was forever lost, indeed never really existed. So home became the fertility of her mind, the seed of her inspiration, which she spread throughout northern Europe.

World War I, with its advent of modern technology which so greatly increased death and destruction, made the need for psychoanalysis all the more acute. The practice began to become more widely accepted by the medical community. According to biographer Peters, she spent a half a year at a hospital in Königsberg analyzing patients and five of the doctors there as well. Peters records one doctor's account of psychoanalysis with Lou. Sitting opposite one another in the semi-darkness, he talked and she listened, speaking only to relate a personal experience that might enlighten him. "She had a very quiet way of speaking and a great gift of inspiring confidence."[3] He was surprised how much he revealed to her, but he "always had the feeling she not only understood everything, but that she forgave everything. I have never again experienced such a feeling of conciliatory kindness, or if you like, compassion, as I did with her."[4] "I confess," the doctor went on, "that the way Lou analyzed me left a deep impression on me and has been a great help to me all my life."[5] She taught him to look at his own shortcomings — to see his "inner scoundrel, and we all have one" — in a way that made him more compassionate towards others.

Lou worked exhaustively at the hospital, and when she returned home, she set up a lay practice there. While Freud continued sending her referrals and they discussed patients at length in letters, Freud often admonished her for the long hours she worked and encouraged her to charge her patients — particularly the wealthy ones — a higher fee. But Lou showed a devotion and dedication to her patients that went beyond the realm of analysis. She repeatedly told Freud of the special joy she derived by sharing in the lives of these people. It sustained her through her old age and added grace to her later years.

In the 1920s, at the age of sixty, Lou began referring to herself as a "little old woman," but her energy was as remarkable as it had been throughout her life, though now devoted to psychoanalysis. From time to time she still wrote fiction, though far less frequently then she had in earlier years.

Livingstone perfectly labels Lou's early fiction "fiction of desire"; the middle years, dating from her relationship with Rilke, "fiction of fulfillment"; and finally the later years were marked by "probing psychic depths and establishing control over them."[6] An allegorical drama called *The Devil and His Grandmother*, published in 1922, showed Lou's wit and Freudian influence. It depicts the devil as a depository of God's dark side — "God had to load all his own filth onto him in order to remain clean and for the sake of a people who cannot bear an unclean God."[7] Livingstone describes "Siblings," written in 1919 and published in 1921, as a "story about the dark passions raging beneath the jocular surface of a household of adolescents."[8] In "The Hour Without God," Lou gives the first fictional account of her loss of God in childhood, as well as revealing a childhood fear of sexuality and the human body.

In 1921, Lou went for an extended stay with Freud and his family. During this time she became close to his daughter Anna. Despite the mother-daughter age gap, Anna felt comfortable enough to talk with Lou about things she couldn't talk about with her own parents. The two even began collaborating on psychological theories. When Anna had emotional problems, Freud would discuss them in letters to Lou, as if Anna were their child.

Old friends: Sigmund Freud and Lou Andreas-Salomé, late 1920s (© Sigmund Freud Privatstiftung).

In 1923, after a near life time of smoking cigars, Freud was diagnosed with cancer of the jaw. He was 67. He would have thirty operations over the course of his remaining years to prevent the disease from spreading. He eventually had to have his entire jaw removed, and was fitted with a prosthesis. Even then he refused to give up cigar smoking. He even confessed to smoking while describing the cancer prognosis in a letter to Lou.

When Freud found out Lou's seventieth birthday had come and passed, he chastised her for not telling him: "Perhaps I would have been glad to tell you on your birthday how greatly I esteem and love you."[9] Despite the reprimand, she replied, his letter gave her "infinite joy!"[10]

During an illness in 1931 she began writing an essay titled "My Thanks to Freud." After reading it Freud told her it was "the finest thing of yours I've read, an involuntary proof of your superiority over all of us."[11] But with the slightest modesty he suggested she change the title to "My Thanks to Psychoanalysis" with his name in the subtitle. "Not everything you deal with is immediately intelligible to me," he told her quite openly, "but I'm not an artist, I could have never depicted the effects of light and color, only hard outlines."[12] Lou replied with humility, "[W]hat a joy it is to me that you approved of my stammering attempts!"[13]

In 1932, she began writing her memoirs, referring to them as a "sketch of my Experiences of Life." Freud replied that he hoped she would tell her side of the Nietzsche story. In reference to Elizabeth Nietzsche's lifelong hostility towards Lou, Freud wrote, "You have put up with everything and have been far too decent; I hope that now at last you will defend yourself...."[14] But she replies she wants nothing more to do with it, "not even in my book."[15]

The entire memoir is arranged not chronologically but by "experiences"— the experience of God, of love, and of friendship. Each experience is expressed in a timeless void, not following any chronological order, but by order of subjective intensity. The structure of the memoir itself gives us insight as to how Lou saw her past — not in a linear fashion but by quality of the bonds she had with God and man. There are lightning-like flashes of insight she had gained about both her own life and life in general. But it is a frustrating read as well, because of the obvious omissions and even distortions in it. Of her stay with Nietzsche in Tauntenburg and Lisbeth's first assault, she says only, "It seems that Nietzsche and I argued a bit at first, over all sorts of nonsense that I still can't understand ... but the subsequent experience was a rich one...."[16] It is difficult to assess why she chose not to clarify the legendary story. Her choice of omission has led biographer Rudolph Binion to believe she was trying to hide the fact that she was rejected by Nietzsche rather than the other way around. That Nietzsche bowed out of the three-way study plan is clear from his letters. And in *Looking Back*, Lou does attempt to make it sound as if Nietzsche were a third wheel in the study plan when, in fact, she desperately wanted him to join her and Rée. Though Binion is far too harsh on Lou, insisting that the proposals from both Gillot and Nietzsche were make-believe, he makes a good point when he suggests that there are remnants of little Ljolja of Petersburg whose fictional tales superseded her reality, and that her fantasy past became somewhat entangled in her real past. Reading her fiction and her memoir side by side certainly shows she was more open in her fiction. But as Binion also points out, *her life was hardly in need of embellishment.*

Lou's memoir ends strangely with a weak attempt to explain why she never had sexual relations with her husband, an explanation that explains nothing. She does however reflect on her numerous affairs, saying that she offered to be forthcoming with Andreas but that he flatly refused to listen. The marriage became shrouded in a "deep and inviolable silence ... a silence from which we never emerged."[17]

As Lou spent her remaining years contemplating her past, Europe was poised for another catastrophe. In 1933, the Nazi party rose to power in Germany. With anti–Semitism and book-burning as mainstays of Nazi power, Freud's books were among the casualties. Freud and his family would later escape to England. Lou was somehow spared harassment, despite the fact she had publicly befriended so many Jews. Perhaps her fame as an esteemed writer or the connection to Friedrich Nietzsche protected her. Lisbeth was ever busy, still sullying Lou's name as well as deliberately distorting her brother's work to fulfill Nazi propaganda.

Descriptions of Lou in her last years show that she continued to fascinate others even then. Her hair still had the shine of its blonde youth. And despite her worsening heart ailment, there was still the presence of a strong, unconquerable nature.

Suffering from breast cancer, Lou underwent a mastectomy in 1935. She survived the operation, but a year and half later she contracted an infection. She died on February 5, only a week away from turning seventy-six. Though she requested that her ashes be buried in her garden, German law did not allow it. Instead, her ashes were buried next to Andreas. The eternal bond between them was, after all, unbreakable.

Afterword

Reflections on an Extraordinary Life

Lou Andreas-Salomé was one of the most influential women Europe ever produced, an extremely active and creative force in the artistic culture of nineteenth century Europe. Her eastern philosophy seemed foreign but profound to the western intellectuals with whom she spent her life. She was many things to many people, but she was ultimately elusive. No one could hold her long enough to reveal her mystery. She was a genius of inspiration — a form of genius that is not always recognized in history books, but nonetheless has great influence. Her genius lay in how she related to herself and others. She cherished her own mind, and followed her own heart, and encouraged others to do the same.

Lou's life was breathtaking in its scope, and lived totally on her own terms. She spent her days working out her own psychological demands, which she herself didn't fully understand. In a sense she rejected the muse role while knowing full well the power it gave her. But her inability to accept any limits or boundaries was only surpassed by her remarkable ability to get the world to comply with her wishes. She never gave up being a pupil or searching for an eastern-style teacher to worship. This willingness to always be a student of great masters gave her an everlasting youth and a unique beauty that had little to do with superficialities.

In her book *A Call to Create*, Linda Schierse Leonard points out the dangers of identifying with the muse: "By equating oneself with the Muse, it is easy to fall into the pitfall of inflation. An attendant danger is to become a mere reflection of another's wishes and desires, thus losing or failing to develop one's own creative center."[1] Leonard cites Scott Fitzgerald's wife and muse, Zelda, as an example of the dangers of identifying with the creative works inspired, which resulted in complete loss of individuality in Zelda Fitzgerald.

Lou was no parasite to genius or fame. Rather, she had an uncanny ability to arrive just *before* a significant moment in intellectual and cultural history, and often acted as a spur to great thoughts and great works. All but Freud became famous *after* she met them. She could not have known that Nietzsche or Rilke would become world-famous, although she recognized the thundering greatness in the former and inspired the poetic genius in the latter. She entered the lives of a group of young playwrights, including Arthur Schnitzler, Gerhart Hauptmann and Frank Wedekind, well before they produced world-famous works. And she entered Freud's circle just when major eruptions would occur that would alter the history of psychoanalysis.

It is a testament to Lou's unique genius that she recognized the trap that lay within the role of the muse. She realized all too well that it is within the nature of woman to mirror and become an object of desire to men. But rather than spend her life as a reflection of Gillot's desires, she let his teachings inspire her to a unique and independent life. Rather than be Nietzsche's disciple, she explored philosophy on her own. Rather than remaining a muse and mentor to Rilke, she embraced her Russian homeland as the missing inspirational element in her own life, and offered the Russian god as a substitute inspiration for Rilke.

It was in the final act of her extraordinary life that she found what she had long searched for. Through psychology she found the elements of her quest — an understanding of self, and a way to give back to the world that which she received in such great abundance: love.

Chapter Notes

Introduction

1. Angela Livingstone, *Salomé: Her Life and Work* (Mt. Krisco, NY: Moyer Bell, 1984), p. 9.
2. Stanley A. Leavy, "Introduction," in Lou Andreas-Salomé, *The Freud Journal* (London: Quartet, 1987), p. 7
3. Mary Kay Wilmers, quoted in introduction to Andreas-Salomé, *The Freud Journal*, p. 9.
4. Rudolph Binion, *Frau Lou: Nietzsche's Wayward Disciple* (Princeton, NJ: Princeton University Press, 1968), p. 32.
5. *Ibid*.
6. H.F. Peters, *My Sister, My Spouse: A Biography of Lou Andreas-Salomé* (New York: W.W. Norton, 1962), p. 271.
7. Binion, p. 312.
8. Helene Klingenberg, "Lou Andreas-Salomé," *Deutsche Monatsschrift für Russland*, Mar. 15, 1912.
9. Rainer Maria Rilke, *The Diaries of a Young Poet*, trans. Edward Snow and Michael Winkler (New York: W.W. Norton, 1997), p. 64.

Chapter 1

1. Binion, p. 68.
2. Lou Andreas-Salomé, *Looking Back*, trans. Ernst Pfeiffer (New York: Marlow, 1991), p.14.
3. *Ibid*.
4. *Ibid*., p. 24.
5. Peters, p. 30.
6. Andreas-Salomé, *Looking Back*, p. 24.
7. *Ibid*., p. 159.
8. *Ibid*., p. 22.
9. *Ibid*., p. 26.
10. *Ibid*., p. 24.
11. *Ibid*., p. 13.
12. *Ibid*.
13. *Ibid*., p. 7–8.
14. *Ibid*., p. 7.
15. *Ibid*.
16. *Ibid*., p. 5.
17. *Ibid*., p. 50.

Chapter 2

1. Livingstone, p. 24.
2. *Ibid*.
3. Binion, p. 15.
4. Andreas-Salomé, *Looking Back*, p. 157.
5. *Ibid*., p. 13.
6. *Ibid*.
7. Johann Wolfgang von Goethe, *The Tragedy of Faust*.
8. Andreas-Salomé, *Looking Back*, p. 156.
9. *Ibid*.
10. *Ibid*.
11. *Ibid*., p.157.
12. Biddy Martin, *Women and Modernity: The Lifestyles of Lou Andreas-Salomé* (Ithaca: Cornell University Press, 1991), p. 35.
13. Andreas-Salomé, *Looking Back*, p. 3.
14. Martin, p. 35.
15. *Ibsen's Heroines*, trans. Siegfried Mandel (New York: Limelight, 1989), p. 101.
16. Andreas-Salomé, *Looking Back*, p. 21.
17. Friedrich Nietzsche, *Selected Letters*

of *Friedrich Nietzsche*, trans. Christopher Middleton (Indianapolis, IN: Hackett, 1996), p. 186.
  18. Livingstone, p. 29.
  19. *Ibid.*
  20. Andreas-Salomé, *Looking Back*, p. 214.
  21. *Ibid.*, p. 20.

Chapter 3

  1. Binion, p. 116.
  2. Andreas-Salomé, *Looking Back*, p. 170.
  3. *Ibid.*, p. 169.
  4. Binion, p. 37.
  5. *Ibid.*, p. 38.
  6. Peters, p. 72.
  7. *Ibid.*
  8. Binion, p. 39.
  9. Andreas-Salomé, *Looking Back*, p. 44.
  10. *Ibid.*
  11. *Ibid.*
  12. Binion, p. 51.
  13. *Ibid.*
  14. Andreas-Salomé, *Looking Back*, p. 44.
  15. *Ibid.*, p. 45.
  16. Livingstone, p. 37.
  17. *Ibid.*, p. 37.
  18. Andreas-Salomé, *Looking Back*, p. 45.
  19. *Ibid.*, p. 46.
  20. *Ibid.*
  21. *Ibid.*
  22. Binion, p. 52.
  23. *Ibid.*

Chapter 4

  1. Friedrich Nietzsche, *Ecce Homo: How to Become What You Are*, trans. Duncan Large (Oxford: Oxford University Press, 2004), p. 88.
  2. Lou Andreas-Salomé, *Nietzsche*, trans. Siegfried Mandel (Champaign: University of Illinois Press, 2001), p. 77–78.
  3. *Ibid.*, p. 79.
  4. *Ibid.*, p. 34.
  5. *Ibid.*, p. 45.
  6. Rüdiger Safranski, *Nietzsche, A Philosophical Biography* (New York: W.W. Norton, 2001), p. 31.
  7. *Ibid.*
  8. *Ibid.*
  9. Friedrich Nietzsche, *The Birth of Tragedy*, trans. Shaun Whiteside, ed. Michael Tanner (New York: Penguin, 1993), p. 16.
  10. *Ibid.*, p. 20.
  11. *Ibid.*
  12. Rainer Maria Rilke, *Duino Elegies and the Sonnets of Orpheus*, trans. A. Poulin (New York: Mariner, 2002), p. 5.
  13. Andreas-Salomé, *Nietzsche*, p. 39.
  14. *Ibid.*, p. 91.
  15. *Ibid.*, p. 40.
  16. H(ugh) A(dam) Reyburn, *Nietzsche: The Story of a Human Philosopher* (London: Macmillan, 1948), p. 130.
  17. Andreas-Salomé, *Nietzsche*, p. 48
  18. *Ibid.*, p. xxxiv.
  19. *Ibid.*, p. xxxiii.
  20. Peters, p. 83.
  21. Andreas-Salomé, *Nietzsche*, p. 9.
  22. *Ibid.*
  23. *Ibid.*
  24. *Ibid.*
  25. Andreas-Salomé, *Looking Back*, p. 47.
  26. Binion, p. 53.
  27. *Ibid.*
  28. *Ibid.*
  29. Friedrich Nietzsche, *The Portable Nietzsche*, ed. and trans. Walter Kaufmann (New York: Penguin, 1976), p. 97.
  30. *Ibid.*
  31. Nietzsche, *Selected Letters*, p. 186.
  32. Binion, p. 53.
  33. Andreas-Salomé, *Looking Back*, p. 167.
  34. Binion, p. 69.
  35. Andreas-Salomé, *Looking Back*, p. 167.
  36. David Farrell Krell, *Nietzsche: A Novel* (Albany: State University of New York Press, 1996), p. 213.
  37. Binion, p. 62.
  38. Nietzsche, *The Portable Nietzsche*, p. 79.
  39. Friedrich Nietzsche, Paul Rée, and Lou von Salomé, *Friedrich Nietzsche, Paul Rée, Lou von Salomé: Correspondance*, trans. Ernst Pfeiffer (Paris: Presses Universitaires de France, 1979), p. 111–112.
  40. Binion, p. 60.
  41. *Ibid.*, p. 61.

42. Nietzsche, Rée, and von Salomé, p. 116.
43. *Ibid.*
44. Binion, p. 58.
45. *Ibid.*, p. 59.
46. Nietzsche, Rée, and von Salomé, p. 136.

Chapter 5

1. Farrell, p. 209–210
2. Nietzsche, *Selected Letters*, p. 185.
3. Nietzsche, Rée, and von Salomé, p. 145–146.
4. *Ibid.*, p. 147.
5. Binion, p. 76.
6. *Ibid.*
7. *Ibid.*
8. Binion, p. 76.
9. Binion, p. 77.
10. *Ibid.*
11. *Ibid.*
12. Andreas-Salomé, *Looking Back*, p. 171.
13. *Ibid.*
14. Binion, p. 77.
15. Andreas-Salomé, *Looking Back*, p. 49.
16. *Ibid.*, p. 49.
17. *Ibid.*
18. Binion, p. 79.
19. *Ibid.*, p. 79–80.
20. *Ibid.*, p. 79.
21. Andreas-Salomé, *Looking Back*, p. 50.
22. *Ibid.*
23. Andreas-Salomé, *Nietzsche*, p. 77–78.
24. Andreas-Salomé, *Looking Back*, p. 50.

Chapter 6

1. Krell, p. 226.
2. Binion, p. 87.
3. *Ibid.*, p. 84.
4. *Ibid.*
5. *Ibid.*, p. 86.
6. Nietzsche, Rée, and von Salomé, p. 197.
7. Binion, p. 88.
8. Andreas-Salomé, *Looking Back*, p. 182.
9. *Ibid.*, p. 182–3.
10. *Ibid.*, p. 183.
11. Binion, p. 88.
12. Nietzsche, Rée, and von Salomé, p. 199.
13. Andreas-Salomé, *Looking Back*, p. 173.
14. *Ibid.*
15. *Ibid.*
16. Nietzsche, Rée, and von Salomé, p. 213.
17. *Ibid.*
18. Krell, p. 225–226.
19. *Ibid.*
20. *Ibid.*
21. Farrell, p. 226–227.
22. *Ibid.*, p. 228.
23. *Ibid.*, p. 229.
24. Livingstone, p.54

Chapter 7

1. Goethe, *The Tragedy of Faust* (author's translation).
2. Nietzsche, *Selected Letters*, p. 199.
3. *Ibid.*
4. *Ibid.*, p. 208.
5. Nietzsche, *The Portable Nietzsche*, p. 149.
6. Nietzsche, Rée, and von Salomé, p. 298.
7. Nietzsche, *Beyond Good and Evil*, p. 87.
8. *Ibid.*, p. 88.
9. *Ibid.*, p. 89.
10. Andreas-Salomé, *Looking Back*, p.174.
11. *Ibid.*
12. Andreas-Salomé, *Looking Back*, p. 51.
13. *Ibid.*
14. Peters, p. 153.
15. Binion, p. 112.
16. *Ibid.*, p. 116.
17. *Ibid.*, p. 132.
18. *Ibid.*, p. 133.
19. Andreas-Salomé, *Looking* Back, p. 53.
20. Livingstone, p. 204.
21. Peters, p. 160.

22. Livingstone, p. 205.
23. *Ibid.*
24. Binion, p. 126.
25. *Ibid.*, p. 128.
26. *Ibid.*, p. 132.
27. Nietzsche, *Selected Letters*, p. 249.
28. Binion, p. 98.
29. *Ibid.*, p. 97.
30. *Ibid.*
31. Andreas-Salomé, *Looking Back*, p. 54.
32. *Ibid.*, p. 116

Chapter 8

1. Andreas-Salomé, *Looking Back*, p. 213.
2. *Ibid.*, p. 127.
3. Livingstone, p. 61–2.
4. Andreas-Salomé, *Looking Back*, p. 124–125.
5. *Ibid.*, p. 125.
6. Livingstone, p. 63.
7. Andreas-Salomé, *Looking Back*, p. 213.
8. *Ibid.*, p. 214.
9. *Ibid.*, p. 213.
10. Livingstone, p. 62.
11. Binion, p. 142
12. Andreas-Salomé, *Looking Back*, p. 55.

Chapter 9

1. Andreas-Salomé, *Looking Back*, p. 214.
2. *Ibid.*, p. 58.
3. Peters, p.188.
4. Warren Maurer, *Understanding Gerhart Hauptmann* (Columbia: University of South Carolina Press, 1992), p. 38
5. *Ibid.*
6. Andreas-Salomé, *Looking Back*, p. 130.
7. *Ibid.*
8. *Ibid.*, p. 131.
9. *Ibid.*, p. 130.
10. *Ibid.*, p. 131.
11. *Ibid.*, p. 130.
12. *Ibid.*, p. 131.
13. *Ibid.*
14. Livingstone, p. 90.
15. *Ibid.*
16. Martin, p. 120.

Chapter 10

1. Friedrich Nietzsche, *Basic Writings of Nietzsche*, trans. Walter Kaufmann, introduction by Peter Gay (New York: Modern Library, 2000), p. 171.
2. Nietzsche, *Selected Letters*, p. 283.
3. *Ibid.*
4. *Ibid.*, p. 284.
5. *Ibid.*, Jan 4, 1889.
6. *Ibid.*, Jan. 1889.
7. *Ibid.*, Jan. 4, 1889.
8. *Ibid.*, Jan.1889.
9. *Ibid.*, Jan. 3, 1889.
10. *Ibid.*, Jan. 15,1889.
11. *Ibid.*, p. 351.
12. *Ibid.*, p. 352.
13. Martin, p. 96.
14. Safranski, p. 316.
15. Andreas-Salomé, *Nietzsche*, p. 12.
16. *Ibid.*, p. 13.
17. *Ibid.*
18. *Ibid.*
19. *Ibid.*, p. 14.
20. *Ibid.*
21. *Ibid.*
22. *Ibid.*, p. 89.
23. *Ibid.*
24. Martin, p. 93.
25. Andreas-Salomé, *Nietzsche*, p. 27.
26. *Ibid.*
27. *Ibid.*, p. 88–89.
28. Siegfried Mandel, "Introduction," in Lou Andreas-Salomé, *Nietzsche*, trans. Siegfried Mandel (Champaign: University of Illinois Press, 2001), p. ixi.
29. *Ibid.*, p. lx.
30. Andreas-Salomé, *Nietzsche*, p. 89.
31. Livingstone, p. 91.
32. *Ibid.*

Chapter 11

1. Rainer Maria Rilke, *Rilke on Love and Other Difficulties*, trans. John J.L. Mood (New York: W.W. Norton, 1975), p. 33.
2. *Literature Resource Center*, http://www.galegroup.com/tlist/sb5102.html.
3. *Ibid.*
4. Andreas-Salomé, *Looking Back*, p. 60.
5. *Ibid.*

6. Lou Andreas-Salomé, *Fenitschka*, in *Fenitschka and Deviations*, trans. Dorothee Einsyein Krahn (Lanham, MD: University Press of America, 1990), p. 3.
7. *Ibid.*
8. *Ibid.*
9. *Ibid.*, p. 4.
10. *Ibid.*
11. *Ibid.*
12. *Ibid.*, p. 5.
13. *Ibid.*, p. 6.
14. *Ibid.*
15. *Ibid.*
16. *Ibid.*
17. *Ibid.*, p. 7.
18. *Ibid.*
19. *Ibid.*
20. *Ibid.*, p. 8.
21. *Ibid.*
22. *Ibid.*, p. 11.
23. *Ibid.*, p. 12.
24. *Ibid.*
25. *Ibid.*, p. 13.
26. *Ibid.*
27. *Ibid.*, p. 19.
28. *Ibid.*
29. *Ibid.*, p. 26.
30. *Ibid.*, p. 27.
31. *Ibid.*, p. 32.
32. *Ibid.* p. 39.
33. *Ibid.*, p. 40.
34. *Ibid.*
35. Stefan Zweig, *The World of Yesterday* (Lincoln: University of Nebraska Press, 1964), p. 20.
36. *Ibid.*, p. 39.
37. Binion, p. 192.
38. Andreas-Salomé, *Looking Back*, p. 65.
39. Binion, p. 190.
40. *Ibid.*, p. 191.
41. *Ibid.*
42. *Ibid.*, p. 192.
43. Zweig, p. 78.
44. Binion, *Frau Lou*, p. 192.
45. *Ibid.*, p. 194.
46. *Ibid.*, p. 195.
47. *Ibid.*
48. *Ibid.*
49. *Ibid.*
50. *Ibid.*
51. Muriel Cormican, "Sex, Sexuality, and Gender: Cultural Critique in the Fictional Works of Lou Andreas-Salomé," Ph.D. dissertation, Indiana University, 1999, p.140.
52. *Ibid.*
53. *Ibid.*
54. *Ibid.*, p. 143.
55. Andreas-Salomé, *Looking Back*, p. 65–6.
56. Roy Pascal, *From Naturalism to Expressionism: German Literature and Society 1880–1918* (London: Weidenfeld and Nicolson, 1973), p. 56.

Chapter 12

1. Rilke, Diaries, p. 4.
2. Andreas-Salomé, *Looking Back*, p. 68.
3. Binion, p. 213.
4. Ralph Freedman, *Life of a Poet: Rainer Maria Rilke* (Evanston, IL: Northwestern University Press, 1996), p. 61.
5. Donald Prater, *A Ringing Glass: The Life of Rainer Maria Rilke* (New York: Oxford University Press, 1986), p. 37.
6. *Ibid.*
7. Freedman, p. 64.
8. Rainer Maria Rilke, *Letters of Rainer Maria Rilke, 1892–1910*, trans. Jane Bannard Greene and M.D. Herter Norton (New York: W.W. Norton, 1972), p. 98.
9. *Ibid.*, p. 99
10. Freedman, p. 10.
11. Freedman, p. 10.
12. *Ibid.*, p. 14.
13. *Ibid.*, p. 15.
14. *Ibid.*
15. Wolfgang Leppmann, *Rilke: A Life* (New York: Fromm International, 1984), p. 41.
16. *Ibid.*
17. Andreas-Salomé, *Looking Back*, p. 69.
18. *Ibid.*
19. Leppmann, p. 68.
20. Frank Baron, ed., *Rilke: The Alchemy of Alienation* (Lawrence: Regents Press of Kansas, 1980), p. 4.
21. Freedman, p. 60.
22. Andreas-Salomé, *Looking Back*, p. 69.
23. *Ibid.*
24. Andreas-Salomé, *Fenitschka and Deviation*, p. 33.

25. *Ibid.*, p. 26.
26. Andreas-Salomé, *Looking Back*, p. 87.
27. Binion, p. 198.
28. *Ibid.*
29. *Ibid.*, p. 202.
30. Andreas-Salomé, *Looking Back*, p. 85.

Chapter 13

1. Rainer Maria Rilke, *Rilke on Love and Other Difficulties*, trans. John J.L. Mood (New York: W.W. Norton, 1975), p. 36.
2. Andreas-Salomé, *Deviations*, in *Fenitschka and Deviations*, trans. Dorothee Einsyein Krahn (Lanham, MD: University Press of America, 1990), p. 51.
3. *Ibid.*, p. 52.
4. *Ibid.*
5. *Ibid.*
6. *Ibid.*
7. *Ibid.*
8. *Ibid.*
9. *Ibid.*
10. *Ibid.*, p. 53.
11. *Ibid.*
12. *Ibid.*
13. *Ibid.*, p. 54.
14. *Ibid.*
15. *Ibid.*, p. 56.
16. *Ibid.*, p. 57.
17. *Ibid.*
18. *Ibid.*
19. *Ibid.*
20. *Ibid.*, p. 58.
21. *Ibid.*
22. *Ibid.*
23. *Ibid.*
24. *Ibid.*
25. *Ibid.*
26. *Ibid.*, p. 59.
27. *Ibid.*
28. *Ibid.*
29. *Ibid.*
30. *Ibid.*, p. 66.
31. *Ibid.*, p. 67.
32. *Ibid.*, p. 69.
33. *Ibid.*
34. *Ibid.*
35. *Ibid.*, p. 75.
36. *Ibid.*
37. *Ibid.*, p. 87.
38. *Ibid.*
39. *Ibid.*, p. 80.
40. *Ibid.*
41. Rilke, *Diaries*, p. 4.
42. *Ibid.*, p. 64.
43. Binion, p. 222.
44. Walter Sorrell, *Three Women: Lives of Sex and Genius* (Indianapolis: Bobbs-Merrill, 1975), p. 165.
45. Rilke, *Diaries*, p. 74.
46. *Ibid.*, p. 75.
47. *Ibid.*, p. 77.
48. *Ibid.*, p. 75.
49. Rilke, *The White Princess*, in *Nine Plays*, trans. Klaus Phillips and John Locke (New York: Frederick Ungar, 1979), p. 180.
50. *Ibid.*
51. *Ibid.*, p. 181.
52. *Ibid.*
53. *Ibid.*, p. 182.
54. *Ibid.*
55. *Ibid.*
56. *Ibid.*, p. 183.
57. *Ibid.*
58. *Ibid.*, p. 181.
59. Livingstone, p. 212.
60. *Ibid.*
61. *Ibid.*

Chapter 14

1. Rilke, *Diaries*, p. 64.
2. Peters, p. 228.
3. *Ibid.*
4. James Billington, *The Face of Russia* (New York: TV Books, 1999), p.128.
5. Andreas-Salomé, *You Alone Are Real to Me*, trans. Angela von der Lippe (Rochester, NY: BOA, 2003), p. 42.
6. *Ibid.*
7. Binion, p. 249.
8. Livingstone, p. 214.
9. In Rainer Maria Rilke, *Book of Hours: Love Poems to God*, trans. Anita Barrows and Joanna Macy (New York: Riverhead, 1996), p. 24.
10. *Ibid.*
11. Rilke, *Book of Hours*, p. 47.
12. Andreas-Salomé, *You Alone Are Real to Me*, p. 38.
13. *Ibid.*

14. *Ibid.*
15. *Ibid.*, p. 38–39.
16. Rilke, *Book of Hours*, p. 24.
17. *Ibid.*, p. 62
18. *Ibid.*, p. 62
19. Andreas-Salomé, *Looking Back*, p. 73.
20. Binion, p. 237.
21. *Ibid.*, p. 238.
22. *Ibid.*
23. Lao Tsu, *Tao Te Ching*, trans. Gia-Fu Feng and Jane English (New York: Vintage, 1972).

Chapter 15

1. Rainer Maria Rilke, *Duino Elegies and the Sonnets of Orpheus*, trans. A. Poulin (New York: Mariner, 2002), p. 5.
2. Andreas-Salomé, *Looking Back*, p. 40.
3. Livingstone, p. 111.
4. *Ibid.*
5. *Ibid.*, p. 112.
6. Andreas-Salomé, *Looking Back*, p. 40.
7. *Ibid.*
8. Rilke, *Letters…, 1892–1910*, p. 40.
9. *Ibid.*
10. *Ibid.*
11. *Ibid.*, p. 40–41.
12. *Ibid.*, p. 42.
13. Andreas-Salomé, *Looking Back*, p. 41.
14. Livingstone, p. 115.
15. Andreas-Salomé, *Looking Back*, p. 36
16. *Ibid.*, p. 72.
17. Rilke, *Letters…, 1892–1910*, p. 37.
18. *Ibid.*
19. *Ibid.*
20. *Ibid.*, p. 38.
21. Rilke, *Diaries*, p. 195.
22. Binion, p. 292.
23. *Ibid.*
24. *Ibid.*
25. *Ibid.*, p. 290.
26. *Ibid.*
27. *Ibid.*
28. *Ibid.*
29. *Ibid.*, p. 301.
30. Rainer Maria Rilke and Lou Andreas-Salomé, *Rainer Maria Rilke, Lou Andreas-Salomé: Briefwechsel*, trans. Ernst Pfeiffer (Frankfurt am Main: Insel Verlag, 1989), p. 54.
31. *Ibid.*
32. *Ibid.*
33. *Ibid.*
34. *Ibid.*
35. Binion, p. 299.
36. Rilke and Andreas-Salomé, p. 54.
37. Binion, p. 299.

Chapter 16

1. Binion, p. 310.
2. *Ibid.* p. 302.
3. *Ibid.*, p. 305.
4. *Ibid.* p. 306.
5. *Ibid.*
6. *Ibid.*, p. 310.
7. *Ibid.*
8. *Ibid.*
9. *Ibid.*
10. Rainer Maria Rilke, *The Notebooks of Malte Laurids Brigge*, trans. M.D. Herter Norton (New York: W.W. Norton, 1992), p. 14.
11. *Ibid.*
12. Rilke, *Letters…, 1892–1910*, p. 122.
13. Andreas-Salomé, *Looking Back*, p. 106.
14. Binion, p. 312.
15. Rilke, *Letters…, 1892–1910*, p. 138.
16. *Ibid.*, p. 139
17. *Ibid.*, p. 140.
18. Binion, p. 313.
19. *Ibid.*, p. 141.
20. *Ibid.*, p. 166.
21. Binion, p. 317.
22. *Ibid.*, p. 318.
23. Livingstone, p. 214.
24. *Ibid.*
25. *Ibid.*
26. Binion, p. 325.
27. *Ibid.*, p. 326.
28. *Ibid.*, p. 327.
29. *Ibid.*, p. 329.

Chapter 17

1. Livingstone, p.153.
2. Klingenberg.

3. *Ibid.*
4. *Ibid.*
5. *Ibid.*
6. *Ibid.*
7. Andreas-Salomé, *Looking Back*, p. 94.
8. *Ibid.*
9. Peters, p. 270.
10. *Ibid.*
11. *Ibid.*, p. 271.
12. Andreas-Salomé, *Looking Back*, p. 104.
13. Sigmund Freud and Lou Andreas-Salomé, *Sigmund Freud and Lou Andreas-Salomé: Letters*, trans. William and Elaine Robson-Scott (New York: W.W. Norton, 1985), p. 7.
14. Andreas-Salomé, *Looking Back*, p. 95.
15. *Ibid.*
16. Freud and Andreas-Salomé, p. 7.
17. Andreas-Salomé, *Freud Journal*, p. 32.
18. *Ibid.*, p. 52.
19. Freud and Andreas-Salomé, p. 8.
20. *Ibid.*
21. Andreas-Salomé, *Freud Journal*, p. 33.
22. *Ibid.*, p. 34
23. *Ibid.*
24. *Ibid.*, p. 35.

Chapter 18

1. Andreas-Salomé, *Freud Journal*, p. 168.
2. Binion, p. 338.
3. Paul Roazen, *Brother Animal: The Story of Freud and Tausk* (New York: Vintage, 1971), p. 5.
4. *Ibid.*
5. *Ibid.*
6. *Ibid.*, p. 9.
7. Paul Roazen, *Freud and His Followers* (New York: Da Capo, 1992), p. 313.
8. *Ibid.*
9. Roazen, *Brother Animal*, p. 19.
10. *Ibid.*, p. 20.
11. *Ibid.*, p. 21.
12. *Ibid.*
13. Andreas-Salomé, *Freud Journal*, p. 51.
14. *Ibid.*
15. Andreas-Salomé, *Freud Journal*, p. 56.
16. *Ibid.*, p. 168.
17. *Ibid.*, p. 101.
18. Peters, p. 280–81.
19. Roazen, *Brother Animal*, p. 39
20. *Ibid.*
21. *Ibid.*, p. 43.
22. *Ibid.*, p. 48.
23. Andreas-Salomé, *Freud Journal*, p. 76.
24. *Ibid.*
25. *Ibid.*, p. 169.
26. *Ibid.*, p. 79.
27. *Ibid.*, p. 79.

Chapter 19

1. Andreas-Salomé, *Looking Back*, p. 149.
2. *Ibid.*, p. 89.
3. *Ibid.*
4. Livingstone, p. 162.
5. Andreas-Salomé, *Freud Journal*, p. 147.
6. Livingstone, p. 163.
7. *Ibid.*
8. Andreas-Salomé, *Freud Journal*, p. 61.
9. *Ibid.*, p. 111.
10. Livingstone, p. 163.
11. Andreas-Salomé, *Freud Journal*, p. 164.
12. *Ibid.*, p. 168.
13. *Ibid.*, p. 124.
14. *Ibid.*, p. 124.
15. *Ibid.*, p. 123.
16. Binion, p. 404.
17. Andreas-Salomé, *Looking Back*, p. 149.
18. Binion, p. 405.
19. *Ibid.*
20. *Ibid.*
21. *Ibid.*
22. *Ibid.*
23. *Ibid.*, p. 406.
24. Freud and Andreas-Salomé, p. 20.
25. *Ibid.*
26. *Ibid.*
27. Andreas-Salomé, *Looking Back*, p. 113–114.
28. *Ibid.*
29. *Ibid.*, p. 113.

30. *Ibid.*
31. *Ibid.*, p. 28.
32. *Ibid.*, p. 150.
33. *Ibid.*, p. 112.

Chapter 20

1. Andreas-Salomé, *Looking Back*, p. 135.
2. *Ibid.*, p. 1.
3. *Ibid.*
4. *Ibid.*, p. 150.
5. Freud and Andreas-Salomé, p. 98.
6. *Ibid.*
7. Roazen, *Brother Animal*, p. 142.
8. Binion, p. 403.
9. *Ibid.*
10. *Ibid.*, p. 421.
11. Rilke, *Love and Other Difficulties*, p. 36.
12. *Ibid.*, p. 36–37.
13. *Ibid.* p. 37.
14. Rainer Maria Rilke, *Letters of Rainer Maria Rilke, 1910–1926*, trans. Jane Bannard Greene and M.D. Herter Norton (New York: W.W. Norton, 1972), p. 35.
15. *Ibid.*, p. 45.
16. Rilke, *Duino Elegies and the Sonnets of Orpheus*, p. 5.
17. Andreas-Salomé, *Freud Journal*, p. 154.
18. *Ibid.*
19. *Ibid.*, p. 156.
20. *Ibid.*
21. *Ibid.*, p. 179.
22. Livingstone, p. 168.
23. *Ibid.*
24. *Ibid.*
25. *Ibid.*, p. 169.
26. *Ibid.*
27. *Ibid.*
28. Livingstone, p. 170.
29. *Ibid.*
30. Leppmann, p. 384.
31. *Ibid.*
32. Andreas-Salomé, *You Alone Are Real to Me*, p. 27.
33. Andreas-Salomé, *Looking Back*, p. 130.
34. *Ibid.*
35. *Ibid.*, p. 135.
36. *Ibid.*, p. 134.
37. *Ibid.*, p. 129.
38. *Ibid.*, p. 135.
39. *Ibid.*
40. *Ibid.*

Chapter 21

1. Livingstone, p. 198.
2. Binion, p. 481.
3. Peters, p. 284.
4. *Ibid.*
5. *Ibid.*, p. 283.
6. Livingstone, p. 216.
7. *Ibid.*, p. 217.
8. *Ibid.*, p. 218.
9. Freud and Andreas-Salomé, p. 191.
10. *Ibid.*
11. *Ibid.*, p. 195.
12. *Ibid.*, p. 196.
13. *Ibid.*
14. *Ibid.*, p. 198.
15. *Ibid.*, p. 199.
16. Andreas-Salomé, *Looking Back*, p. 49.
17. *Ibid.*, p. 131.

Afterword

1. Linda Schierse Leonard, *The Call to Create: Celebrating Acts of Imagination* (New York: Harmony, 2000), p. 3.

Bibliography

Published Works

Andreas-Salomé, Lou. *Amor, Jutta, die Tarnkappe.* Frankfurt am Main: Insel Verlag, 1981.
_____. *Fenitschka and Deviations.* Trans. Dorothee Einsyein Krahn. Lanham, MD: University Press of America, 1990.
_____. *The Freud Journal.* Trans. Stanley A. Leavy. London: Quartet, 1987.
_____. *Ibsen's Heroines.* Trans. Siegfried Mandel. New York: Limelight, 1989.
_____. *Looking Back: Memoirs.* Trans. Ernst Pfeiffer. New York: Marlow, 1991.
_____. *Nietzsche.* Trans. Siegfried Mandel. Champaign: University of Illinois Press, 2001.
_____. *You Alone Are Real to Me.* Trans. Angela von der Lippe. Rochester, NY: BOA, 2003.
Appignanesi, Lisa, and Forrester, John. *Freud's Women.* New York: Basic, 1992.
Baron, Frank, ed. *Rilke: The Alchemy of Alienation.* Lawrence: Regents Press of Kansas, 1980.
Billington, James. *The Face of Russia.* New York: TV Books, 1999.
Binion, Rudolph. *Frau Lou: Nietzsche's Wayward Disciple.* Princeton, NJ: Princeton University Press, 1968.
Cormican, Muriel. "Sex, Sexuality, and Gender: Cultural Critique in the Fictional Works of Lou Andreas-Salomé." Ph.D. dissertation, Indiana University, 1999.
Diethe, Carol. *Nietzsche's Women: Beyond the Whip.* Berlin: Walter de Gruyter, 1996.
Freedman, Ralph. *Life of a Poet: Rainer Maria Rilke.* Evanston, IL: Northwestern University Press, 1996.
Freud, Sigmund, and Lou Andreas-Salomé. *Sigmund Freud and Lou Andreas-Salomé: Letters.* Ed. Ernst Pfeiffer. Trans. William and Elaine Robson-Scott. New York: W.W. Norton, 1985.
Klingenberg, Helene. "Lou Andreas-Salomé." *Deutsche Monatsschrift für Russland,* March 15, 1912.
Krell, David Farrell. *Nietzsche: A Novel.* Albany: State University of New York Press, 1996.
Leonard, Linda Schierse. *The Call to Create: Celebrating Acts of Imagination.* New York: Harmony, 2000.
Leppmann, Wolfgang. *Rilke: A Life.* New York: Fromm International, 1984.
Livingstone, Angela. *Salomé: Her Life and Work.* Mt. Krisco, NY: Moyer Bell, 1984.
Martin, Biddy., Biddy *Women and Modernity: The Lifestyles of Lou Andreas-Salomé.* Ithaca: Cornell University Press, 1991.
Maurer, Warren. *Understanding Gerhart Hauptmann.* Columbia: University of South Carolina Press, 1992.
Nietzsche, Friedrich. *Basic Writings of Nietzsche.* Trans. Walter Kaufmann. Introduction by Peter Gay. New York: Modern Library, 2000.
_____. *Beyond Good and Evil.* Trans. Walter Kaufmann. New York: Vintage, 1989.
_____. *The Birth of Tragedy.* Trans. Shaun Whiteside. Ed. Michael Tanner. New York: Penguin, 1993.
_____. *Ecce Homo: How to Become What You Are.* Trans. Duncan Large. Oxford: Oxford University Press, 2004.
_____. *The Portable Nietzsche.* Ed. and

trans. Walter Kaufmann. New York: Penguin, 1976.
———. *Selected Letters of Friedrich Nietzsche.* Trans. Christopher Middleton. Indianapolis, IN: Hackett, 1996.
Nietzsche, Friedrich; Rée, Paul; and von Salomé, Lou. *Friedrich Nietzsche, Paul Rée, Lou von Salomé: Correspondance.* Translated Ernst Pfeiffer. Paris: Presses Universitaires de France, 1979.
Pascal, Roy. *From Naturalism to Expressionism: German Literature and Society 1880–1918.* London: Weidenfeld and Nicolson, 1973.
Peters, H.F. *My Sister, My Spouse: A Biography of Lou Andreas-Salomé.* New York: W.W. Norton, 1962.
Prater, Donald. *A Ringing Glass: The Life of Rainer Maria Rilke.* New York: Oxford University Press, 1986.
Reyburn, H(ugh) A(dam). *Nietzsche: The Story of a Human Philosopher.* London: Macmillan, 1948.
Rilke, Rainer Maria. *Book of Hours: Love Poems to God.* Trans. Anita Barrows and Joanna Macy. New York: Riverhead, 1996.
———. *The Diaries of a Young Poet.* Trans. Edward Snow and Michael Winkler. New York: W.W. Norton, 1997.
———. *Duino Elegies and the Sonnets of Orpheus.* Trans. A. Poulin. New York: Mariner, 2002.
———. *Letters to a Young Poet.* Trans. M.D. Herter Norton. New York: W.W. Norton, 1993.
———. *Letters of Rainer Maria Rilke, 1892–1910.* Trans. Jane Bannard Greene and M.D. Herter Norton. New York: W.W. Norton, 1972.
———. *Letters of Rainer Maria Rilke, 1910–1926.* Trans. Jane Bannard Greene and M.D. Herter Norton. New York: W.W. Norton, 1972.
———. *Nine Plays.* Trans. Klaus Phillips and John Locke. New York: Frederick Ungar, 1979.
———. *The Notebooks of Malte Laurids Brigge* Trans. M.D. Herter Norton. New York: W.W. Norton, 1992.
———. *Rilke on Love and Other Difficulties.* Trans. John J.L. Mood. New York: W.W. Norton, 1975.
Rilke, Rainer Maria, and Andreas-Salomé, Lou. *Rainer Maria Rilke, Lou Andreas-Salomé: Briefwechsel.* Trans. Ernst Pfeiffer. Frankfurt am Main: Insel Verlag, 1989.
Roazen, Paul. *Brother Animal: The Story of Freud and Tausk.* New York: Vintage, 1971.
———. *Freud and His Followers.* New York: Da Capo, 1992.
Safranski, Rüdiger, *Nietzsche, A Philosophical Biography.* New York: W.W. Norton, 2001.
Sorell, Walter. *Three Women: Lives of Sex and Genius.* Indianapolis: Bobbs-Merrill, 1975.
Tsu, Lao. *Tao Te Ching.* Trans. Gia-Fu Feng and Jane English. New York: Vintage, 1972.
Zweig, Stefan. *The World of Yesterday.* Lincoln: University of Nebraska Press, 1964.

Notes on translations

Translations of letters in the French edition of *Friedrich Nietzsche, Paul Rée, Lou von Salomé: Correspondance* are by the author.
Translations of *En Route*; *Amor, Jutta, Die Tarnkappe; Ruth; Rainer Maria Rilke, Lou Andreas-Salomé: Briefwechsel,* and the article "Lou Andreas-Salomé" in *Deutsche Monatsschrift für Russland* are for the author by Romona Bernhard.

Index

Adler, Alfred 162–163, 165
Albert-Lasard, LouLou 184
Alexander I (Tsar) 10
Andreas, F.C. 1, 65, 66–71, 75, 78–79, 87, 103, 113, 115, 116, 123, 126, 129, 130–133, 134, 137, 140, 142, 144, 145–146, 147, 148–149, 151, 174, 175, 185–187, 191, 192
Aphrodite 44
Apollo (Apollonian) 35–37, 67, 76, 100, 163
Aristotle 27
Athena 24, 158, 161

Basel 35, 38, 42
Bayreuth 44, 47, 49
Beer-Hofmann, Richard 96–99, 103, 112, 171, 180, 186
Bergman, Ingrid 110
Berlin 17, 55, 58, 61, 62, 65, 75, 87, 95, 108, 116, 130, 141, 147, 148, 151, 152, 167
Beyond Good and Evil 32, 60, 84–85, 175
Biedermann, Alois 25
Binion, Rudolph 1, 41, 50, 62, 63, 64, 69, 112, 142, 145, 146, 150, 180–181, 191
The Birth of Tragedy 35–38, 67, 75
Bjerre, Poul 158, 159
Bonn 147
The Book of Hours 134, 150
Botticelli 116, 122, 124
Brahms, Johannes 95
Buber, Martin 153, 164
Bülow, Frieda von 95, 96, 104, 105, 106, 113, 116, 133, 152–153
Burckhardt, Jakob 81

Café Griensteidl 96, 97
Caro (Lou's aunt) 16–17, 20, 21, 22, 55, 69, 118, 132
Charles University 109
Children of Man 128
Christ 38, 106, 107, 127, 131, 150
Confucius 25
Cormican, Muriel 102, 103

Dalton, Herman (pastor) 17, 19, 21
David-Rhonfeld, Valerie von (Vally) 109
Daybreak 38
Dep, Ellen 161
Deutsch, Dr. Helen 179
Deviations 22, 117–121
The Devil and His Grandmother 189
Dionysus (Dionysian) 34, 35–37, 67, 76, 81, 82, 85, 100, 163, 166
Dohm, Hedwig 135–136
Dostoevsky, Fyodor 121–122, 143
Drozhzhin, Spiridon 140–141
Duino Elegies 182–183, 184–185

Ebner-Eschenbach, Maria von 129
"En Route" 113
Endell, August 116, 123
Eros 44, 164

Faust 21
Federn, Paul 165
Fenitschka 89–94, 111, 125
Fitzgerald, Zelda 193
Förster, Bernhard 49, 83
Freedman, Ralph 107, 110
Freie Bühne 75, 76, 79, 103
Freud, Anna 189
Freud, Sigmund 1, 3, 4, 13, 15, 24, 35, 37, 85, 89, 94, 100, 112, 121, 142, 157, 174, 176, 179–181, 182, 186, 189–192, 194
Frisch, Martha 166

Garborg, Arne 76
Gast, Peter 56, 61, 82, 151
The Gay Science 38, 40, 54
Gelzer, Heinrich 49
Gillot, Hendrik 9, 17, 18–24, 26, 28, 29–30, 40, 49, 54, 55, 63, 67, 68, 69–70, 75, 87, 93, 98, 111, 117, 118, 119, 132, 134, 145, 147, 159, 178, 179–181, 185, 188, 191, 194
God (Christian) 4, 9, 11, 14–17, 19, 20–24, 25–26, 32, 34, 38, 39, 51, 60, 62–65, 75,

207

84–86, 98, 106, 108, 126, 134, 135, 140, 151, 178, 180–181, 183, 185, 188, 189, 191, 194
Goethe, Johann Wolfgang von 20, 21, 25, 34, 59, 75, 158
The Gospels 25
Göttingen 147, 148, 149, 151, 152, 161, 174, 175, 176, 177, 183

Hart, Julius and Heinrich 76
Hauptmann, Gerhart 76–78, 86, 88, 142, 194
Heller, Hugo 158
Hitler, Adolph 83
Hofmannsthal, Hugo von 96, 97
Holz, Arno 76
Homer 36
"The Hour Without God" 15, 189
The House (Das Haus) 145, 151
Hugo, Victor 25
Human, All Too Human 38, 54
"The Human as Woman" ("Der Mensch als Weib") 135–136

Ibsen, Hendrik 23, 76, 79–80
Ibsen's Heroines 79–80

"Jesus der Jude" 99
Joyce, James 33, 37, 75
Jukovsky, Count Paul von 48
Jung, Carl 35, 95, 161, 163, 165–166, 173
Jutta 99–103, 180

Kaufmann, Walter 33
Kay, Ellen 150, 153
Kierkegaard 20
Kinkel, Gottfried 26
Klimt, Gustuv 152
Klingenberg, Helene 158–159
Kremlin 130–131
Kühnemann, Eugen 76

"The Lay of the Love and Death of the Cornet Christoph Rilke" 135, 181
Ledebour, Georg 78–79, 87, 186
Leipzig 55–58
Leonard, Linda Schierse 193
Leppmann, Wolfgang 110
Livingstone, Angela 24, 63, 85, 128, 133, 151, 173, 174, 184, 189
Loewi, Hilde 179
Lonely People 76–77
Looking Back: Memoirs 191
Löwengarten 42
Lucerne 42, 61

Ma 133, 142
The Magic Cap 152
Mahler, Alma 95, 152

Mandel, Siegfried 38, 85
Marie (Andreas' mistress) 151
Mariechen (Andreas' daughter) 151
Martin, Biddy 80
Meysenbug, Malwida von 26–30, 38, 41, 47, 54, 64
Monte Sacro 41–42, 49, 51, 61
Moscow 130, 138
Munich 87, 99, 104, 105, 106, 109, 115, 126, 174, 175, 184
muse 1, 3, 24, 35, 44, 77, 105, 110, 115, 124, 125, 134, 149, 152, 193–194

Napoleon 10, 150
Narcissus 3, 15, 172–174
Naturalism (Naturalists) 76, 88, 103
Naumburg 54, 64, 83
Nazism 157, 192
Nicholas I, Tsar 10
Nietzsche 83–86
Nietzsche, Elizabeth (Lisbeth) 47–50, 52, 53, 54, 58, 60, 64, 83, 86, 103, 160, 191, 192
Nietzsche, Friedrich 1–5, 24, 27, 29–65, 67, 75, 79, 80–86, 87, 93, 100, 103–104, 106, 110, 112, 149, 158, 160, 162, 163, 169, 170, 174–176, 183, 185, 191, 192, 194
The Notebooks of Malte Laurids Brigge 148

Oedipus 13, 36, 37, 180
Oedipus complex 13, 37
"Old Age" 145
Orta 41, 57
Out of an Alien Soul 98
Overbeck, Franz 42, 45, 64, 82, 83
Overbeck, Ida 42, 45, 54

Paris 56, 58, 87, 89–91, 95, 119, 142, 147, 185
Parsifal 38, 44
Pascal, Blaise 20
Pascal, Roy 104
Pasternak, Leonid 131
Peterof 132
Peters, Dr. Carl 95
Peters, H.F. 61, 62, 77, 95, 131, 146, 159, 188
Petersburg *see* St. Petersburg
Pfeiffer, Ernst 50, 57, 152
philosophy 3, 4, 20, 25, 27, 29, 34, 35, 38, 41, 50–52, 54, 55, 56, 59–60, 64, 65, 69, 76, 83–85, 104, 109, 136, 151, 161, 181, 193, 194
Pineles, Friedrich (Zemek) 112, 141–142, 143, 144–147, 149, 151, 152, 153, 186
"The Problems of Love" 129
psychoanalysis 85, 158, 160–162, 166–170, 175, 179, 181, 182, 186, 188, 189, 190, 194

psychology 3, 4, 27, 33, 76, 80, 85, 90, 117, 153, 159, 162, 165, 173, 174, 194
Pushkin, Alexander 10

Rank, Otto 171
Rée, Paul 27–31, 38–58, 60–61, 64–65, 70, 75, 79, 103, 113, 143, 146, 186, 191
Reformed Protestant Movement 171
religion 3, 4, 14, 16, 20, 21, 25, 26, 27, 34, 35, 40, 51, 60, 62, 75, 87, 95, 105, 124, 161, 182, 183
"Religion and Culture" 124
Rig Veda 25
Rilke, Josef 107–108
Rilke, Rainer Maria 1, 4, 24, 33, 35, 37, 77, 105–116, 122–144, 145, 147–152, 159, 160, 169, 175, 181–185, 186, 189, 194
Rilke, Sophia (Phia) 106–108, 183
Roazen, Paul 166, 167, 169, 170, 179, 180
Rodin, August 142, 148, 185
Rodinka 141
Rohde, Erwin 64
Rome 26–28, 30–31, 38, 40, 61, 81, 149–150
Ruth 20, 87, 98

Safranski, Rüdiger 34, 83
St. Petersburg 10–12, 14, 15, 17, 18, 21, 29, 33, 44, 45, 53, 63, 70, 75, 96, 97, 122, 125, 126, 132, 141, 147, 176, 191
Salomé, Eugene von (Jenia) 12, 44–45, 122, 125
Salomé, Gen. Gustav von 10–15, 21, 40, 41, 117
Salomé, Louise von (Lou's mother) 9–11, 13–14, 17, 19–21, 25–29, 33, 39–42, 44
Salomé, Robert von 12, 177
Salten, Felix 96, 97
Sartre, Jean-Paul 33
Schill, Sofya 138–140
Schmargendorf 133, 134, 142, 146
Schnitzler, Arthur 96–99, 103, 180, 194
Schopenhauer 20
Schulz, Carl von 62
sexuality 4, 44, 63, 68–69, 88–90, 93, 94, 102, 103, 104, 105, 111, 124, 145, 146–147, 161, 162–164, 178, 189, 191
"Siblings" 180–181
Sonnets to Orpheus 184
Sorell, Walter 124
Spinoza, Baruch 20, 38
Stein, Henrich von 64, 65

Stibbe 44, 45, 47, 48, 54, 55, 56, 61
Stöcker, Helene 69
Strauss, Richard 95
Strindberg, August 76, 81
Struggling for God (Im Kampf um Gott) 61, 62–65, 98

Tao Te Ching 25, 136
Tauntenburg 50, 64, 191
Tempelhof 75
Third Congress (Vienna) 161–162
Thurn und Taxis, Maria von 182
Thus Spake Zarathustra 41, 51, 59–60, 84–86, 104
Tolstoy, Leo 10, 76, 131–132, 138–139, 141, 150
Tönnies, Ferdinand 62

Übermensch 32, 40, 59, 60, 75, 85, 183
Ulmann, Liv 110
University of Basel 35, 38
University of Vienna 164, 166
University of Zurich 4, 25, 76

Victorian Age 4, 69, 99, 161, 174
Vienna 56, 58, 87, 95–99, 102, 103, 112, 129, 142, 152, 157, 158, 160–161, 163, 167, 168, 171, 174, 175, 177, 179, 180, 182
Vienna Congress of Psychoanalysts 161
virginity 68, 98, 128
Visions of Christ 106
Volga 142
Voltaire 20
Volynsky, Akim 113, 116

Wagner, Cosima 35, 38, 81–82
Wagner, Richard 32, 34, 35, 37–38, 44, 47–49, 52, 82
Wedekind, Frank 87–90, 92, 94, 99, 194
Weimer Congress 161
Westoff, Clara 143–144
The White Princess 126–128
will to power 163
World War I 78, 166, 176, 188

Young Vienna (*Jung Wein*) 96–97, 102–103, 129, 171

Zurich 4, 9, 25–26, 39, 76, 89, 90, 95, 133, 136
Zweig, Stephan 95, 98

www.ingramcontent.com/pod-product-compliance
Ingram Content Group UK Ltd.
Pitfield, Milton Keynes, MK11 3LW, UK
UKHW041918140426
5217IPUK00013B/217